Stirring the Pot

Africa in World History

SERIES EDITORS: DAVID ROBINSON AND JOSEPH C. MILLER

James C. McCann
Stirring the Pot: A History of African Cuisine

Forthcoming:

Peter Alegi
African Soccerscapes: How a Continent Changed the World's Game

John M. Mugane
The Story of Swahili

Charles Ambler
Mass Media and Popular Culture in Modern Africa

Stirring the Pot

A History of African Cuisine

James C. McCann

OHIO UNIVERSITY PRESS

in association with the

OHIO UNIVERSITY CENTER FOR INTERNATIONAL STUDIES

Athens

Ohio University Press, Athens, Ohio 45701
www.ohioswallow.com
© 2009 by Ohio University Press
All rights reserved

To obtain permission to quote, reprint, or otherwise reproduce or distribute material from
Ohio University Press publications, please contact our rights and permissions department
at (740) 593-1154 or (740) 593-4536 (fax).

Printed in the United States of America
Ohio University Press books are printed on acid-free paper ⊗ ™

16 15 14 13 12 11 10 09   5 4 3 2 1

Library of Congress Cataloging-in-Publication Data
McCann, James, 1950–
  Stirring the pot : a history of African cuisine / James C. McCann.
    p. cm. — (Africa in world history)
  Includes bibliographical references and index.
  ISBN 978-0-89680-272-8 (pb : alk. paper)
  1. Food habits—Africa. 2. Food preferences—Africa. 3. Cookery, African. 4. Africa—
Social life and customs. I. Title.
  GT2853.A35M37 2009
  394.1'2—dc22
                    2009035723

To Peter Georgouses (Northwestern '71)

Anthropologist of food, cook, and friend

He died much too soon

CONTENTS

ILLUSTRATIONS

Figures

Maps

Tables

SERIES EDITORS' PREFACE

The field of African history has developed considerably over recent decades, but its discoveries and insights are rarely acknowledged outside the continent. In this series we seek to make African history accessible to courses in world history, the history of the Americas, and the histories of other regions. We are aiming to reach advanced secondary school students, college/university undergraduates, and general readers. In modern settings still rife with the residues of centuries of slaving and racial stereotyping, we hope that these descriptions of Africans at work, at home, and engaged in sport and cultural activities will bring out the universal human experience that Africans have expressed in their own particular ways. Too often the media and textbooks still seek to make Africa accessible by resorting to inappropriate modern meanings—"tribes" glossed condescendingly as "ethnicities," or complex African polities reduced to stereotyped "kingdoms" and "empires"—or by the pervasive coverage of diseases, political disorder, and destitution. Africans through their histories and cultures bring great diversity to the human experience and enrich us all, and it is that enrichment we seek to suggest in this series.

The titles in the series are intended for teaching and for stimulating further inquiry and comparison. Our authors therefore present their topics on accessibly modest scales. They provide references to academic works for specialists from other world regions who want to pursue the literature for Africa on their topics. For teachers and students, these short books offer a variety of primary source materials relevant to each topic, including images, firsthand accounts, and Web resources. Instructors can both teach basic historical methods to their students and learn about the range of unfamiliar sources that Africanists have tapped.

The inaugural volume in the series aims to appeal to "hungry" students as they confront unfamiliar cuisines and reflect on the virtues of the home cooking they are leaving behind. Africans, as James McCann explains through examples ranging from the plains of Zambia to the mountains of Ethiopia, grew up eating a variety of cuisines and cooking dishes no less varied or loaded with all the sentiments of home and family. For people raised eating particular dishes since infancy, foods that might appear monotonous or even unpalatable to the McDonald's generation held an appeal comparable to the charm that McNuggets exert on children today. Cuisines in Africa, McCann shows, can be politicized as effectively as soul food or *nouvelle cuisine* in Europe or the United States. In the end, the similarities in the universal human experience of commensality overwhelm the contrasts in whatever people may consume, here or there. Therein lies the food for thought in McCann's reflections on gustatory pleasures and creativity in cookery. He makes the basic point of the series: all of us in the global community share much more than we realize, and appreciating the differences brings its own reward. This volume, we hope, will draw students into the "African" and "Ethiopian" restaurants appearing everywhere, as the modern diaspora brings immigrants to cities all around the world. All of them are hungry—like their predecessors—for the tastes of home. Instructors know that students who eat together may be lured to learn together as well, and McCann's bibliography will introduce them to the considerable range of African and neo-African recipes available in cookbooks to prepare for a characteristically collaborative African class supper.

The second title in the series, *African Soccerscapes,* will bring Peter Alegi's take on African manifestations of the global game of football at the moment that the 2010 World Cup is played in the Republic of South Africa. The intriguing story of culture, politics, and commercialization is one we hope students will find instructive in integrating Africa into broader patterns of the world's history.

David Robinson
Okemos, Michigan

Joseph C. Miller
Ivy, Virginia

ACKNOWLEDGMENTS

This book has its origins in a list of topics suggested for a new series by Ohio University Press by Joseph Miller and David Robinson for studies of Africa's place within world history. One of the topics they proposed was what they called African foodways. To me, that topic evoked an immediate emotional response: it was an opportunity to explore a new dimension of history and would be a logical extension of work I had just finished on the history of corn (maize) in Africa. That work, *Maize and Grace: Africa's Encounter with a New World Crop*, had encompassed agriculture, language, ecology, and culture in Africa and the wider Atlantic world. This topic of African food and cookery promised to do that, and more. In this book, I am seeking a broad audience. For some readers African cookery and cuisine may a new phenomenon. And for others, even though it may be a quite well-trodden path, it is one that previous writers, especially historians, have not thought about as a way of looking at history and historical change.

Research for this book has been an adventure, in market stalls in Accra, Ghana, in Addis Ababa restaurants, at the back tables of roadside bars, in Zimbabwean farm compounds, in a Venda farmer fair in South Africa, in Caribbean groceries in Cambridge, Massachusetts. It has been an exploration of primary knowledge, among cooks, eaters, and in discussions about mothers' stews. In addition to historical sources, I have been drawn into literature, film, and grocery stores—all as different kinds of texts. The list of acknowledgments is therefore eclectic. My work began with a year's research fellowship at the W. E. B. DuBois Institute of Harvard University, aided by its supportive staff and the remarkable and lively set of 2005–2006 fellows. Those include Skip Gates, Lisa Gregory, Lidet Tadele, Claudine Reynaud, Maria Frias, Stanley Engerman, Phyllis Taoua, Harry Garuba, Adisa Ogunfolakin, Samuel Ngayhembako, Noel Twagiramungu, Barbara Rodriguez, Roquinaldo Ferreira, James Hefner, Melina Pappademos, and especially Bobby Donaldson. Lesley Burkett was my Harvard-based research assistant.

In Ethiopia I had encouragement and specific inspiration from Heran Serekebrhan, Tekalign Wolde Mariam, and Shiferaw Bekele. In London I had advice and ideas from John Parker, Izabela Orlowska, and my friend Ahmed at the Calabash restaurant in Covent Garden. In Boston John Hutchison, Jennifer Yanco, Chris Annear, Robyn Metcalfe, Tom Glick, and Diana Wylie had ideas and connections. Key U.S.-based contacts included Judy Carney, Fran Osseo-Asare, and Daphne Miller. In fall 2006 I taught a quite remarkable cohort of students who researched their own topics in a seminar on food as a window on cultural change, economic development, and precolonial history: these students included Brian Casady, Ari Fogelman, Melissa Graboyes, Natalie Mettler, and Chelsea Strayer-Shields. Ilona Baughman from Boston University's program in gastronomy read the manuscript and offered helpful advice. From the sidelines my friend and remote sensing guru Asnakew Kebede shared roadside and farmhouse food and drink, always piquing my curiosity.

As always, my thanks go to my family: to Libby and Martha as they grow into young womanhood, and to Sandi, who had the idea for this book a long time ago.

Stirring the Pot

MAP 0.1 Contemporary Africa. *Map by Claudia K. Walters. Source: http://exploringafrica.matrix.msu.edu/images/capitals.jpg*

Introduction

African Cooking and African History

Culture began when the raw got cooked.
—Felipe Fernández-Armesto, *Food: A History*

Yameftehay guday, chewna berbere lay
(A solution lies in salt and spice)
—Proverb written on the back windscreen
of a motorbike taxi in the market town of
Welkite, Ethiopia

IN 1887, on a mountaintop overlooking Addis Ababa, her kingdom's new capital, Queen Taytu Bitul laid out a magnificent feast for her guests. She had prepared pots of mutton stew, roasted beef, spiced soups, peppered pea sauce, minced meat sautéed in butter flavored by exotic spices, all accompanied by rivers of honey wine. The scents of the simmering stews, the buzz of the assembled guests, and the tableau of elegant presentations were part of an elaborate theater of political ritual, but the food itself had not only taste, aroma, and texture, but also historical meaning. The act of the feast, I would argue, had as much to do with the meaning of the cooking as with taste of the food itself. What can we learn about history from understanding the cookery? This book examines the deeper historical evidence and the meaning of food and cooking in African history.

Food as a topic in African history adds taste and texture to events and personalities. There are two possible approaches to discussing it. The first is to consider the daily struggle for sustenance, whether in the African origins of humankind or, in modern times, in the famines that have devastated regions of Africa such as Ethiopia, Niger, and Sudan. This approach has value in addressing Africa's economic woes and their human consequences, but it emphasizes struggle and heartbreak at the expense of recognizing Africa's fundamental energy and creativity in the history of its cooking and its solutions to life's problems.

The second approach, the one I adopt, is to consider cooking and cuisine as a creative composition at the heart of all cultural expressions of ourselves as humans. Historically, and in Africa until recently, food has grown, literally, under our feet or as animals that we herd or hunt, and until recent times families prepared meals from the bounty they could create from the lands and waters where they lived. They thus ate in the rhythm of the seasons, the bearing of wild fruits, the movements of fish, the timing of harvests, and the migrations of animals in the wild.

So I want to explore cuisine in Africa as something conceived, cooked, and consumed, first around home fires, cooking pots, griddles, and spits, and later in market stalls and restaurants and at political events where food expressed power. Eating together, commensality, was thus not just nutrition but also a measure of human values, linking communities of kin, neighbors, and friends around tastes and sequences of taste expressing who they were on a daily basis: in a word, cuisine.

The focus of the book is therefore on what African peoples composed to eat throughout the centuries on a wide variety of their landscapes, seasons, and historical exchanges. The combinations of textures, flavors, and techniques of preparation they created, and when and with whom, thus expressed their agility in keeping up with their times, their struggles, and their opportunities. A central theme here is that food is a marker of cultural identity. It tells us who we are, how we grew up, about our memories and the history we share. Africa is no different in that respect than other world areas, yet what are those things that make Africa's history of food distinctive? Empress Taytu's feast (described further in chapter 3) is one example. The book explores more of these as they appear in the historical record.

In Africa, as in other world areas, cookery is a stage for performance (by the cook) and audience (family, neighbors, and guests), who respond by eating and appreciating it. In Africa, women were almost always the performers, and techniques of cooking remained women's specialized knowledge. Women cooked in the home, but in Europe and in many world areas the art itself became the privilege of a literate, male, class, dominated by professional guilds as a kind of priestly knowledge. African food preparation, in contrast, has, until recently, been consistently a woman's daily domain rather than a distinct profession. Like other forms of oral performance that combined creativity with consistency of reproduction, erudition in cooking in Africa could take place via both the memory of individuals and that of groups of people as their shared cuisine—but only very recently via written recipes. While written recipes became important in literate societies and among the elite classes in Europe, Asia, and the classical world, cooking and cuisine in Africa was more fundamentally an oral art in societies that preserved traditions and history via both the spoken and unspoken word. African griots from the Mali empire have become famous for their ability to recall the details of political history and its cultural meaning. Like griots, Africa's cooks have long demonstrated a remarkable capacity for oral memory that combines experience, practice, and replicability.[1]

The African cuisines that we encounter today express history and a blending of local ecologies and public cultures. Cooking displays itself in the elaborate political structures of empire as well as free cultural interchange between neighbors, mothers, and daughters, and among social classes within villages and across larger cultures and geographies. African cuisines were and are not simply the result of what outsiders brought, but the formative imperial experiences of political history in Mali, Ethiopia, and Asante. Ideas about cooking and ingredients were more often intra-African sharing of ideas than, as some Western food scholars say, purely the result of European colonial and cultural domination in the late nineteenth and twentieth centuries.[2] African cooking showed distinctive qualities of technique and innovation in adapting new farm crops (maize, peppers), trade items (salt or seeds), and more perishable ingredients borrowed from neighbors (leafy vegetables, fruits, exotic spices).

Yet inequality and political domination do often appear in the culture of cooking. Pasta, French-style baguettes, and colonial curries appeared in African cities shortly after colonial rule arrived in the early 1900s. Distinctly African experiences, such as state formation in the West African forest-savanna in the seventeenth century and the Horn of Africa, and maritime empires at the Cape of Good Hope, promoted the processes of migration, the formation of class hierarchies, cultural overlays, and social borrowing that were fundamental to the emergence of the cuisines of Africa over time. The rise of global agricultural ecologies and systems of trade in the post-Columbian mercantile period brought Africa major foods like maize, cassava, tomatoes, and potatoes. African forms of these foods later spread back across the Atlantic and into Europe and Asia. The exchange between Europe and Africa that metastasized into formal colonial rule by European powers in the late nineteenth century also affected food and cooking in ways that expanded European food systems in Africa, but later also exposed Europeans themselves to African and Asian techniques of cooking and specific food preparations like curries, gumbos, porridge with green leafy relishes, and samosas.

Each of these actions of cultural exchange, especially ritual feast cycles within African societies and religious cultures, had implications for food and cooking. A dominant theme in these cases, as in many nonindustrial societies, was the idea that filling the belly and fulfilling the ritual require-ments of a meal constituted the cook's primary goal, rather than food as an aesthetic pleasure. In those African societies where everyone had the same diet regardless of station in life, food's preparation and consumption did not mark rank in power or social class. This pattern of what we might call culinary equality is what the well-known Cambridge anthropologist Jack Goody in the 1950s found among the LoDagaa and Gonja people of northern Ghana, leading him to conclude that Africans did not have a properly defined "cuisine," or what he called stratified food-consumption habits. In his view, while food in these African societies had ritual meaning, beyond meeting a biological need, it did not achieve a status of beauty in which people took pleasure in both variety and sophisticated ingredients and preparation. African cooking, he concluded rather narrowly, was mun-dane and unremarkable. He argued prematurely that cuisine occurred only in societies that were historically literate and used the plow as a primary tool of agriculture.[3] Goody's argument was impossibly narrow. Parts 2 and 3 of this book directly challenge this idea in describing a range of African culinary cultures and the elaborate ways that Africans (women in particu-lar) cooked and presented their own foods in a brilliant array of techniques and taste. Part 4 describes how these ideas have moved out of Africa and affected what people eat in the world as a whole.

Cuisine as a Historical Phenomenon

Webster's Third International Dictionary defines cuisine rather simply as "a manner of preparing food." One food scholar, however, makes the more nuanced and elegant observation that cuisines are more precisely "formal and symbolic ordering of culinary practice."[4] I want to expand that definition considerably by using cuisine to denote a distinct and coherent body of food preparations based upon one or more starchy staples, a set of spice combinations, complementary tastes, particular textures, iconic rituals, and a locally intelligible repertoire of meats, vegetables, and starchy textures. Most importantly, these elements form a structure of both preparation and presentation that makes a meal. In the modern developed world that sequence might consist of a hamburger, fries, and a Coke, while in Africa it might more likely mean a dish of pounded yam, fish, and garden egg (eggplant), or one of the many other combinations of a starch and sauce that show local ingredients and taste.

African cooking is a part of the universal human experience. Sauces, oils, herbs, and spices add flavor and texture to primary ingredients and remove food "from the state of nature and smother it in art."[5] A cuisine is thus a collection of dishes and meals that mark a distinct culture much in the way that styles of dress, music, or dance do. Cuisines behave like language families in that they are bodies of knowledge and practice "mutually intelligible" between several societies, locations, and ethnic identities.[6] People tend to know intrinsically what they consider food, its taste, and how to eat it—or what is not edible. For some, food means rice, and for others it means maize porridge. The taste, textures, and sequencing of peoples' food shows history, geography, and ideas shared within and between cultures. Moreover, the act of cooking is not merely a mechanical skill, but a special form of knowledge. Cuisinal concoction (in other words, cooking) is an accumulation of collective experience, experiment, and observation in the use of various forms of heat (dry heat, immersion in water, sautéing) that release sugar and transform carbohydrates and meat fibers into digestible form. Cooking and food preparation is an application of both knowledge and accumulated experience that has historically been a fundamentally oral skill, and one quite specific to women.

Tracing the origins and the character of African culinary history, and identifying African cuisines as products and reflections of African agricultural, cultural, and economic history, requires a breakdown of the idea of cuisine. What, in fact, is cuisine, as opposed to cooking or the simple idea of foodways? Sidney Mintz, the distinguished anthropologist of the Caribbean and of food commodities (sugar, coffee, tea, Coca-Cola), argues that cuisines

> are never the foods of a country, but the foods of a *place*. . . .
>
> . . . What makes a cuisine is not a set of recipes aggregated in a book, or a series of particular foods associated with a particular setting, but something more. I think a cuisine requires a population that eats that cuisine with sufficient frequency to consider themselves experts on it. They all believe, and *care* that they believe, that they know what it consists of, how it is made, and how it should taste. In short, a genuine cuisine has common social roots; it is the food of a community—albeit often a very large community.[7]

My argument in this book reflects my own sense of cuisine as a product of two factors: first, dominant political cultures, such as empires, including African ones; and second, cultural exchange (via trade, intermarriage, or religious conversion). These factors in terms of food and cooking include a history of ingredients, their procurement and use in cooking, styles of cooking, and also the social context of the presenting and consuming of cooked food. Meals consumed by Africans were both public (banquets or restaurants) or private (family or household) occasions in which preparing food and acquiring the right ingredients put in play a body of symbols, economic possibilities, and the political structures that underlay them. People ate all of this during a meal, whether they were Senegalese, Ugandan, or Sudanese, though they obviously did not dwell on deeper meanings with every mouthful.

With the notable exception of southern Ghana, the selling of food in public places, such as restaurants and market stalls, was a twentieth-century phenomenon in Africa, a much more recent development than elsewhere in the world. The Ethiopian feast described earlier is an example of food as ritual rather than as a commercial good. But Africa's contributions to world culture now are part of the international phenomenon of cooking in restaurants and homes throughout the world. How and when African woman's knowledge came to express itself in this way is part of the larger story of African history as world history.

This book distills bits of evidence from agronomy, archaeology, anthropology, ethnobotany, linguistics, and cultural history into a story of the history, geography, and styling of food in Africa. The consideration of taste, color, and texture—what scholars call hermeneutics—has mattered a great deal in this story. In many parts of Africa a meal was not a meal without the sensation of fullness in the belly produced by glutinous staples like pounded yam, maize porridge, rice, and millet—foods not well known in northern Europe or North America. These factors in African cooking and foodways have also changed over time with the inclusion of new materials and new ideas via Africa's global trade contacts, the forced migration of slavery, and the seeking by Africans of new lives in new places. Of course they adjust, but they also tend to bring their own ideas about foodstuffs and how to cook them edibly. While the story told here will acknowledge premodern African innovations in the production, processing, and presentation of what they eat, this book emphasizes the centrality of global contacts in framing Africa's foods in the last half millennium. African cooking shows the continent's cultures' unique engagements with neighbors and its place in the world, flanked by two oceans and the Mediterranean Sea, and containing its own landscapes of forest, desert, and savanna. And, of course, its cities.

How Distinctive Is the History of African Cookery?

Combinations of ingredients and structures of cooking are not carried in the genes, but come from historical experiences shared among peoples and across generations. Not all countries or nations have a distinctive "cuisine," though they sometimes try to invent them for political reasons.[8] Cuisine is a product of history, and a meal is a conjuncture of time, place, particular ingredients. It is the powerful act of cooking that draws the physical and sensory elements together. In Africa there are a number of obvious examples of cuisines—Ethiopia, southern Ghana, Senegalese, southern Nigeria, the Cape of Good Hope—that show such a meeting. In those places and cultures a type of cooking involves the layering of ideas, daily rituals of eating, ingredients, and methods of assembling foods for both public and private meals that transform cooking and food into what we then call a cuisine. "Culture began when the raw got cooked," as the historian Felipe Fernández-Armesto has said. Mutually intelligible traditions of cooking are like similar languages with which people can communicate across borders and between political groups that were otherwise in competition. These areas existed in places like the Nile Valley, along the Indian Ocean rim, and later in colonial kitchens where Africans cooked for European colonial employers in their homes or hotels.

Like its geology and its distinctive plants and animals, Africa's cooking exhibits regional character. But it also shows broad historical themes of continuity that we can also see in dress, music, and language. Restaurants in London's Covent Garden or Paris's Rive Gauche that claim an African cooking theme and cultural milieu more often than not have a hybrid menu that mixes a number of national cuisines and quite separate traditions of African cookery via signature dishes like Ghana's groundnut stew (with a rich peanut sauce), Senegal's *thiebou dienn* (rice and fish), and Ethiopia's *doro wet* (buttery, peppered chicken stew) that would never actually appear together in a kitchen in Africa. These new African restaurants cherry-pick dishes from around the continent rather than presenting the coherent cultural and historical settings behind a true cuisine. Few African cooks would recognize these dishes as having common elements of style or taste that would make them part of a thing called African cuisine. Ethiopian-Swedish chef Marcus Samuelsson learned his craft in Europe and America but has now studied African cooking styles around the continent to bring to his New York restaurant's creative menus. While African-inspired, those menus do not represent a single coherent cuisine that Africans ate in past times. My argument here is that there has not historically been such a cuisine, and that Africa in fact has produced a number of distinct cuisines that deserve recognition and celebration on their own terms.

If there is, however, a common theme that marks African cookery, it lies in African cooks' adaptation and indigenization of staples and ingredients collected from encounters with other world edible ecologies (for example, bananas, maize, cassava, Asian rice, capsicum peppers) and oceanic trade networks (the Indian Ocean, the Atlantic Rim, the Red Sea, the Persian Gulf) that contributed spices, herbs, and fruits to Africa's bowls, mortars, and cooking pots.

Structure and Key Themes of the Book

I have organized this book around themes and regional geographies of cookery in Africa. The first two chapters describe the basic local components available to African cooks in the two or three millennia before the current era, including the origins and genetic endowments of foodstuffs from Africa's ecology. Chapter 1 describes the distribution of starches and staples used as the base of Africa's cooking, especially the role of Africa's own staples of grains—rice, sorghum, millet, and teff. Chapter 2 looks at key staple foods borrowed from other world areas, like maize, cassava, bananas, and Asian rice, and considers the effect of the arrival of New World capsicum peppers, which "democratized" flavor in a remarkable transformation of African cooking. Hotness and spice became a trademark for many (though not all) types of African cooking.

Contact with world regions like the Indian Ocean rim (from at least the first century CE) and the Atlantic world (after 1500) brought many more challenges and opportunities that African cooks built into their stews, porridges, and breads until the eve of the twentieth century. At that point Africans began to adapt these local cuisines to even wider worlds. The pressures of European colonialism and colonial rule by the twentieth century often forced Africans to sacrifice variety and nutrition for empty calories and strategies of survival to endure the strain. They also began to add the exotic food habits of their rulers, just as the rulers began to adopt foods and ideas from their own colonies, including regions of Africa.

Parts 2 and 3 of this book examine the adaptation of African cooking to a new world in which Africans dealt with their role as subjects of colonies and as citizens of modern nations. Part 2 (chapters 3 and 4) describes one of Africa's most celebrated traditions of cooking, that of the Ethiopian highlands. Ethiopia, unlike most of Africa, did not endure colonial domination but built its own nation from a multiethnic empire—and food was a part of that process. Part 3 identifies other regions that have historically evolved distinctive and coherent cuisines: West Africa (chapter 5) and the central and southern African maize belt and maritime coasts (chapter 6). In those places cuisine was not so much the product of modern nations as of regions that shared common ecologies and histories.

Part 4 (chapter 7) traces the diffusion throughout the world of these African traditions of cooking in the era of North American slavery and the wider African diaspora in Latin America and the Caribbean, which influenced the European and American communities with whom Africans and their descendants interacted.

Readers should notice a number of interwoven themes about African cooking and culinary cultures. The first of these is the dynamism of African foods and the broad geographic reach of ingredients over the years 1500–2000. Another is the extent to which cooking constitutes a particular body of gendered knowledge—Africa's cooks, who built distinct repertoires of methods, processing, and presentation, were women. In African societies bachelors do cook—but not creatively and rarely well. Women, on the other hand, share their knowledge with one another and over generations via practice and oral transmission rather than in written form (at least until very recently). And again, food, like dress, music, and art, carried deeper structures of cultural identity that formed a marker of group coherence and solidarity—food helps define who we are.

Historical Sources on African Cooking

Each of the book's chapters highlights food and cooking as it appears in several types of primary historical sources. The raw materials of the historian's craft are correspondence, published observer accounts, or archaeological artifacts. But what are the raw materials of a study of cooking? One set of valuable primary sources is description by external observers. Travelers who tell us in written accounts about the exotic peoples and landscapes they encountered in Africa also faced the daily task of feeding themselves by "shooting for the pot" when on trek or relying on the hospitality of their hosts in villages or royal courts. Travelers away from royal courts or elsewhere on the continent fed themselves on trek or were fed at the homes and courts of local hosts. They only occasionally describe the preparation of the food they consumed. Food, like sex, was part of their experience but not the stuff that their Victorian or home mission audiences were interested in reading about. Modern audiences are very different.

Later, during the years of colonial rule in the early to mid-twentieth century, foreign residents, as anthropologists, colonial officials' wives, or travelers, watched what African women did hunkering around the compound hearth, moving about the kitchen, or standing at the mortar and pestle. These observations appear as cookbooks, informal lists of local dishes, or formal ethnographic studies by outsiders. In the case of imperial Ethiopia, for example, a key observer was the emperor's physician, from Russian Georgia, whose interests in nutrition, the emperor's and empress's health, and his own daily life allowed him to comment authoritatively on "les cordons bleus éthiopiennes" as well as the culinary preferences of the empress, who took a great interest in cooking and imperial hospitality. The historian gleans evidence from these sources carefully, since the writers were often short-term visitors who had little stomach for local flavors or techniques or had to work hard to tolerate foods that seemed exotic to their palettes and bellies.

Indigenous primary historical sources generated by African societies themselves are richly embedded in both oral and written forms of expression. They include fixed texts of oral traditions (such as the *Sundiata* epic of Mali), songs, or written religious texts (in Arabic, Hausa, or Ge'ez languages). Though these texts had other purposes and rarely comment on what people ate or how they prepared it, there are key exceptions. The Ethiopian imperial chronicler who described Queen Taytu's feast in 1887 showed her influence on his observations and described the food prepared for the feast in deep sensual detail of sights, smells, and taste. In *Sundiata* we learn that the young Sundiata, who would be the founder of the thirteenth-century Mali empire, displayed his physical prowess in pulling down a baobab tree so that his aged mother could gather the leaves for her cooking pot. Ifa *orike* (oral verses from southwest Nigeria) refer to food and crops, though they rarely offer the details of cookery.[9] But such insights preserved in indigenous historical sources on what Africans ate in the past and how they cooked are few and far between. For many, food was a matter of everyday life that no one bothered to record for posterity in the usual ways.

When all is said and done, the most revealing primary historical sources about cooking are, in fact, recipes. Recipes are a peculiar form of historical text, being rather awkward written summaries of oral knowledge always in some state of change and adjustment. The transcribing of that knowledge as a formal recipe by missionary women or a literate middle class violates, in a sense, their original flexible and creative oral character. Cooking practices are in fact gendered (female) historical oral transcripts that combine ingredients (spices, starchy staples, meats, beans/peas, fruits, leafy vegetables, roots), cooking techniques (boiling, frying, smoking, baking), and relishes of leafy vegetables that comprise dishes and a cuisine.

The young learned the art of cooking by listening and watching mothers, aunts, relatives, and neighbors. Recipes (written or oral) also imply accepted ideas about color, texture, and flavor combinations acceptable to cultural practice of both performance (cooking) and audience (those who eat a meal). Written recipes are strange things. They are intended for strangers to use in future times and, maybe, in foreign places. But for the historian they are valuable as markers of accumulated experience of those generations of cooks who have gone before.

Each of these recipes cited in chapters here, of course, is an attempt to duplicate a performance of the individual cook's skill and choices. A dish that appears in a oral demonstration to a young woman or in a fixed written recipe in a mission wives' or Peace Corps cookbook presents its own historical testimony of historical exchange, gathered wild local materials, agriculture, livestock husbandry, and, in some cases, male hunting. Oral communication maintains an important element of ambiguity that allows each cook to adjust or personalize the concoction across generations or time. The African American food writer and novelist Vertamae Smart-Grosvenor refers to the improvisational nature of African American cooking as "vibration cooking," reflecting the idea that measurements and combinations are not fixed texts but open to individual style.[10] That fact is doubtless true of all cooking, but Africans have maintained the oral form more thoroughly than other world areas. Yet, like jazz, what appears to be a free form was actually a deeper structure understood by the performer and by the informed within the audience. Its essential orality was carefully preserved and passed on via performance, practice, and the response of those who appreciated the final result and encouraged the cook to repeat the performance. A dish like groundnut stew with fish, chicken, or beef eventually evolved into different forms as its popularity spread around a number of West African cooking cultures.

The oral transcripts of women's accumulated experiences passed between neighbors and family—and between generations; African American writer Maya Angelou, for example, recalled this in her own life: "Mother brought out a recipe for Jollof rice that I had sent her from Ghana. She unfolded the letter and read, 'Cook about a pound of rice, sauté a couple or three onions in not too much cooking oil for a while, then put in three or four or five right-sized tomatoes.'"[11] Here, the recipe sent to the mother in America conveys the ambiguity of the oral version that the daughter observed in situ in Ghana. The subjectivity of "right size" and "not too much" suggests the role of the individual cook's judgment. I have included such a context in chapter 4 to contrast a published recipe (by a male author) with a woman's oral rendition to me, including her voicing of the sound "tuk tuk" made by the sauce itself as it simmered to a certain thickness.

Each chapter of this book thus contains a mix of ideas, images, and text from these primary sources: recipes, photos, engravings, and external observations. For each theme and region the book suggests dynamics of change as well as the deeper-seated structures of continuities of flavor, aroma, and texture. For each of these the historical evidence differs in its presentation of the sensual aspects (taste, sight, smell, and texture) and the process of concoction (boiling, baking, frying, smoking, and so on). The texts presented here consist, inevitably, of a number of foreign observations of what were, to the writers, exotic ingredients and methods. As historians we rely on outsiders to tell us what they saw, and what they ate. Local foods were, to these outsiders, strange, not mundane, and only maybe worthy of note. For each of these regions, moreover, there is a need to understand the dynamics of change in African regional cookery as well as the globalization of diet and foods through migration and commercialization. When did canned tomato paste become a required ingredient? Or a cube of chicken bouillon? Finally, the globalization of African culture, including the growth of a powerful cultural production in diaspora, appears here as a collective expression of distinctive types of African cuisine (Ethiopia) or an amalgam of New World culture and African culinary aesthetics (Caribbean, Creole, African American).

Bon appétit (or, as they say in Addis Ababa, "Good appetite").

Basic Ingredients

You are where you eat.

Africa's culinary history is written on both its natural and its human landscapes. What African women cook, serve to their households and their guests, offer to the public in ritual events, and proffer in public eating establishments reflects the genetic endowments of the continent's forest, grassland, marine, and riparian (riverside) ecologies, but it is also a presentation of African's ingenuity of ideas, ingredients, utensils, and sequence of eating. African cuisine is a plural and not a singular phenomenon: the cookery of the continent presents multiple personalities over space and over time. In some places, like Zanzibar and southern Nigeria, spices and pepper dominate the palette, while in South Africa's rural highveld the bulky blandness of local maize porridge offers a fullness that satisfies. What accounts for those differences? And the historian's question is: how has African cooking changed over time?

Part 1 of this volume identifies the raw materials of African cookery and their distribution across Africa's physical

FIGURE 1.1 Stirring the pot, nineteenth-century engraving. *Source: Theophilious Waldmeier, Erlenisse in Abessinien in den Jahren 1858 bis 1868 (Basel, 1869), 139*

landscape, as well as the historical chronology that brought particular concoctions into the everyday meals consumed by farmers, urbanites, traders, soldiers, kings, and herders. African cooks initially made their meals from ingredients and additives presented by nature where they lived, but over time their choices grew to incorporate those things that came via trade with neighbors and from across oceans or from other ecologies of forest, desert, and savanna. The end result was not only the mundane daily fare of subsistence but also the culturally elaborated cuisine of feasts, rituals, and elite classes.

CHAPTER ONE

Seasons and Seasonings

Africa's Geographic Endowments of the Edible

Rhythm of the Seasons

What Africans in the preindustrial era ate and when they ate it was, as in all cultures, a compromise between individual choice, cultural preference, and the vagaries of nature. Africa's physical environment and climate imposed on it a distinctive annual rhythm—that of the seasonal calendar of climate, movement, and human ritual. In the temperate zones of the world, growing seasons and cycles of life respond most directly to fluctuations in temperature, but Africa's rhythms of life reflect the availability of moisture, especially rainfall. The shifting of the seasonal rain-bearing turbulence on an annual basis sets a general two-part pattern of seasons, one wet and one dry. The movement of the turbulence over what is known as the Intertropical Convergence Zone brings rainfall to regions north of the equator from June to September (the northern summer) and then to regions south of the equator from December to March (the southern summer).

The onset of the rains has a remarkable visual effect. Within two weeks, brown and seemingly lifeless landscapes turn green as seeds germinate and chemical reactions within soils make nutrients available to plants. Livestock—cattle, goats, sheep, camels—regain their vigor and regenerate both sinew and fat. Camel's and cow's milk becomes more plentiful. In the dry season that follows, the wet-season fields ripen for harvest, pasture grasses shift into dormancy, and livestock (and their human minders) migrate to pasture nearer permanent water sources. Where the equator crosses near the Tanzania/Kenya border, this seasonal change brings one of the planet's most dramatic effects, the great annual seasonal migration of wildlife in the Serengeti Plain. As rainfall moves with the season, grazing wildlife—wildebeest, impala, kudu, gerenuk—and the carnivores that follow their prey move north to seasonal pastures in the summer and back south at the end of the rains when the pasture itself retreats into dormancy. For pastoral people like the Masai in East Africa, the Fulani in West Africa, and the Herero in the southwest, it is young men who follow their cattle's seasonal needs. For the Somali and the Afar in the Horn of Africa, it is the movement of their camels and goats that motivates those annual rhythms.

Africa's sharp contrast between wet and dry seasons is the most unforgiving of any continent, and the seasons have imposed on many African societies a harsh "hungry season" that runs from the end of the rains until the fall harvest. Stocks of stored grain and tubers dwindle, and households often turn to collecting wild plant foods or insects or rely on hunting for protein or saleable meat. Some of those foods of seasonal scarcity now paradoxically appear in modern cookbooks as delicacies.[1]

At opposite ends of the continent, in areas like South Africa's Cape and northern Algeria, a wetter and more temperate Mediterranean climate prevails, making wine, citrus, and grain production possible. European settlers were attracted to these areas, which also provided both markets and cheap local labor.

Why did certain foods evolve in certain places? At least part of the answer is the seasonal availability of certain foods and local solutions to the problem of what people ate and when. In the 1930s, British anthropologist Audrey Richards recorded the diet and foodways of the Bemba people of Northern Rhodesia (Zambia). Her work showed clearly that what African people ate—and what African women cooked—changed radically through the year depending on the patterns of rain, movements of livestock, and Africa's peculiar shifts from wet to dry as the seasons changed. As a young woman anthropologist in a professional field dominated by men, Richards began to explore an unusual approach to social anthropology: she first observed women as the managers of nutrition and then tried to understand cooking itself. Her book *Land, Labour, and Diet in Northern Rhodesia* was to become a classic in social anthropology as a whole and in the field of food studies in particular. Her description of the seasonality of food in that era is an important primary historical document produced by a colonial government attempting to understand the material culture of its colonial subjects.

It also reflects a seasonal rhythm lost in an industrialized world where supermarkets homogenize the annual cycle. Her findings are presented in table 1.1.

TABLE 1.1 SEASONALITY OF FOODS, BEMBA (ZAMBIA)

	Wet Weather			Cold Weather				Hot Weather			Wet Weather	
	Jan.	Feb.	Mar.	Apr.	May	June	July	Aug.	Sep.	Oct.	Nov.	Dec.
Gardens												
Millet				------	xxxx	xxxx	xxxx	xxxx	xxxx	xxxx	------	------
Maize			------	xxxx	xx--							
Kaffir corn					------	xxxx	xx					
Curcubits	xx	xxxx	xxxx	----								
Groundnuts				---	xxxx	xxxx	xxxx	xxxx	xxxx	------	------	
Legumes (fresh)		---xx	xxxx	xxxx	xxxx	xx---						
Legume leaves		---	xxxx	xxxx	xxxx	xxxx	xxxx	xx---				
Sweet potatoes				xxxx	xxxx	xxxx	xxxx	xxxx	xxxx	xxxx		
Bush												
Wild spinaches					------	xxxx	xxxx	xxxx	xxxx	------		
Mushrooms	xxxx	xx									------	xxxx
Orchids						---	xxxx	xxxx	--			
Fruit												
Meat								xxxx	xxxx	xxxx		
Fish	------			xxxx	xxxx		xx	xxxx	xxxx	----	xxxx	xx
Caterpillars	xxxx	------	------	------						------	xxxx	xxxx
Ants etc.									xxxx	xxxx		
Honey				xxxx	xxxx	xxxx	xxxx			xxxx	xx	

xxxxxx   supplies plentiful
------   supplies scarce

The lines indicate the length of time the average Bemba uses each foodstuff, either because it ripens during that particular month; or, in the case of game and fish, can be trapped then; or because he has only planted sufficient for the supply to last for a given number of months. For instance, maize could be made to last to twelve months of the year, but the ordinary Bemba only grows enough to use it fresh during two, and therefore this period only is shown as a line. Dried relishes are not shown. Caterpillars swarm at different periods in different districts and hence are marked from November to April.

Note, in the table, the preharvest scarcities of the January–March period in central Africa (what was to become northern Zambia). Richards notes the increased consumption during those months of collected wild but edible foodstuffs like caterpillars, ants, and honey. She observes:

In effect the people have a harvest season from May to September in which millet, beer, green food, ground-nuts, pulses are plentiful, and meat in some areas, and the diet is therefore ample and probably varied. This is followed by a dry season (October–November) in which millet and beer are still available but green vegetables scarce or non-existent. The wild fruits are much liked, but only for about a month or six weeks. Meat and fish are obtainable in these months also, but only in certain districts. At the beginning of the rains, November and December, the diet changes. Millet is already beginning to be short, and mushrooms and caterpillars are the main standby as additional relishes. In the late rains millet is practically non-obtainable, and gourds and occasional maize cobs are often the only available foods. Thus the diet changes completely in composition from one season to another.[2]

Though Richards gives us an accurate rendering of what she observed in landlocked central Africa, this description of Bemba diet offers little insight into cookery or the culinary imagination at other times and places in Africa. Would that we had such rich descriptions for other areas as well.

As mentioned earlier, both the seasonal climate and the political calendar of Africa's great empires determined in many ways what Africans ate in a particular place. The seasonality of moisture in the African climate affected not only the abundance and variety of food, but also disease, migration of humans and livestock, the timing of military campaigns, and ritual cycles of politics and religion. Kings and their subjects feasted at harvest time, but tightened their belts during the hungry season. Each of these actions by rulers or by citizens, especially the ritual feast cycle, had implications for food and cookery. Most tropical diseases, whether epidemic or endemic, were also seasonal events. Military states, like the Zulu, generally organized raids and large military campaigns during the dry season, when their soldiers were free from agricultural work and enemy harvests were in storage. Roaming armies of young men fought their rivals but also foraged among the enemy village granaries and corrals. In many cases, camps of women followed the armies to cook the spoils on campfires, a pattern of mobility that encouraged simplicity of both tools and ingredients.

Other African societies adapted to seasonality in ways that reflected a food system with meat or fish as a greater part of the mix than in the Bemba diet that Richards describes. The historian Diana Wylie, working from accounts of contemporary observers, has described the nineteenth-century Zulu diet. A clear rhythm of seasonality is evident in her reconstruction, but with the subtle differences of a society where cattle were a more important symbolic and nutritional focus than in Richards's Bembaland:

> The staples of an ordinary nineteenth-century Zulu diet were fermented milk, cereals boiled as porridge, and cultivated vegetables, eaten twice daily, first after milking and then before sunset. Zulus spoke of solid and watery foods. People stored their food by fermenting in the form of thick sour milk (*amasi*) and sorghum beer. Sour milk—extraordinarily rich in cream where the cattle grazed on long grass, but low in yield after the calves sucked—was ideally the basis of each of the two meals eaten daily. Only children drank fresh milk. Beer was a seasonal delight, the postharvest reward for a good season's crops. People ate boiled or roasted maize every day, supplemented by pumpkins, beans, taro root, and sweet potatoes. The consistency of the porridges depended mainly on how coarsely the grain was ground and for how long it was boiled. When the grain and vegetable supply ran short in late winter and early spring, that is, between June and August, people scoured the bush for wild spinaches (*imifino*), gathering greens perhaps three or four times a week in the spring, drying some leaves for winter meals when they might have to ration themselves to one daily meal. While looking for *imifino*, they could also hunt for bitter herbs to help their stomachs accommodate the radical shifts in diet brought by the changing seasons. Meat was rarely served. . . . By-products of a slaughtered beast produced highly prized dishes of fatty dumplings and sausages and congealed blood. Only at such times and few others did nondairy animal fat enter Zulu diet.[3]

Although the Bemba diet of the 1930s and the nineteenth-century Zulu food culture seem unremarkable and monotonous compared to that of Cape Town and the East African coastal ports (see chapter 6), both Bemba and Zulu diets were then undergoing change through contact with the wider world of neighboring people, economic forces, and European intruders. And though southern African societies like the Zulu and Bemba are quite different in cultural and economic terms, by the mid-nineteenth century their foods were more cosmopolitan than one might think. They included adopted New World plants like maize and groundnuts (although not yet cassava; see below). Both societies consumed maize as a vegetable snack on the cob in the milky green stage, but not yet as a rough milled flour used boiled in porridges. Millet (for Bemba) and sorghum (for Zulu) were the dominant grains historically, and as rural peoples not yet drawn into an urban orbit, both the Zulu and Bemba cooks also had access to a natural world of wild plants, game, and seasonal insects. Locusts, ants, and cater-pillars were treats that broke the seasonal monotony, as Richards recorded meticulously in her seasonal food chart. The rural diets depicted by Richards's pioneering study and Wylie's more recent one were distinct from an older maritime and cosmopolitan culinary culture of the coastal areas of the Indian Ocean and Atlantic Rim, where fish, fruit, and spicy curries with coconut milk brought a wide variety of flavors to local diets.

A Chronology of African Cuisine

Three distinct periods shaped the cookery of Africa in the twentieth cen-tury and first decade of the twenty-first. The regional systems of food types and cooking described in part 3 of this book were in one way or another the results of historical changes that brought together ingredients, particular oral knowledge, the practice of how to cook, what consumers expected, and, finally, culinary communities that came to recognize themselves as having a common cuisine. The three periods are described below.

Africa in the World, c. 1500 CE

Africa's culinary history begins with its edible palette of possibilities in in-gredients derived from hunting, gathering, agriculture, and herding. While Africa is now universally understood to be the place of humankind's origin, our knowledge of its agricultural history of food is more limited than that of other world areas. Although sub-Saharan Africa was home to three dis-tinct zones in which food production arose (the Sahel zone, tropical West Africa, and the Ethiopian highlands), Africa had fewer endowments than other parts of the world in genetic materials of plants and animals available for domestication. This is particularly true in the distribution of the fifty-six large-seeded grass species (the ancestors of wheat, barley, rice, and rye) that made up the raw material from which humans could domesticate cereals. West Asia, Europe, North Africa, and England had a total of thirty-three

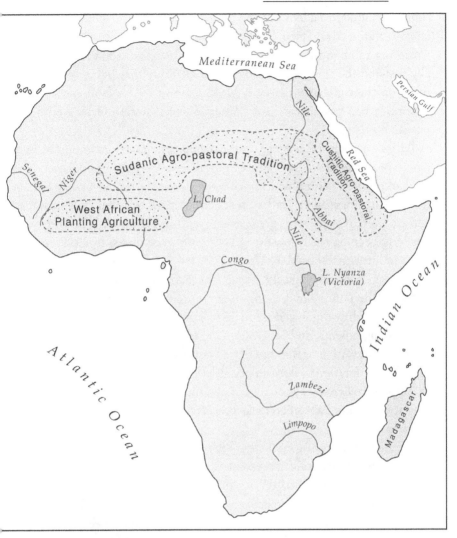

MAP 1.1 African agricultural innovation. *Map by Claudia K. Walters*

species; the Americas had eleven; and sub-Saharan Africa had only four. As for large domesticated mammals, Africa was the genetic homeland of only the Nile Valley's donkey, while the Fertile Crescent of Mesopotamia was home to four (goat, sheep, pig, and cow).[4]

A simple list of Africa's limited genetic endowments of the flora and fauna of food sources, however, belies the dynamism of Africa's wider physical and human geography. If Africa had fewer building blocks of food supply, its ability to adopt outside foods was its greatest skill. Ironically, of course, humankind itself had its earliest florescence in Africa, where gathering and hunting activities sustained human food sources and eventually fostered the skills in foraging and agriculture that humans took with them on their global expansion. More relevant for its food and culinary history, Africa has always been part of a global system of biological and human exchange.

Africa's globalization is not a new phenomenon, and its importation of new types of food was not an exception. Africa's human population, and its cooking pots, combined the continent's own peculiar initial gifts of nature with ingredients and culinary ideas of others that they absorbed and adapted, usually with great energy and imagination. The continent has long been on the receiving end of world trade in goods, ideas, and genetic endowments related to Africa's culinary larder. Interactions took place across penetrable ecological borders (the Sahara), along natural corridors of trade (the Nile Valley), along ocean currents (the Indian Ocean Rim), and along tightly organized trade networks (the Red Sea/Persian Gulf) of peoples, ingredients, and ideas about cooking. In more recent times (after 1500 CE), the Atlantic Rim has played perhaps the largest role as a result of the forced migration of African peoples to the New World along with their tropical ingredients and cookery ideas. These pathways enabled activities that at some times absorbed ideas peacefully and at other times took them by force.

Africa's culinary engagements with the wider world in the early pre-Atlantic period were sometimes subtle and often profound. When Europeans first arrived at the coasts of West Africa and East Africa before 1500, they found a huge range of "foreign" crops and fruits already well adopted by African farmers and cooks. Each of these geographic connections flavored African cookery, influencing the evolution of distinctive African cuisines in differing regions. Each chapter of this book describes a cornucopia of ingredients that cooks adapted, filtered, and adjusted to make regional cuisines marked by their own culinary philosophies and the iconic dishes that are part of their identity. Transcripts of this accumulated and dynamic knowledge—otherwise called recipes—demonstrate the history of African cookery as a form of distinctive technical and aesthetic practice. From the Mediterranean world (including Egypt) Africa received citrus fruits, chickpeas, wheat, barley, onions (including garlic and shallots), Asiatic rice, dates, goats, sheep, and cattle, either from across the Sahara or via the Nile

Valley. Other Mediterranean foods included figs, melons, pomegranates, and cucumbers. From the Indian Ocean and Asian connections had come Asian yam, coconuts, mangoes, ginger, bananas, and rice (see chapter 2). Some of these had even originated in Africa and returned in new forms.[5] Contacts with the monsoonal trade of the Red Sea and Persian Gulf brought coconut palms, sugarcane, cloves, cocoyams, and, indirectly, maize.

Africa also accepted certain cooking techniques, such as brewing coffee from Yemen and steaming couscous from North Africa, but rejected others, such as cooking rice in fat, typical of Arab and Spanish cookery. The result was a smorgasbord of possible ingredients, techniques, and taste combinations from which African farmers and cooks selected and innovated as ecological, political, and economic factors brought cultural and aesthetic adaptations of many kinds.

The Columbian Circulation as Culinary Benchmark, 1500–1900

Dynamic forces were already at play when European maritime and naval technology in the fifteenth century expanded trade across global oceans and transformed forever humankind's cooking larder. Over time there was much to choose from and lots of ways to cook it. Africa's farmers and its cooks were active participants in that moveable feast. Food writer Linda Civitello, in an evocative but misleading image, refers to the opening of the Atlantic world in the late fifteenth century as "the collision of Eastern and Western Hemispheres." Environmental historian Alfred Crosby coined the term "Columbian Exchange," which stuck in the literature and public vocabulary but implies that the exchange was ordered and bilateral.[6] But it was not so much a European-led event as it was a process, the initiation of a long-term swirl of material culture on a colossal scale, with Africa front and center in the biological buffet that resulted.

The Atlantic biological circulation involved a number of key foods from the New World, Africa, the Mediterranean, Europe, Asia, and the Pacific, as shown in the lists in table 1.2. These lists, and others, of Columbian Exchange materials are somewhat misleading in that they distort the swirls, eddies, and recirculation of genetic materials, the lumpy transfer of knowledge between cultural groups and economic classes, and Africans' role as sources, consumers, and adopters overall. This is particularly true of human agency and intellect, the role of African farmers and cooks. In fact, until the 1830s the Atlantic exchange brought three to four times more Africans to the New World (as captives) than Europeans, and the ships carrying those

TABLE 1.2 THE ATLANTIC CIRCULATION (COLUMBIAN EXCHANGE)

Foods from the New World to Africa

Animals	Vegetables/Spices	Grains, Legumes	Fruits
turkey	allspice	kidney bean	avocado
muscovy duck	green beans	navy bean	cacao
	soy beans	maize	papaya
	capsicum (peppers)	cassava (manioc)	pineapple
	pumpkins	peanut (groundnut)	tomato
	potatoes (Irish)		guava
	potatoes (sweet)		
	sunflower		

Foods from Africa (including the Mediterranean) to the New World

Animals	Vegetables/Spices	Grains, Legumes	Fruits
donkey	cowpeas (black-eyed peas)	sorghum	watermelon
	okra	millet	lemon
	coffee	African rice	orange
	malagueta pepper (grains of paradise)	sugarcane	banana (via Asia)
	yam	teff	
	olive		

Africans often brought African domesticated food crops with them, including rice, okra, watermelon, yams, and black-eyed peas.[7] Perhaps more importantly, those African captives brought the knowledge of tropical cultivation, food preparation, and medicine to the New World. Geographer Judith Carney makes this point effectively regarding rice:

> The development of rice culture in the Americas required more that the movement of seeds across the Atlantic. In Virginia rice was planted and discarded as a potential export crop by whites because cultivation with rainfall was low yielding and European milling methods could not produce a whole-grained product. In the Carolina colony blacks implemented another way of growing rice, in high-yielding wetland environments, and introduced the mortar and pestle for milling. Rice cultivation in the Americas depended on the diffusion of an entire cultural system, from production to consumption.[8]

This last point (about consumption) points directly to the issue of cookery, where Africa's contribution to the New World's methods of cooking rice has been profound, continuing right into the twenty-first century. Africa was thus instrumental in shaping how the New World cooks—then and now (see also chapter 7).

Africa's Colonial Period in Culinary Practice

Africa's formal colonial experience stretched from roughly 1885 through the mid-1970s, an era when European powers ruled colonies in sub-Saharan and North Africa. Afro-European cultural and economic interaction in places like Angola, Mozambique, and South Africa and along the West African coast, however, had been long established during the mercantile age (roughly 1500–1850) that preceded formal colonial rule. While the impact of Europe on Africa in the colonial era was profound in terms of language, the creation of economic dependency, and the formation of new national identities, the precise effect of these factors on food and cookery is less well understood.

Food writer Linda Civitello asserts rather recklessly that "much of modern African cuisine is the colonial cuisine that Europeans forced on Africa in the nineteenth century." This is why, she says, "there are croissants and baguettes in Ivory Coast in West Africa, spaghetti in Ethiopia and Eritrea on the east, and curry and chutney in British east and west Africa."[9] Her observations are true of elite urban culture, formal restaurants, and expatriate homes perched in elite urban neighborhoods in postcolonial Africa, and perhaps what one can buy in a modern supermarket in Addis Ababa or Ouagadougou. But the far more salient reality was not the introduction of the French baguette, but the colonial period's role in the expansion of scale of trade, centralization of power, and the emergence of national political life, which influenced Africa's kitchens and food stalls in a global marketplace of new ingredients, industrial foods, and consumer tastes for Coca-Cola, Uncle Ben's rice, and Maggi broth cubes.

But the movement of ideas about cooking, class preferences for wheat bread, sweets, and industrialized canned goods flowed in two directions, not just one. Food historian Filipe Fernández-Armesto argues for a very different view of the culinary effects of imperialism:

> No source of influence in cookery . . . has exceeded imperialism. Empires can sometimes be powerful enough to enforce a metropolitan taste on a peripheral area, and they usually promote human migration and colonization. These in turn transmit eating habits alongside other aspects of culture, or reeducate the

palates of expatriates who become vectors of new tastes when they return home. The tides of empire run in two directions: first the flow outwards from an imperial center creates metropolitan diversity and "frontier" cultures—cuisines of miscegenation—at the edges of empires. Then the ebb of imperial retreat carries home colonists with exotically acclimatized palates and releases the forces of "countercolonization," dappling the former imperial heartlands with enclaves of sometimes subject peoples, who carry their cuisines with them.[10]

Fernández-Armesto has in mind more than the twentieth-century European colonization of Africa; he also includes the Ottoman Turks, the Dutch in the East Indies, imperial China, and the Islamic effects on the Mediterranean, among others. In this book it will also become evident that empires, states, and religious movements in Africa like Ethiopia, Asante, Oyo, and Benin promoted a mix of cookery, ideas, ingredients, and forms of consumption of particular Africa-based cuisines.

The influence of colonial rule on Africa did not involve merely formal political domination; it also included the work of missionaries, the establishment of schools, and the circulation of different peoples in colonial society. The effect in food and cooking, however, was not a transfer in toto, but a more subtle and layered infusion into and out of different parts of the non-Western world. So a far more fundamental measure of the effects of European colonial rule on food and cooking is in the unintended consequences by which ingredients, cooks, and ideas circulated under the radar of formal programs like mission schools and teacher training. Here is an example of gendered communication about cookery during the Jeanes School Program in Kenya colony of the 1920s and 1930s, a program that trained male teachers but also asked wives to join in the colonial effort by attending classes in sewing, gardening, and proper hospitality. The actual result was an informal exchange of ideas about cooking and cuisine that the colonial officials had not planned, as Zipporah M'Mwirichai, a wife of one of the male participant teachers from central Kenya in the 1930s, recalled:

> I was always nervous sitting in those classes [in European hospitality] because I did not follow what we were learning. I was not able to understand the teacher. I always waited for the free time or the weekend to ask other women to show me how to do the sewing or to explain to me what the teacher had said. This way, I

was able to learn faster. What I most liked was cooking, but not the *mzungu* [white European] foods. I wanted to know how the other women from different parts of the country cooked their foods, and I also showed them how we cooked our foods. By the time we were through with the training, I could cook rice, fry my foods with onions, cook *ugali* [maize porridge], and fish and chicken. Some women learnt my way of mixing maize and beans to make [a] family meal. I learnt more things by visiting the women in the village than I learnt from those classrooms. I had trouble keeping measurements of flour, sugar and butter when we were taught to make cakes. One evening while we practiced our baking, we figured out how to estimate the measurement by using our hands and eyes, not spoons. The *mzungu* teaching was full of mathematics, we wanted simple things.[11]

This recollection suggests two of the arguments made in this book. First, it indicates the importance of the contact between different food cultures (e.g., maize-based, rice-based) and language groups (e.g., Kikuyu, Luo, Swahili), in this case within the Kenya colony. Second, it provides illuminating testimony of the oral nature of the transfer of knowledge about types of food and types of cooking as dynamic and active—the "vibration" cooking described by American Vertamae Smart-Grosvenor.[12] Measurements, ingredients, and innovation by consensus among women took place as an active process alongside emerging ideas of what it meant to be Kenyan, Nigerian, or Ghanaian.

The emergence of colonial cuisines was a common occurrence in Africa and in other world regions like British India, Dutch Indonesia, and French Algeria. From these colonial collisions came hybrid dishes—Scottish kedgeree (salmon and rice), Cape bobotie (ground lamb baked in a béchamel cream sauce), or Algerian ratatouille (with couscous)—using ingredients that moved between colonial and local kitchens. These new concoctions had new flavors, colors, and tropical pizzazz. Anthropologist Arjun Appadurai makes the case for the emergence of an "Indian" cuisine as a culinary consensus that emerged "because of, rather than despite, the increasing articulation of regional and ethnic cuisines." He argues that in the pulsating ideas about cultural identity in emergent nations like Kenya or India, cosmopolitan cultures in urban areas interacted "dialectically" with local parochial expressions rather than simply mixing willy-nilly. "Especially in culinary matters," he asserts, "the melting pot is a myth."[13] What he means in plainer language is that the emergence of a new type of cookery was not a random mixing of many types but an interaction of flavors, textures, and ingredients that reflected power relations, encounters between social classes, and the creation of a middle class that cooked in multiple identities. This phenomenon, visible in India in the post–World War II era, affected African cookery in the 1980s and continues today in cosmopolitan areas like London, Washington, Paris, and Houston, where African-themed restaurants are becoming common.

A similar view holds that there are three types of imperial—as distinct from colonial—cuisines: (1) cuisines of the colonized areas themselves, which sweep ingredients, styles, and dishes from all over the regions of conquest into a central menu; (2) colonial cookery, which juxtaposes the food of elite colonists from the home country with the styles of local cooks and concubines; and (3) the "counter-colonial" effect, whereby the food culture of the imperial country is exposed to the cookery and foods of the subject people when the latter migrate to the imperial center.[14] The first type is exemplified by the Indian cuisine most visible in the cookbooks of Madhur Jaffrey, the actress whose books popularized Indian cooking across the West and India itself. A second type, similar though less globally visible, can be seen in Kenya, Malawi, and Nigerian national cookbooks compiled by expatriate women.[15] The third type is certainly visible in the Indonesian *rijsttafel* of Amsterdam, Indian takeaway shops in London and Manchester, or the Vietnamese restaurants of Paris or Everett, Massachusetts.

Africa's influence in Europe is a far more recent phenomenon of the postcolonial period than South Asian or Southeast Asian cooking or even the migration of Tex-Mex cuisine to Europe via America. The most visible examples of African cuisine are Ethiopian restaurants, which appeared in most major cities of Europe and North America in the 1980s. Yet cookery and a recognizable cuisine from Europe's former African colonies, like Nigeria, Cameroon, or Angola, is not yet a common part of the cosmopolitan restaurant scene. Why?

One possible reason is that the effect of the colonial experience in Africa differed substantially from that in India, Vietnam, or Indonesia. In the case of Asian cuisine, the category of "curry" associated with a blend of Indian Ocean spices used in meat and vegetable stews and using sweet and hot accompaniments of chutneys and pickles is a concoction of the Indian colonial experience, rather than imported wholly from local Indian traditions.

In East Africa, colonial curry dishes spread to the coast and inland towns more than British cookery did; samosas are much more common than Cornish pasties in East Africa. The curries found in the coastal cuisines of eastern and southern Africa are versions of the hybrid dishes assembled by the British and Indian armies and adapted among trading communities along the Indian Ocean rim. In places like Lamu, Malindi (in Kenya), or Maputo (in Mozambique), dishes like goat curry, curried black-eyed beans, and curried chicken are a regular feature of local menus, but more for a commercial audience than in the home cooking of Kenyan workers or the Mozambiquan women who process cashew nuts in a local factory. These dishes and taste/texture combinations are the results of historical interactions between trade of spices and trading communities and local cooks who knew how to prepare them.

Cooks in colonial households occupied a middle ground between local knowledge and the culinary expectations of their employers. Those connections link colonial Africa to a wider geography of colonial settings more than to Europe itself. For example, food writer Harvey Day's multivolume cookbook *Curries of India* includes dishes from Indonesia, Iran, Turkey, Malaya, and Thailand under the category of curry.[16] *The Malawi Cook Book,* published in 1979, is a compilation of recipes by three British expatriate women that includes sections on soups, fish, edible insects, meats, chicken, salads, desserts, and household hints. We know little about these women themselves, but their cookbook tells us something about the culinary world they came from and the one they came to inhabit. Its recipes include a full range of the culinary geography of the British empire: Irish stew, chicken Maryland, Assamese fish curry, kedgeree, *mtedza* (groundnut) chicken, and a wild poultry dish called duck hartebeeste.[17] Unlike these colonial culinary cultures, however, African cookery's influence has taken place less in the public sphere of the upscale urban restaurant than in the daily cookery of the Caribbean, southern United States, and Latin America.

Africa's cookery, or more properly cookeries, evolved historically as the product of a lively stew of culture, place, and migration within a wider world of politics, power, and human interaction. Africa's cooks were among the more subtle intermediaries of those dynamics. Even though, as women, they were marginal to formal politics at the regional, national, and household levels, they were the custodians of an oral culture of concoction that drew on local and exotic ingredients and formulae to transform raw materials into cultural meaning in taste, texture, and aroma.

CHAPTER TWO

Staples, Starches, and the Heat of Atlantic Circulation

> Starch is the source of energy which has supplied most people for recorded history, but it is inefficient until it is cooked. Heat disintegrates it, releasing sugar which all starch contains. At the same time dry heat turns dextrins in starch brown, imparting the comforting look we associate with cooked food.
>
> —Felipe Fernández-Armesto, *Food: A History*

> Bemba, after leaving their country to work in urban areas in the south, say they find it difficult to adjust themselves to the maize flour "mealie meal" they are given there. One old man probably too fixed in his gastric habits to become adapted to town life said, "Yes, first I ate through one bag of [maize] flour and then a second. Then at last I said, 'Well, there it is! There is no food to be found among the Europeans.'"
>
> —Audrey Richards, *Land, Labour, and Diet in Northern Rhodesia*

THIS CHAPTER sets the foundation of African regional cuisines and foodways by describing the historical geography of starch, a seemingly mundane element of what African people eat, now and in the past. The epigraphs above illustrate two ways of understanding that fundamental part of cooking. The Bemba man quoted by anthropologist Audrey Richards in the late 1930s concisely expressed a fundamental fact that distinguishes human food and cookery from mere chemistry: starchy staples in most cultures are based in the concept of fullness, what it feels like to have "eaten." All cultures have their chosen starches: the middle-class North American "meat and potatoes" diet, Asian cuisines' preference for rice over wheat bread, the Central American preference for maize. African cuisines and cookery follow a well-marked geography of starchy staples like rice, cassava, maize, plantain, and yam. That geography includes not only the list of available grains (maize, rice, sorghum, millet), and root crops (yams, cassava, cocoyam), but also cultural preferences for what constitutes a proper and filling meal, based more on the texture of a particular glutinous starch than on its taste, and far more than on a meal's meat, fish, vegetable, or spice components. Even in areas that provide a choice of starchy staples, local culinary cultures have strong preferences for a particular type. For example, Ghanaians typically prefer *fufu* made from pounded yam, while in areas like southern Nigeria and western Congo many prefer fufu made from cassava, plantain, rice, or a mixture of these.[1] These choices reflect the history of ecology, cultural geography, and changes in individual tastes over time.

Starchy staples usually offer calories and variation of texture, but actually little in the way of taste. Starches are . . . bland. Yet they provide an essential factor of texture, shape, and bulk that frames other components of a meal and is in fact the defining feature of the culinary culture. Depending on the culture, it may be the stickiness of rice (East, Southeast, and South Asia), or the yeastiness of wheat bread (Europe), or the heavy starchiness of potatoes (Latin and North America), or the gritsy texture of maize porridge (northern Italy, Serbia, Eastern and Southern Africa) that makes a meal.

Africa historically has embraced a number of starchy staples, though their historical geography reflects innovation in endemic African crops: it was African rice, or yam, or sorghum, versus starchy staples adopted and embraced from other world areas, such as maize and cassava (New World), *Oryza sativa* (Asian rice), or plantains/bananas (Southeast Asia, Indonesia), that African farmers quickly adapted to local farm ecologies. African cooks quickly followed the farmers' lead in incorporating new starches. We may never know whether it was the farmer or the cook who played the larger role in choosing the new foods to grow. But a study of cuisine is about the end results of the labors of farmers, herders, gatherers, and cooks.

The Native American maize dish called grits is a peculiar lesson about African cooking and its history. Native American cooks routinely soaked their maize in an alkaline wood-ash solution to remove the hull, a process called *nixtamalization*. The lye-soaked maize kernels then have the more common name of hominy.[2] Hominy ground and then boiled became the iconic American dish called grits. African cooks, by contrast, never adopted the making of hominy, preferring to grind and boil their maize into the dish that Italians called polenta, or what Americans would call cornmeal mush (see chapter 6). Here was one cooking technique that did not move with its starch. It raises a perplexing question we might not be able to answer. African cooks had learned soaking for cassava and using wood ash, but why did they not adopt that for maize?

African Grains: Millet, Sorghum, and Teff

The simplicity of the following recipe may mask much deeper currents of history and human action.

Vuswa bya nwa-huva (Shangaan Millet Porridge)—South Africa

750 ml water
1 liter millet flour

Pour 625 ml water into a small bucket. Add 750 ml millet flour, stir, and leave to ferment overnight. Bring 125 ml water to boil, add fermented mixture, and cook for 10–15 minutes. Add 250 ml millet flour and cook for 15 minutes.[3]

Flour and water (and maybe a bit of salt) are as fundamental to cooking as one can imagine.

Three indigenous African grain crops—millet, sorghum, and teff—made the transition from wild grasses to domesticated food at the hands of Africans who collected seed grains of local wild grasses as food, planted the best of those grains as seed, and continued over generations to select from those domesticated grains the characteristics that best suited their tastes and farm ecologies.

Language tells us a great deal about the history of food and cooking in Africa, where borrowings and invention of nouns and verbs referring to agriculture can be used to reconstruct the early history of grains in Africa. UCLA historian Christopher Ehret has been a pioneer in using grains as a measure of Africa's innovations in agriculture. His complex but intriguing studies posit three major African regions where historical innovations in food grain occurred. From these areas came key grain staples, such as sorghum and millet, that spread to the diets and emerging cuisines of the Mediterranean, India, Korea, Japan, and China well before 2000 BCE.[4] In those world areas sorghum and millet were important for local food ecologies and climatic regions where rice or wheat did not grow, especially before maize's arrival around 1500 CE from the New World. These African grains were particularly important because their domestication in Africa gave them selected traits of drought resistance and storability, and because they provided a rich source of B vitamins. Whole grains of sorghum contain 12 percent protein starch (equal to wheat), 4 percent fat, and 4 percent minerals, a vital mix to sustain humans. These African sorghums and millets spread eventually to Asia and southern Europe as basic parts of the diet of Venice, India, and Ming China.

Other African grains stayed closer to home. African millets and millet-like cereals include small-grain types: finger millet (*Eleusine coracana*), pearl millet (*Pennisetum glaucum*) and endemic African cereals, fonio (*Digitaria exilis*) from West Africa, and teff (*Eragrostis tef*) from the Ethiopian highlands. These grains are especially nutritious because their small size means that the entire grain is consumed, unlike wheat or rice, which humans often process to remove their bran. African grains offer sources of protein, iron, and calcium. Moreover, their tiny size means the small space between grains allows little oxygen for insect pests and mold to survive and propagate, so that that they can be stored for a long period without damage. In humid Africa's climate zones, this was a major advantage. After all, storage was the stage between the farmer's field and the cook's fire.

Both sorghum and millet were also important in Africa for the production of alcohol in the form of beer and spirits. Ironically, sorghum's greatest influence in Africa is in places where the influence of Islam and its proscription against alcohol is greatest: Egypt, Sudan, eastern and northeastern Ethiopia, northern Nigeria, and the Sahelian countries of Niger, Mali, Chad, and Burkina Faso.[5] In many of these areas, pre-Islamic and syncretic religious practice recognized the value of beer, which was fermented grain consumed as food. Beer was tolerated even after the coming of Islam. Later, distilled spirits, which reduced the grain to almost pure alcohol, proved socially, if not nutritionally, important.[6] Nevertheless, in some areas of Africa the spread or revitalization of Islam, under which alcohol is nominally forbidden, brought a decline in the growing of certain grains, including sorghum, whose major use had been for producing beer and local "white lightning" alcoholic spirits.

FIGURE 2.1 Malawi sorghum fields. *Photo by author*

In the more arid ecologies of the Sahel and southern Africa, these grains were most of all the base of porridges or gruel served with meat or vegetable sauces to make a meal. Since sorghum, millet, and teff do not contain gluten, bread made from them is unleavened, and over the course of the twentieth century they lost favor with some African urban elite populations that had adopted wheat bread. Millet and sorghum porridges, made by boiling either grains or milled flour from those grains, were the key staples of most areas that at some point in the twentieth century switched to maize porridges under the local names of *ugali, miele pap, sadza, bidia, nsima,* or *upswa* (see chapter 6). Along the West African coast, along the escarpment of the Ethiopian highlands, and on the veld in southern Africa, sorghum quickly lost ground in the twentieth century to maize (see below) in the years after its arrival from the New World. Along the West African coast, for example, maize replaced sorghum in the 1700s within a century of that New World crop's arrival via the Atlantic trade. That transformation for the rest of Africa took place in the twentieth century.

In other places, however, the African staple foods had true staying power. In Ethiopia the indigenous grain teff is still the primary base for the local flat, spongy bread called injera. Figures II.1 and 4.5 indicate how little injera's preparation has changed over time.

African Rice

Jollof Rice (Sierra Leone Version)

3 cups long-grain rice
Meat or chicken stew
2 small cans tomato puree
Salt to taste
6 cups water

1. Prepare the meat or chicken stew.
2. Put water, salt, and tomato puree in a saucepan and bring to a boil.
3. Add half of the meat stew and bring to boil again.
4. Clean and wash rice. Add to the boiling liquid. Cover and boil rapidly stirring occasionally as the grains swell.
5. Cook until the rice is soft and the tomato and gravy are evenly distributed throughout.
6. Serve with the rest of the meat or chicken stew and some boiled cabbage or other green vegetable.[7]

This recipe from a 1970s cookbook assembled by a Sierra Leonean woman modifies an iconic West African dish by adopting canned tomato paste, but adheres to the more fundamental principle of Jollof rice as a one-pot dish later reinvented in New World Creole cuisine as the classic New Orleans jambalaya. In this dish it is the texture of the rice simmered in the sauce that defines its character, rather than the fish, meat, or chicken added according to the choice of the cook or what she happened to have on hand.

In the 1970s, botanical research on the world origins of domesticated rice reached a consensus that only two genetically distinct varieties existed: *Oryza sativa* from Asia and *Oryza glaberrima* from Africa. The African version appeared over a broad region of West Africa from Senegal to Liberia (and a small part of Ghana) along the coast and inland for more than a thousand miles to Lake Chad. In fact, African rice was probably domesticated first on the freshwater wetlands of the Niger River in Mali by 300 CE, from whence it spread to coastal estuaries and the rain-fed highland area between Guinea and Sierra Leone, where it became a staple crop well before the arrival of New World crops after 1500.[8]

It is no accident that the domestication of African rice and its spread as a food crop coincided with the history of the Mande people and the formation of great West African empires—Ghana, Mali, and Songhay—near the watersheds of the Niger and Senegal rivers. Early European travelers along the West African coast commented on the local foods and often mentioned rice prominently in particular cultural or ecological areas. Valentim Fernandes, a Portuguese traveler, noted in the period 1506–10 about the Gambian Mandinka (Mande) people who lived in the hinterland of the old Mali empire: "They eat rice, milk, and millet. . . . Poor people who don't have sweet potatoes [yams], have rice. . . . Their food is like that of the Wolof [of Senegal] except that they eat more rice and they have so much that they take it to sell and exchange, also [palm] wine, oil, and meat and other foodstuffs. Because this Mandinka land is very rich in food like rice and millet, etc."[9]

Rice therefore existed alongside other staple crops in Africa's culinary past. Fernandes also noted that along the tidal river floodplains of the Senegambia area "twice they sow and twice they harvest rice and millet etc., knowing they will harvest in April and in September, and when they gather in the rice then they sow yams and these they cultivate year round."[10] So while African diners may have preferred to eat rice, African farmers in this part of the continent hedged their bets by planting yams. African rice, however, also had a global appeal. By the middle of the eighteenth century, amateur naturalist Benjamin Vaughan of Hallowell, Maine, had collected and sent African rice to Thomas Jefferson in Virginia for experimental cultivation at his Monticello plantation. It failed there but eventually found a home in the wetlands of the South Carolina colony.

African rice, similar to other rice varieties, produces almost twice the protein content of wheat per unit of land and slightly more than maize.

Like other true grains, rice is rich in B vitamins and contains complex carbohydrates (starch and fiber).[11] The key to rice's nutrition and characteristics as a food, however, is its processing and cooking. Processing involves threshing, milling, and winnowing. Unlike the processing of the European grains wheat, rye, and oats for flour, the processing of rice is intended to produce grains without breakage. Women use a mortar and pestle with a skilled tapping and rolling motion that minimizes breakage of the individual grain and yields white rice by removing the bran and germ from the soft endosperm.[12]

The evolution and selection of the personality of West African rice as food, however, probably owed as much to the preferences of the women cooking it as to the characteristics of the plant itself or even the techniques of processing. West African cooking of rice favored a method that yielded separate grains of rice rather than the sticky clumps preferred in East Asian cooking. The rice would be boiled for ten to fifteen minutes, the excess water would be drained, and the pot would be removed from the heat and the grains allowed to absorb the remaining moisture. The crusty caramelized residue along the edges of the pot was a particularly popular snack for children; in Cuba (once African "red" rice had migrated across the Atlantic), the residue was known as *respa*. Judith Carney points out that this method not only yields separate grains but also would have saved the scarce wood that women had to collect from the historically wood-scarce landscapes of West Africa's middle Niger Valley.[13]

Carney also points out key distinctions between African—and African diaspora—methods for rice cookery and the cooking aesthetics of both Asia and the Mediterranean. Asian rice dishes, for example, use short-grain rice types because their sticky endosperms cling to one another and make eating with chopsticks easier. Mediterranean rice-cooking methods, such as Italian risotto, Arab pilafs, Persian rice, and Spanish paella, use oil or animal fats to sauté the rice grains prior to slow cooking. The cooks who practiced these methods favored short- to medium-grain varieties of rice, such as Italian arborio, which produce more individual grains and thus make use of spoons or forks preferable. But it was African women who developed the method of cooking rice (meaning long-grain rice) that came to be preferred by most New World cooks. Guatemalan *arroz precocido*, a rice grain variety preferred in Mexico and Central America, for example, is parboiled and resembles its African cousin—not suitable for chopsticks—since using the hands to scoop up the rice and sauce was efficient and more common in West Africa.

Carney's pioneering study *Black Rice* points out the African contribution to American cookery:

> Thus more than the cultivation of rice took root in the Americas. Rice culture embodied a sophisticated knowledge system that spanned field and kitchen, one that demanded understanding the diverse soil and water conditions of seed survival along with cooking methods for consumption. The transformation of rice from field grain to food depended on yet another knowledge system perfected by African women, that of milling cereal by hand. During the colonial period rice milling involved a skilled tapping motion for removing hulls without grain breakage. This female knowledge system served as the linchpin for the entire development of the Carolina rice economy. For without a means to mill rice, the crop could not be exported.[14]

The rice that reached African cooking pots in pre-Columbian times included not only the long-grain varieties, Asian types (*Oryza sativa*) that arrived via a number of trade networks, including the trans-Saharan trade with the Arab/Berber Mediterranean. Asian rice reached East Africa as early as the ninth century, when the Indonesian migrants who began to populate Madagascar brought Asian *sativa* rice with them. These adoptions included types that European visitors would describe as "as fine as that of Valencia and very white," suggesting an Asian type found at the Gold Coast that local traders had received indirectly via India.[15] Rice contacts and exchanges from Asia seem to have been continued into more recent times. A variety known as "Carolina gold" came to Sierra Leone in the 1840s with West Africans who liberated themselves from the slave ship *Amistad* and returned to their homeland after release from captivity in New Haven, Connecticut. That type was a white Asian variety that proved very popular with West Africans, who liked both its color and its high yield compared to the local *glaberrima* type.

Rice thus appears as a favorite African starch in various forms in areas such as Senegal, Sierra Leone, Liberia, and part of Ghana, while in many areas by the mid-twentieth century imported Uncle Ben's Converted Rice ("converted" means parboiled in the West African style) had already emerged as a postcolonial affectation in urbane diets and cookery. That result shows not just current globalization but also a longer history of cooks, farmers, and household diets.

Yams (*Dioscorea cayenensis* and *Dioscorea rotundata*)

The historical linguist Christopher Ehret tells us that what he calls the "West African planting agricultural tradition" had its foundation in the indigenous African yam before 5000 BCE. The homeland of this African root crop tradition was West Africa's woodland savanna zone, where natural forest clearings would have provided an ideal setting for yam cultivation.[16] In turn, the yam-fed concentration of population in otherwise carbohydrate-poor forest ecologies formed the basis of the powerful political and artistic cultural complexes of West Africa, such as Benin, Ife, and Akan (including the Asante people of Ghana). The yam, in fact, nurtured a set of related culinary traditions that raised the cooking of root crops to an art of the edible.

A native West African plant, the white yam grew in forest areas under the careful tutelage of farmers who built mounds, planted root cuttings, protected young tender tendrils, and hoed the mounds to keep down the weeds. Yams may be big, ranging from thirty to one hundred pounds, or they may be the size of New World sweet potatoes, which they resemble and are sometimes confused with (though the two root crops are genetically unrelated). They also contain from 15 to 40 percent starch, much less than cassava, another root crop common in West and Central Africa (see below). The common English term "yam" comes from *nyami*, the name used commonly in West African languages. In French it is *igname*, and in Spanish, *ñame*.

As the central starchy staple food of the forest zone that stretches from Guinea to the Congo, the yam also had a role in the human life cycle. The Nigerian novelist Chinua Achebe tells us that in his home Ibo culture the yam had a special place: "Every child loved the harvest season. Those who were big enough to carry even a few yams in a tiny basket went with the grown-ups to the farm. And if they could not help in digging up the yams, they could gather firewood together for roasting the ones that would be eaten there on the farm. This roasted yam soaked in red palm-oil and eaten in the open farm was sweeter than any meal at home."[17] Yams in the forested zones of West and Central Africa are consumed roasted, boiled, fried, and pounded. The version pounded in the mortar becomes fufu, a thick mass that takes on a gelatinous consistency as the starch particles break down under pounding by the pestle. For southern Ghanaians, yam fufu is the pinnacle of a meal; the stew that accompanies it is secondary to the satisfaction offered to the eater by the fufu itself.[18] In southwest Nigeria, *asaro* (yam pottage) is among the most popular concoctions, the flavors of fish and tomatoes being added to the mashed yam. This one-pot dish combines the starchy bulk of the yam with the classic blend of fish chunks and powdered crayfish as a thickening agent. Powdered shellfish as a sauce thickener is a formula found throughout West African cooking, as well as in Louisiana Creole dishes. The recipe below is thus a historical text unto itself. The ingredients show a deeper culinary philosophy in the inclusion of a complex mix of the Atlantic world (tomatoes, chilies, and palm oil).

Patten doya (Nigerian Yam Pottage)

1 small tuber of yam
1 medium smoked dried fish
4 large tomatoes
1 large onion
50 g ground chili
100 g ground crayfish
6 tsp palm oil
600 ml water or stock
salt to taste

Peel the yam and cut into medium-sized chunks. Wash, place in a clean pot, add the stock and other ingredients, season with salt. Cover and cook for 20–30 minutes until the yam is soft. Stir gently, adjust seasoning, and serve hot. The yam pottage should be thick and moist.[19]

There are two types of indigenous yams in West Africa, and additional varieties from Asia appeared in the 1500s via the Atlantic trade, eventually becoming part of the culinary and agricultural repertoire.[20]

That yams were an indigenous crop long associated in West Africa with deep meanings in religious and civil authority is clear in societies whose historical roots are in forest ecology. In the Asante kingdom the annual Odwira festival, in which surrounding kingdoms and villages brought tribute to the Asantehene (king), was a celebration of the yam harvest and the end of the hungry season.[21]

Yam also displayed its ritual power in other West African societies, like southeastern Nigeria's Ibo culture, where politics played out at a village level, without kings or formal hierarchy. The yam's maturity marked the season of abundance and celebration of the harvest in works of classic anthropology. James Frazer, in his pathbreaking 1890 study of human culture *The Golden Bough,* chose to feature the eating of yam at Onitsha, in Ibo country, as a ritual as well as culinary act:

FIGURE 2.2 Asante Odwira festival (yam harvest). *Source: T. Edward Bowdich, Mission from Cape Coast Castle to Ashantee, ed. W. E. F. Ward (London: Frank Cass, 1966)*

Each headman brought out six yams, and cut down young branches of palm-leaves and placed them before his gate, roasted three of the yams, and got some kola-nuts and fish. After the yam is roasted, the *Libia,* or country doctor, takes the yam, scrapes it into a sort of meal, and divides it into halves; he then takes one piece, and places it on the lips of the person who is going to eat the new yam. The eater then blows up the steam from the hot yam, and afterwards pokes the whole into his mouth, and says, "I thank God for being permitted to eat the new yam"; he then begins to chew it heartily, with fish likewise.[22]

Achebe's fictional village of Umofia in his novel *Things Fall Apart* also celebrated that moment of both culinary and ritual significance:

The feast of the New Yam was held every year before the harvest began, to honor the earth goddess and the ancestral spirits of the clans. New yams could not be eaten until some had been offered to these powers. Men and women, young and old, looked forward to the New Yam Festival because it began the season of plenty— the new year. On the last night before the festival yams of the old year were all disposed of by those who still had them. The new year must begin with tasty, fresh yams and not the shriveled and fibrous crop of the previous year. All cooking pots, calabashes and wooden bowls were thoroughly washed, especially the wooden mortar in which yam was pounded. Yam foo foo and vegetable soup was the chief food of the celebration.[23]

Whether as the symbolic stage of ritual or the sticky, starchy spheres of fufu that satisfied village elders, yams constituted the heart of the cuisinal community in Iboland and elsewhere in forested West Africa.

In addition to its role as food, yam as a plant was central to the psyche of Achebe's Ibo village of Umofia. We also get a glimpse of other foods that accompanied it in the field (and presumably later on the table):

Yam, the king of crops, was a very exacting king. For three or four moons it demanded hard work and constant attention from cock-crow till the chickens went back to roost. The young tendrils were protected from earth-heat with rings of sisal leaves. As the rains became heavier the women planted maize, melons and beans between the yam mounds. The yams were then staked, first with little sticks and later with tall and big tree branches. The women weeded the farm three times at definite periods in the life of the yam, neither early nor late.[24]

FIGURE 2.3 Yams in Accra (Ghana) market stall, 1975. *Photo by author*

Maize

Maize porridge rivals wheat bread as perhaps the most universal staff of life on planet earth. Its African versions are spread across the continent under many names. What is *nsima* in Malawi is *mealie pap* in South Africa, *sadza* in Zimbabwe, *ugali* in Kenya, and *gunfo* in Ethiopia.

Nsima (Malawian Thick Maize Meal Porridge)

1 cup *ufa* (maize meal) for two persons
2–3 cups of water for each cup of *ufa*

Use a wooden spoon to stir the *nsima*. Heat the water in a saucepan until lukewarm (test by letting a drop fall on the back of the hand). Mix a little of the *ufa* with the lukewarm water, stirring well to avoid lumps. Bring to a boil, stirring well, then lower the heat and let it boil gently. The mixture should then look like a thin, transparent porridge. Sprinkle the remaining *ufa* over, a little at a time, stirring continuously. Keep stirring until the *nsima* is smooth. Serve in a dish accompanied by meat, fish, or vegetables.[25]

Zea mays (maize or corn in North America) was the probably the first New World food plant brought to Africa, and certainly the food source with the quickest and widest impact. Though its first arrival in Africa in West Africa or at the Nile Delta (via Venetian commerce) does not appear in the historical record, its impact was immediate in some areas; in others it was delayed by a century or more.

Maize's adoption in Africa is not a single story, but a complex mosaic of farms', villages', and regions' choices and preferences. Maize's journey from an exotic visitor in the sixteenth century to a thoroughly African crop by the seventeenth century in West Africa was also a long one, as it went from vegetable to grain, from garden to field, from curiosity to staple. The first documentary reference to maize's presence in Africa may be that of an anonymous Portuguese pilot in 1540 who described already well-established cultivation on the Cape Verde Islands: "At the beginning of August they begin to sow grain, which they call Subaru [*zaburro*], or in the West Indies mehiz [*sic*]. It is like chick pea, and grows all over these islands and along the West African coast, and is the chief food of the people."[26] On the island of São Tomé farther south, another Portuguese pilot in the mid-sixteenth century reported that the island's slave traders fed their captives on "zaburro, which we call maize in the western islands and which is like chickpeas."[27] Dutch traveler and writer Olfert Dapper in 1668 remarked that maize had earlier been carried from the West Indies to São Tomé and thence to the Gold Coast, where he saw it as a common food: "First of all there grows there Turkish wheat, which the Indians call mays and which was first brought from the West Indies where it is plentiful by the Portuguese to the Island of Saint Thomas and which was distributed thence along the Goldcoast for cosumtion [sic] by the blacks."[28]

By the middle of the seventeenth century, European references to maize in settings in West Africa became commonplace. Shipping logs describe maize on West Africa's Gold Coast beginning in the early 1600s. By the late seventeenth century, maize had largely replaced both millet and sorghum along the West African coast—a remarkable transformation. Presumably, West African farmers had already been exploring the new plant's possibilities as food and as a farm crop that filled a distinctive ecological niche in the crop cycle. The native grains simply could not match maize's ability to produce massive amounts of food in a short growing cycle. By the eighteenth century, maize was the principal *céréale cultivée* in the region. In 1795 Mungo Park found that the people around the Gambia River cultivated it in considerable quantities. In fact, only in two areas of the Gold Coast, the Volta River Delta and coastal Axim, did rice remain the dominant cereal preferred by both farmers and cooks.[29]

Pieter de Marees' fanciful 1607 engraving depicting distinctive plants of West Africa shows maize ("le Mays ou Blè de Turquie") front and center, among sugarcane, rice, millet, beans, peppers, and various spices (see fig. 2.4). His image is implausible as a sketch of a single farmer's field, but is probably an accurate view of the contents of a West African woman's cooking pot.

In southern Africa, however, maize may not have arrived at the Cape by 1652, when Jan van Riebeeck of the Dutch East Indies Company did not report seeing it there on his arrival, despite his hope of identifying new local food sources for the Company's fledgling settlement. In fact, as part of his plan to feed Dutch East India Company slaves, settlers, and port workers, in 1658 he asked for maize seed to be sent from home to test its value at his planned maritime supply station at the foot of the Cape's Table Mountain.[30]

In Africa as a whole, maize took its place within farm plots finely tuned to the vagaries of Africa's capricious climate and old soils. The new crop accounted for a nutritional boost for population growth and concentration.

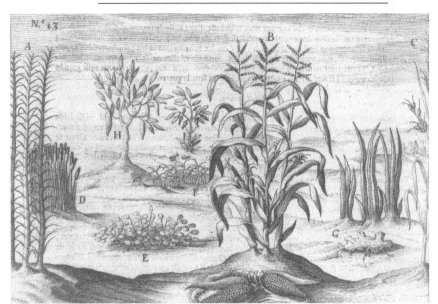

FIGURE 2.4 First engraving of maize in Africa, c. 1540. *Source: Pieter de Marees, Description and Historical Account of the Gold Kingdom of Guinea (1602) (Oxford: Oxford University Press, 1987)*

Maize, however, differed nutritionally from African true grains like sorghum, millet, and rice, since in a strict nutritional and physiological sense it is a vegetable rather than a grain. Maize offers vitamins A, C, and E, but lacks the lower B vitamins. It is high in carbohydrates but low in usable protein, lacking especially amino acids lysine and tryptophane; the leucine in maize blocks the human body's absorption of niacin, a vitamin whose absence causes protein deficiency.[31] It is not clear, however, how many of these qualities appealed to cooks and mothers concerned with daily meals. Perhaps maize's versatility as a cooking staple was even more appealing to women than its personality as a field crop. Historical records do not reveal much about that aspect of male-female relations, unfortunately.

The arrival of this New World stranger offered benefits that were immediately obvious to farmers: traditional grain yields in Africa were less than half those in Asia and Latin America, reflecting the obstacles of aridity and poor fertility in many parts of Africa. Maize and other New World crops such as cassava, cocoyams, and potatoes helped redress that imbalance in key parts of the continent. Unlike New World farmers, who depended heavily on maize as a primary starchy staple, most African farmers adopted maize initially as an early maturing vegetable niche crop tucked within a complex cropping system that relied on intercropping, rotation, and swidden ("slash-and-burn") techniques of managing soil fertility.

The names African peoples gave to the new food plant suggest it was named by farmers, not cooks. While European observers compared the maize they first saw in Africa to chickpeas (i.e., they saw it as a food), Africans tended to compare it to sorghum the plant, choosing apparently to focus on the appearance of the plant itself rather than the shape of the kernel, its taste, or its qualities in a cooked form. When young stalks emerge from the soil, the sorghum plant is almost indistinguishable from maize, even to the expert's eye. It is not entirely clear if the farmers who named the plant were men or women, though the cooks were presumably women, as they are in many, though not all, African societies.

Naming the stranger, the new crop, was in each society a process of trying to make the exotic more familiar. In addition to the purely African patterns, it was most common in the Old World to use a name for an already known grain combined with popular ideas about where it might have come from. The perception of maize as a kind of sorghum was a frequent influence on African names for the plant, and references to a distant place or the notion of "from the sea" would often be added. In highland Ethiopia, Semitic speakers called maize *yabaher mashela* (Amharic) or *mashela baheri* (Tigrinya), both terms meaning "the sorghum [from] the sea." Similarly, in Malawi, Chichewa speakers called it *chimanga* ("from the coast"). On the East African coast, by contrast, the Kiswahili term is *muhindi* ("[the grain] of India"). The only African localities to use *burro* or *aburro*, borrowed terms derived from the Portuguese *milho zaburro*, were two early sites of Portuguese trade: El Mina on the Gold Coast, the earliest Portuguese permanent trading station on the West African coast and the place where a young Christopher Columbus practiced his first Atlantic navigation; and Mozambique, where the Portuguese had early contacts with Indian Ocean ports. In the Gold Coast's Akan family of languages, *aburro* (also spelled *aburo*) is maize, and Akan speakers also describe overseas countries as *aburokyire* ("countries where maize comes from"). At the mouth of the Congo River in the mid-sixteenth century, local Kikongo speakers called maize *maza mamputo* ("grain of the white man"); similarly, Mande speakers in Senegambia called it *tuba-nyo* ("white man's grain"). From Egypt south and along the trade route south to Lake Chad, local words for maize, especially Hausa and dialects of the Fulfulde language, derived from the root *masa* (or *masar*, i.e., Egypt), describing maize's likely direction of introduction to the region.

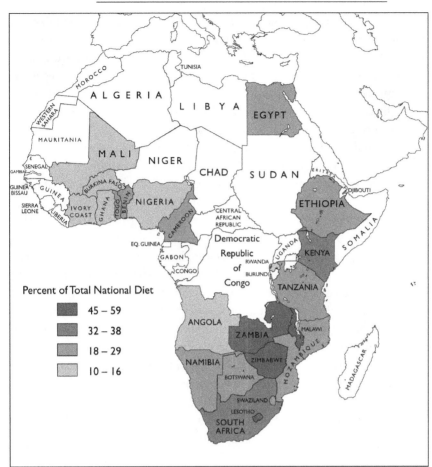

MAP 2.1 Maize consumption percentage

The Bambara in Mali use *maka*, a word that suggests maize's introduction by pilgrims returning from the *hajj* (pilgrimage) to the holy city Mecca, or *kaba*, a word that also designates sorghum. In more recent times it has been women who gave local names to new varieties of maize, though they seem to have done so more as farmers than as cooks.[32]

Whatever the names it went by, maize's twentieth-century spread as Africa's favorite grain crop for farmers also made it the favorite starchy food for local pots. Map 2.1 suggests the extent to which maize became central to food systems in eastern and southern Africa in the second half of the twentieth century.

From the point of view of maize as food and a culinary component, the primary personality shift of maize from a New World plant to an African staple was its morphing from a vegetable eaten as a garden snack in the preharvest days to a grain processed from ground meal into cooked food—*kenkey* in southern Ghana, *ugali* in Kenya/Uganda, mealie pap in South Africa, *sadza* in Zimbabwe (see chapter 6). Fresh roasted maize, however, was a vegetable snack rather than a cooked staple porridge that it would become in much of Africa by the early twentieth century. In Ethiopia it never made the transition to a primary starchy staple, though, as in most parts of Africa, maize at the green, milky stage could be boiled or roasted on charcoal embers on street corners for a tasty snack that also filled the belly at a lean time of year.

As a staple of regional cookeries, maize contributed its own set of tastes and textures. The stiff porridge mentioned above might vary somewhat by regions or even by the variety of maize. The original maize types that reached the South African coast, the Nile Valley, and the Horn of Africa were the flint maizes with hard starch endoplasms that most current African consumers prefer for their texture and women prefer for their grindability; it has less wasted chaff than other types. At the Gold Coast the floury types that came directly from Latin America were grindable but also fermented well, contributing a sour taste when fermented in a batter and then steamed in the husk and served with West African meat/fish stews and vegetables. In still other areas, maize provided the base material for both distilling local white-lightning liquor and brewing beer, drinks that African wives in earlier times would have made from millet, barley, sorghum, or rice.

An eighteenth-century description of a steamed maize and millet "bread" from the Gold Coast near the castle of El Mina:

> In the Evening the Women set-by the Quantity of Corn thought necessary for the Family the succeeding Day, which is brought by the Slaves from the Barn or Granary without the Village, though some have their own Storehouse at home. This Corn the Women beat in the Trunk of a Tree, hollowed for that Purpose like a Mortar, or in deep Holes of Rocks allotted for that Use, with wooden Pestles. They then winnow and grind it on a flat stone, as our Painters do Colours. Lastly, they mix it with Flour of Millet and knead it to a Sort of Dough, which they divide into small, round Pieces, as big as a Man's Fist, and boil in a large Earthen Pan full of Water, like Dumplins.[33]

This recipe was almost certainly an earlier version of the southern Ghanaian staple kenkey, a tamale-like lump made from fermented maize paste boiled in husks.

FIGURE 2.5 *Kenkey* (fermented and steamed maize meal). *Photo by author*

Cassava

Cassava is second only to maize as Africa's favorite staple. Despite its relatively slow adoption of the root crop (compared to maize, for example), Africa now produces more cassava than the rest of the world combined, even though about 70 percent of the continent's total production of cassava takes place in Nigeria, Congo, and Tanzania.[34] Cassava appears in the diet of forty African countries. For farmers the spread of cassava, both historically and in more recent times, has been for the following reasons:

- It adapts to poor soils on which other crops fail.
- It is easily propagated by stem cuttings.
- It resists drought, except at planting time.
- It resists locust damage.
- It has a high yield (ten metric tons per hectare) and is a low-cost source of calories.

- It can be planted at any time of the year.
- Cassava roots can be left in the ground and harvested from six to forty-eight months from harvest.[35]

Cassava (also called manioc and tapioca) arrived in West and Central Africa through Portuguese trade links to Brazil in the sixteenth century. Although it did not have its full effect in many areas until the nineteenth or twentieth century, it reached Angola and the mouth of the Congo River by the late sixteenth century, was a staple food in southern Gabon by 1612, and was abundant on the island of São Tomé by 1619. In 1644 the Dutch traveler Dapper testified that cassava in the Niger Delta (at an area in southeastern Nigeria called Warri) was already being ground into flour and made into a type of bread.[36]

Cassava comes in several varieties, often labeled as sweet or bitter, though each contains poisonous cyanogens (prussic acid) that require careful processing to make it safe for human food consumption. Slow adoption by women was likely partially a result of the tedious and labor-intensive processing requirements. The use of water or heat (roasting, boiling, or sunshine) to remove cyanogens seem to be a historical mix of technology transfer from New World women to African women as well as a substantial bit of local invention, trial and error, and accumulated local experience. Eventually, these methods included some combination of peeling, grating, fermenting, and toasting or by soaking in water for four or five days and then sun-drying to eliminate the poison. Sweet-type cassava roots are low in cyanogens, are mealy after cooking, and are usually eaten raw, boiled, or roasted in an open fire. Bitter cassava varieties have a higher dose of poison, are waxy after cooking, and are processed by peeling, grating, and or toasting the root pieces. Depending on the texture they desire, women might also soak or boil the roots and then sun-dry them.[37] Figures 2.6 and 2.7 show some of the process.

Cassava in African cookery offers its starchy staple food in five forms: fresh roots, dried roots, pasty products, granulated products, and leaves. Each cook may mix these forms with other local staples such as plantain, yam, cocoyam (taro), or sweet potato. The tastes and textures can vary from sticky and sour to a bland grainy porridge made from flour.

Cassava fills the belly, but its value lies in its carbohydrates (it is one of the foodstuffs highest in carbohydrates) rather than its overall nutritional qualities (see fig. 2.8). The roots contain only 1–2 percent protein and are

FIGURE 2.6 Cassava processing in West Africa, eighteenth century. *Source: Paul Erdman Isert,* Voyage en Guinée et dans les îles Caraïbes en Amérique *(Paris: Karthala, 1989)*

FIGURE 2.7 Cassava soaking, southwest Sudan, 1981. *Photo by author*

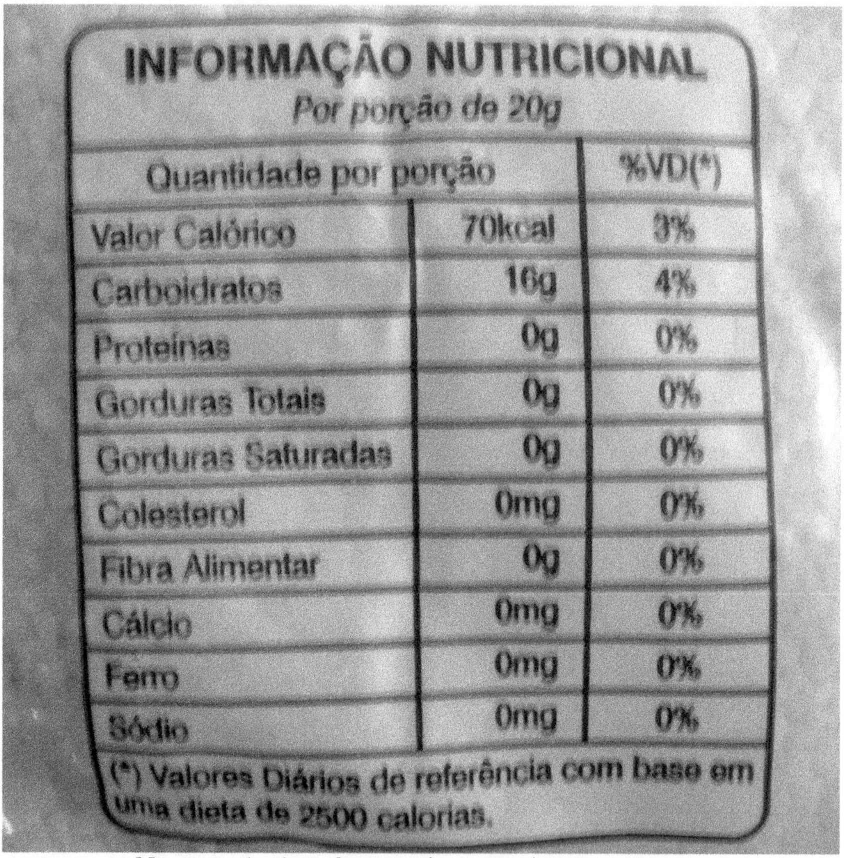

INFORMAÇÃO NUTRICIONAL		
Por porção de 20g		
Quantidade por porção		%VD(*)
Valor Calórico	70kcal	3%
Carboidratos	16g	4%
Proteínas	0g	0%
Gorduras Totais	0g	0%
Gorduras Saturadas	0g	0%
Colesterol	0mg	0%
Fibra Alimentar	0g	0%
Cálcio	0mg	0%
Ferro	0mg	0%
Sódio	0mg	0%

(*) Valores Diários de referência com base em uma dieta de 2500 calorias.

FIGURE 2.8 Nutritional value of cassava (as tapioca). *Photo by author*

also low in minerals. Peeling of the root for processing further reduces the protein content, since part of the protein is in the roots' skin. Cassava root contains calcium and vitamin C, but large proportions of its thiamin, riboflavin, and niacin are lost during processing.

Gari (Nigerian Roasted Cassava Meal)

The cassava roots are dug up and peeled. They are then washed and soaked in water for two hours. The roots are then grated and placed in tightly woven but porous bags; weights are placed on the bags for three days to eliminate much of the water. The contents of the bag are spread out to dry in the sun for several hours. When dry, the grated cassava is then sifted and dry roasted a little at a time, in a large pot over a fierce fire. A few drops of palm oil may be added for colour and flavor.[38]

Gari, as seen in the recipe above, is an example of a grated and toasted cassava starchy food that is particularly popular in the local cookery of Ghana and southern Nigeria, where it is also the most common form in which cassava is sold. The standard method used in Nigeria tranforms the raw cassava material and its culinary chemistry. To prepare the gari, women peel, wash, and grate the raw root into a pulp. The pulp is then put in a porous sack and weighed down by a heavy object, so that it can ferment and lose its excess moisture. When women then toast the pulpy mass in a pan (sometimes with palm oil), the gari loses its cyanide content but retains its distinctive sour, fermented taste. How sour or what texture is a matter of local preference: Yoruba in Western Nigeria prefer the sour type, but Ibo in the east like a blander version. Toasting gari gives it a longer shelf life, ideal for shipping from rural areas to urban markets.[39]

Together with cassava roots processed as a starchy staple, cassava leaves form a major part of the cook's repertoire in areas like Sierra Leone, or in Congo, where women concoct dishes like *pondu* (cassava leaves, onion, and dried fish) and *saka-medesu* (cassava leaves and beans), taking care not to overharvest the leaves and damage the growing roots. Cassava leaves have a nutritive value similar to green leafy vegetables: vitamin A (carotene), vitamin C, iron, and calcium; they are richer in protein, in fact, than the roots of the plant. Pounding the leaves in a mortar and then boiling them with groundnuts, fish, and oil eliminates the cyanide traces and makes them safe as a relish for gari, rice, or yam.[40]

Plantain (*Musa paradisiaca*)

Plantain appeared in Africa even earlier than in the New World, making its way to Madagascar and thence to East Africa in the latter half of the first millennium CE as part of the botanical and human settlement of the Indian Ocean rim. It spread into moist areas around the Great Lakes in western Kenya, Tanzania, Rwanda, and eastern Congo. Unlike Africa's indigenous grains, which were first collected in a wild form and then domesticated on Africa's small farms, plantain spread across Africa's forested and moister landscapes purely as a product of human action rather than through pollination or natural dispersal of seed. Plantain, like other bananas, grows fast, reaching as much as seven meters in a year, and responds to human efforts to propagate it by farmers' deliberate transplanting of stems (suckers).

Known as *matooke* in Uganda and western Kenya, *ndizi* in eastern Congo, and *ndeze* in Mozambique, the plantain is a close relative of the sweet banana.

But African plantain is starchy rather than sweet and prepared in the green form by boiling, steaming in its own leaves, pounding as fufu, frying in oil, or grilling on charcoal. Here is an example of a boiled version:

*Ndeze (*Mozambiquan Plantain*)*

1 kg high-quality green plantain
1 kg stewing beef
2 coconuts
2 onions sliced in rounds
3 tomatoes chopped
juice of half a lemon
salt
pepper

Peel the bananas; scratch them to loosen the natural liquids and cut lengthwise and in half. Cut the meat into chunks and boil until cooked. Season with salt. Prepare the coconut milk by grating and pouring with hot water twice to extract the coconut milk. Add the lemon juice to the first pouring. In a pot place a bottom layer of sliced bananas, then a layer of meat, then onion, tomato, salt, and pepper. Cover with the second pouring of coconut milk and cook until the water is boiled off. Add the first pouring of coconut milk and cook until the sauce thickens.[41]

In coastal Mozambique the dish *ndeze* (green bananas with coconut) is an example of plantain in a one-pot dish. In this dish, only the salt can claim a fully African ancestry, yet the flavor and conception combine aesthetics, ecology, and knowledge that is distinctively Mozambiquan.

In the era before the arrival of maize and cassava, plantain was, along with rice, sorghum, millet, and yams, critical to feeding African populations. In West Africa, plantain was less important than root crops as a staple, but nonetheless added to the potential cooking ingredients of moister and forested areas. Drier areas were better suited to grains like millet, sorghum, and African upland rice. In the Great Lakes area, the low-labor and high-yield characteristics of plantain likely played a significant role in the rise in the late eighteenth and nineteenth centuries of compact and power-ful kingdoms like Buganda that competed with livestock and grain-based neighboring kingdoms. Some historians argue persuasively that it was the productivity of plantain gardens in equatorial Africa that allowed the popu-lation expansion of the great Niger-Congo peoples (i.e., Bantu-speaking groups) who came into contact with grain-producing people at the forest's northern and southern edges. Unlike yam, cassava, or maize, plantain cultivation appeared in areas with fairly rich soils and dense human settlement, and especially in moist forest zones of West and Central Africa.

Like other nongrain starchy staples, plantain can present itself either as a snack or as the core texture element for a meal with stews and sauces. Cooked plantain is high in carbohydrates (97 percent), low in fat (1 percent), and low in protein (2 percent), while, like many fruits, high in vitamins A and C. Fried plantain using palm oil or other oils is found almost everywhere plantain appears. In some other areas, plantain flour appears as the starchy ingredient in local versions of fufu. In Nigeria, fried plantain is *dodo* (fig. 2.9).

The story of Africa's starchy staples and their distribution over time and space strongly indicates the dynamism of the spread of foodways across the continent historically. The decline of indigenous grains—sorghum, millet, and fonio—in the past century marks a contrast with the spread of those crops into world food systems in the Mediterranean, India, and East Asia. At the same time as Africa's own sorghum and millet spread into other world areas, African foodways have appropriated other starchy staples—maize, cassava, Asian rice—from other parts of the globe into their fields and pots. Those

FIGURE 2.9 *Dodo* (fried plantain) Nigerian style. *Photo by author*

staples mark the feel, the weight, and the texture of what African women prepared, shared, and presented on the occasions of high ritual as well as the daily meal. The spread of the flavor and fire of peppers, also an acquisition from the Atlantic World biome followed, and perhaps preceded the movement of the blander New World starchy staples into African cookery. We now consider the spread of the peppers that became a defining feature of the heat and color of what many African cooks stirred in their cooking pots.

Capsicum: The Democratization of Heat and Flavor

If Africa's culinary geography of texture rests on the consistency and bulk of its bland starchy staples, its most ubiquitous staple marker of flavor is that of the capsicum pepper, otherwise known as *chilli, pimiento, berbere, harisa, piri-piri,* or red pepper. For many areas of Africa we cannot imagine sauces and meats without the distinctive qualities of capsicum peppers in one form or another. In some African cooking, powdered pepper, fresh chopped chilies, and crushed pods and seeds are required ingredients. In other regions' food they make no appearance at all historically, though urban cooking of the twentieth century has made them ubiquitous from Khartoum to Durban and from Mombasa to Lagos. In the Venda region of South Africa, for example, peppers are found only as imported American tabasco in upscale urban restaurants in Polokwane (Petersburg), while just to the north in Malawi, fresh chopped green chilies appear as a condiment on virtually every restaurant table. In some African settings, powdered peppers evoke pure heat, while in others they combine with garlic, ginger, salt, and other ingredients to create a virtuosity of flavor.

Capsicum peppers can trace their lineage from a plant native to the New World (tropical South America) that expanded its range into the Old World, especially in the tropics in Africa, southeast Asia, Szechuan China, and India, after the opening of the Atlantic world. The capsicum peppers that had the greatest effects on global flavors (and heat) were *Capsicum frutescens* and *Capsicum annuum.* The *C. frutescens* category includes tabasco, a type processed commercially in North America, and bird's-eye peppers, a small red type found especially in Ethiopia and parts of East Africa. The Ethiopian type is known there as *mitmita,* and the verb describing its effect on the tongue is the same one used for scalding with hot water or red-hot coals—but its taste is much sought after by true aficionados (like me). The *C. annuum* category includes most other types of red and hot peppers, including paprika and jalapeño.

FIGURE 2.10 Drying capsicum. *Photo by author*

Virtually all of these varieties of capsicum (except sweet bell peppers) contain capsaicin, a lipophilic chemical that causes a strong burning sensation to the mouth of the eater. The amount of capsaicin varies in each type of pepper, affecting their volatile balance of heat and flavor. Virtually all mammals (except for some humans) find the burning sensation unpleasant and avoid contact with it. Birds, however, are unaffected and appear to be attracted by the bright colors and vitamin A in the flesh of the fruit. The presence of capsaicin, therefore, may well be a plant adaptation that repels mammals but attracts birds that will spread the seeds widely, an effect quite different than the purely deliberate human propagation of the grains, tubers, and maize that arrived in Africa from the New World. Bacteria may also have an aversion to capsaicin, since dishes spiced with hot powdered capsicum have a longer life in storage than those without it, a fact well known to experienced cooks in the tropics.

It seems likely that pepper seeds and dried pods spread around Africa and the Indian Ocean world via Arab, Indian, and Portuguese traders who brought them from the Mediterranean and India and directly from Brazil, Mesoamerica, and the Caribbean.[42] The seeds were durable, easily stored, and gave great value as trade items in markets like Zanzibar, Cairo, and São Tomé. European travelers to Cuba in the 1500s already knew the power of the "aji-aji" peppers that inflamed *ajiaco criollo*, the favorite dish of the native Cubans, which included many types of root staples, meats, and hot peppers.[43]

Once capsicum seeds had reached Africa, farmers there were able to breed and select their favorites. Capsicum peppers are a garden-based annual crop that farmers can modify by seed selection and home-grown seedlings over successive seasons to refine the characteristics of color, flavor, and size that they most desire for the market or the pot. Farmers may also obtain the peppers by collecting the volatile fruit from "volunteer" plants whose seeds have been spread by vitamin A–seeking birds.

The rapid adoption of capsicum heat and flavor into cuisines in West Africa, the Horn of Africa, and maritime cultures along Africa's coasts may not have been the first introduction of heat and spice to local tastes. Both African and Indian cookery probably had included long-distance trade items like black pepper (from India), malagueta pepper ("grains of paradise," native to West Africa), and ginger, sources of pungent flavors that predated New World capsicums. In the late 1500s, when Portuguese in Ethiopia complained about the local food served to them being too spicy to eat, it seems likely that that chemical heat was due to the presence of locally available flavoring ingredients like ginger, black pepper, and coriander, used heavily in elite pots, rather than New World capsicum, which would later become common in even the poorest household fare. Capsicum peppers changed African cooking because they democratized the fiery flavors; capsicum plants came from easily stored seeds that could be grown locally, or at least regionally, more cheaply and simply than the previously used spices.[44] Capsicum peppers, either in fresh form or processed into powders, thus were not a new flavor sensation, but one that farmers could produce for the market and their own use in kitchen gardens managed by women. The nature of peppers, both as plants and as spice, broadened access to them for more than elites and their cooking pots.

PART TWO

Stirring the National Stew
Food and National Identity in Ethiopia

Part 1 of this volume set the stage for Africa's cooking, the assembling of its basic ingredients—such as starchy staples and spices—and the continent's culinary place in the post-Columbian world. Part 2 focuses more specifically on the role of food and cooking as both the symbol and the substance of a national identity, in this case Ethiopia. Chapter 3 offers a glimpse of a culinary moment, Queen Taytu's 1887 feast, when food and food ritual were a means to display an attempt to make a nation. Chapter 4 more fully traces the historical record of food in Ethiopia, the movement toward a national cuisine, the interweaving of food with politics, and an international audience.

FIGURE II.1 Injera baking, 1974. *Photo by author*

CHAPTER THREE

Taytu's Feast

Cuisine and Nation in the New Flower, Ethiopia, 1887

> There were brought large jars containing spiced butter that was the
> color of the yellow Adei flower; they presented clay pots full of spices
> from beyond the sea, blended *awazē* [red pepper paste], ginger and
> cloves. . . .
>   Also, on that day the nobility were astonished, remarking
> how the many new dishes were superior to those of previous days.
> . . . Emperor Menilek and Wayzero Taytu should not be thanked
> principally for this feast for it was a miracle of Our Mother Mary.
>
>   —Gabra Selasse, *Tarika zaman za-dagmawi Menilek: Negusa
>   nagast za-Ityopya*

IN 1887, a year after the founding of Addis Ababa, Ethiopia's modern capital, Queen Taytu Bitul launched an ambitious plan for a feast to
consecrate the city's new church of Entoto Maryam, which stood on the
mountaintop overlooking the new city from the northeast. The scale of
her culinary project was enormous in its slaughtering of over five thousand
oxen, cows, sheep, and goats; stockpiling of clay pots of spiced clarified
butter by the hundreds; assembling of spices gathered from the best regions
of the new empire. The event also featured the engineering of "rivers" of *tej*
(honey wine or mead) that literally flowed into the site on specially made
wooden troughs from warehouses uphill from the banquet hall. Beyond
the impressive scale of the feast, however, was the event's elaborate use of
cooking, expressed in the variety and volume of the dishes prepared, the

FIGURE 3.1 Ethiopian feast, painting by court painter Fre Heywet, c. 1900, currently held by the Staatliches Museum für Völkerkunde, Munich. *Source: Elisabeth Biasio,* Majesty and Magnificence at the Court of Menilek: Alfred Ilg's Ethiopia around 1900 *(Zurich: NZZ, 2004), 58*

variety of tastes, and the invention of a particular combination of foods. In making food into ritual, Queen Taytu understood the value of presentation, of sequence, and of the meaning of food and feast as political theater. But she understood as well that subtleties of food and cooking itself mattered too. For Taytu the assembly of the theater of empire included the invention of cuisine as a part of empire and nation.

Through this event, the queen was also presenting an integrated show of food preparation to a new urbanizing elite in the process of building a new public political culture for a new nation and national identity. Her husband Menilek's goal was to modernize the Orthodox Christian Abyssinian kingdom by creating a large, multiethnic empire focused on Addis Ababa as capital in the region of Shawa. Taytu's feast was also, perhaps, a way to demonstrate to the old aristocracy that Addis Ababa was a fitting site for a national capital; the feast's culinary triumph was a political signal as well. In September 1887, Menilek and Taytu were on the verge of imperial ascendancy and ready to assert a new Ethiopia with a new, more inclusive political culture. A thousand kilometers from the Italian-occupied Eritrea and the Sudanese Mahdist forces pressing on the western border, Menilek's Shawa, in the central highlands, was positioned to control key trade routes. In 1882, Menilek's Shawan army had won a key battle for access to the southern regions and their coffee, gold, ivory, and slaves. And in January 1887, the army had conquered the eastern market town of Harer, opening Shawa up to access to Red Sea ports and Harer's rich agricultural land.

Over five days in a cool and damp September Taytu spread out her feast under a tent at the Entoto Maryam church compound behind the palace on the mountain above the newly settled Addis Ababa. The event was not just an exercise in public ritual and an assertion of public authority (her husband, Menilek would not actually become emperor for another two years). It was also a gastronomic blueprint for a new urban culture that was self-consciously grand and culturally inclusive—to a degree.

The preparation of food and the ritual of the feast were as important as the food itself. And the context of a meal's ritual political, religious, and social meaning was embedded within the subtleties of language. In the Amharic language of the queen's kingdom, a large feast assembled for political purposes was a *gibir* (a term that also implied taxation/tribute, serfdom, or farmer); an invitation to special guests to eat was *daggese* (with many specialized variations regarding hospitality, e.g., *yasirg daggese,* or wedding feast); a *gibzia* (from the verb meaning "to invite") was a general

FIGURE 3.2 Queen (later Empress) Taytu Bitul. *Source: Gabra Sellase,* Tarika zaman za-dagmawi Menilek: Negusa nagast za-Ityopiya *(Addis Ababa: Berhanena Salam Press, 1966 EC)*

term for a party involving food and drink. *Qedasse* (Eucharist) was the consumption of ritual bread as Christ's body, fundamental to church ritual. The chronicler Gabra Selasse, who wrote the account of the event, used the terms *daggese* and *gibir* interchangeably, suggesting that the ritual meaning of the feast was both political and religious in its intent. The consecration of St. Mary's Church and the event's sophisticated food preparation were a clear demonstration of Addis Ababa's maturity and its recognition by the grace of St. Mary herself. The 1887 feast combined all of these elements of ritual and public hospitality since it consecrated a church, marked her husband Menilek's political ascendancy, and reinforced political ties by providing an elaborate menu drawn from a diverse ethnic landscape.

The culinary ritual organized by Queen Taytu was a preamble to Menilek's coronation as emperor two years later. The feast itself took place on the space between the new church compound and the adjacent royal buildings on the southeast. Though the event might have appeared chaotic to a casual observer, it was a highly orchestrated phenomenon. Court official Kebede Tesemma's description of the feast shows the elaboration of space for such events, with assigned seating based on rank, affiliation, and affection (see fig. 3.3).

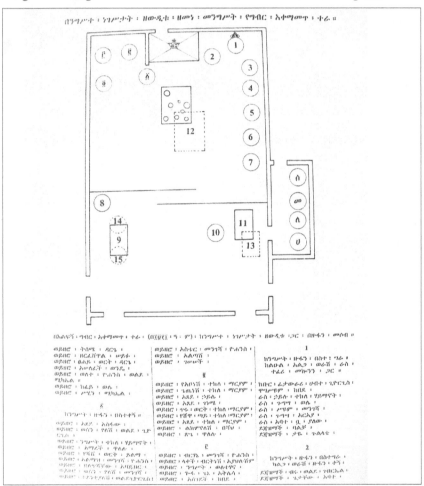

FIGURE 3.3 Feast rank placement in Menilek's court, c. 1918. *Source: Kabada Tessema,* Ya Tarik Mastawasha *(1971)*

FIGURE 3.4 Taytu and Menilek wine tasting, c. 1890. *Source: Biasio*, Majesty and Magnificence at the Court of Menilek

The feast was also remarkable for the unprecedented detail of description in the royal chronicle of its achievements in cookery. Much of the sensual nuance in the chronicle was an indication of the enormous influence of the *Nigist* (queen), whose forceful personality and political skill were evident in marriage arrangements as well. In Ethiopia, unlike France, the culture of cooking was a woman's domain, controlled at its apex by Empress Taytu herself.

Queen Taytu's life story embodied an amalgam of ethnic and regional identities and life experiences, and prepared her exquisitely for overseeing both the food and the ritual symbolism of the feast. As a young woman moving frequently among the mutually intelligible cultures of highland Ethiopia, she must have learned about domestic arts as well as regional politics. Born about 1850, Taytu was a child of a mother from the old northwest imperial city of Gondar and a father from the northwest highlands (Simen) whose ethnic ancestry was Oromo from the mixed Muslim and Christian east (Yejju, in Wollo). Her father had lived in the northern Tigray region, linked by his sister's marriage to a Tigrayan noble family. Taytu was thus a composite of Ethiopia's historical regional identities and cultural traditions. For her the ethnically and geographical diverse nuances of food and its presentation were second nature.

Her exposure at a young age to Ethiopia's rich cultural diversity of religion, language, and ritual life must have influenced her greatly. As a child, Taytu lived with her mother in a Gojjam monastery near the Blue Nile River, where life was simple and daily food tasks a necessity. There she probably learned to winnow grain with a circular wicker basket, grind peas into flour, and dry red pepper pods, ingredients for the hand-milled wheat bread, thin lentil stews, and roasted grains prepared for male priests of the church. After several failed political marriages, in 1883 she married Menilek, then *negus* (king) of Shawa, at a time when he was busy supervising the expansion of Shawa's territory onto new ethnic turf to the east and southwest, and had ambitions for making his kingdom of Shawa the seat of a new Ethiopian empire. Taytu's maturity (she was about thirty-three) and her polyglot background gave her a powerful voice at court and a broad view of Ethiopia's regional diversity. There is also evidence that Queen Taytu was intimately involved in the cooking of the court's most elaborate dishes. Although raised on the plain fare of the monastery, by the 1880s she was well aware of the integral role of food and drink in the workings of power and authority. By the time she reached the status of queen, she had developed a keen eye for detail in spicing a dish and had developed a sweet tooth, as well as a taste for champagne and red wines—Bordeaux reds and Châteauneuf du Pape.

The feast, held on the holiday of Maryam in mid-September 1887, gave her an opportunity to bring together her knowledge, skills in cookery, and sense of overlapping cultural identities. The feast drew together—as did Menelik's Ethiopia itself—tastes, ingredients, and aesthetics appropriated from traditions of the highland Christian kingdom and from many local cultures of an emerging multiethnic landscape. The new national identity she oversaw incorporated a polyglot human landscape over which she superimposed new manners of dress, language, and religion as markers of membership. Food was a part of that identity. "Ethiopian" food, which emerged on the international stage as a recognized cuisine by the late twentieth century, was thus actually the product of a managed historical process of change in Ethiopia itself.

Empress Taytu's 1887 feast was therefore a signal event. The meaning of that event was a product of its scale, the range of ingredients summoned, the equipment deployed, and the timing of its accomplishment. The feast was thus one of the first acts that presented the new center of the Ethiopian state and its assertion of a site from which Menilek (and Taytu) sought to build a new political culture and claim a new national identity both within Ethiopia and for the benefit of the nation's new emergence on the international scene. It was also a moment when Menilek and Taytu's Shawa region expressed its own sense of prosperity and identity via the material culture of culinary preparation and presentation. These elements became the foundation of an inclusive national cuisine. Cooking and politics were intertwined, at least in intent, at this historical moment.

The scale of the event was massive. The chronicler tells us that the *das* (ceremonial tented banquet hall) was so large that a horse could pass through it easily at a gallop. The expansive tent complex connected the emperor's private quarters (*elfign*) and included five special areas for baking *injera* (Ethiopia's flat, spongy bread), cooking the *wet* (stews), storing honey wine (*tej*), and separately preparing the mutton and beef. Five hundred baskets of injera stood at the ready, as did forty-five large clay jars of tej. Three hundred *messob* (woven basket tables), each covered with red fabric (probably imported via Muslim Harer along with the ornate basketry), provided distinctive place settings for those closest to the royal couple, who were perched on an elevated table and behind curtains at the far end of the tent. Another five hundred baskets filled with injera stood ready to serve the multitude of other honored guests spread out at benches and woven basket/ tables below them. Massive clay jars of butter and of ground red pepper "paraded" by throughout the day. While the chronicler tells us in one passage that the number of cattle and sheep slaughtered was "innumerable," he calculates the number elsewhere as precisely 5,395. He also tells us that the "sea" of honey wine flowed "like a torrent" from twelve pipes (six on each side of the banquet hall) from a reservoir in a house near the chapel. Visitors to the Entoto Maryam church today can imagine this structure, which stood just inside what is today the church's busy front gate.

The chronicle's description of preparations and of the event's overall conception makes it clear that the feast was a national project as well as a sumptuary event that enticed the senses of the guests. The ingredients and the equipment marshaled for the feast's dishes were a graphic demonstration of the geographic reach of Menilek's domain, and its ambition. They also demonstrated choices about inclusion in—and exclusion from—the building of an African polity during Africa's colonial era. The newly conquered town of Harer in the east was Muslim-dominated and therefore, according to Orthodox Christian belief, could not be a direct source of food for Taytu's Christian feast. Nonetheless, Harer did matter in the national equation and served as a source for the utensils, metal cauldrons, decorative cloth, and basketry used to cook and present the dishes to the guests. From Jimma, a Muslim kingdom to the east and an ally of Menelik's, King Abba Jafar sent kerosene lamps, cloths for the tables, and special honey the color of the flowers of that region. The chronicle tells us that along with multicolored carpets imported from the Red Sea, the feasting hall and royal seating were "dazzling" to the eye and from a distance appeared like a flowered meadow spread before the king and queen.

In preparation, the workers scurried about preparing seating while women from the kitchen authoritatively sampled the bubbling stews and adjusted the spiced butter to achieve the aroma and crimson color that meant it was just right. Among the scents wafting out of the cooking sheds, one powerful smell must have dominated. Powdered red capsicum pepper (*berbere*) for stews and for *awaze* and *delleh* (types of pepper paste) came from the queen's own lowland holdings in Bulga, Geren (both in northern Shawa), and Yejju (her family land in southern Wallo, two weeks' ride to the north). It had been prepared in previous months and delivered in large clay jars (*gan* and *ensera*) to the palace. Honey at the royal court came from all parts of the Shawan kingdom, or had been paid as tribute in kind from areas like Gera (in the southwest's Gibe valley) and the vassal kingdom of Jimma, which produced honey distinctive for the variety of its color and flavor.

The sensory effects of the feast were, according to the chronicler, overwhelming: the inside of the tent was lit by the mixed brilliance of kerosene lamps, thin yellow beeswax candles, and torches held by male servants dressed in white togas meaningfully wrapped in distinctive styles to show their social rank. The smells of the honey wine and the fresh injera caused, the chronicle tells us, "faintness of the heart." The aromatic and pungent spices used in special mixtures with cayenne pepper to prepare the berbere reflected not only the Horn of Africa's historical trade networks but also the political grasp of the empire itself. While each private elite household had its own mix of spices and the powdered red pepper (Menilek and Taytu's was a state secret), berbere contained a mix of ingredients in particular proportions: garlic, ginger, pounded shallots, rue, basil, cloves, cinnamon, cardamom, grains of paradise (malagueta pepper), and bishop's weed (*Carum ajowan*). But it was cayenne pepper (*Capsicum frutescens*) and related chili pepper varieties that offered the distinctive fiery flavors and preservative power to stew, meats, and sauces. These peppers, rare and much prized in the 1600s, had become by 1887 a staple crop of the empire's lowlands and Rift Valley conquests.

By the mid-nineteenth century, many of these spices derived not just from overseas trade but from southwestern forest ecologies, areas that Menilek had conquered or absorbed in the 1880s. These spices flavored not only the stews (*wet*) and special breads (*ambasha*, baked with black cumin, *tequr azmud*) but also the clarified butter (*nit'r qebeh*) that the empress's cooks used to sauté meats and flavor rich shallot-based sauces. Wealthy landowners in the capital and key agricultural regions coveted particular agricultural zones since their own food supplies came from their own rural feudal land holdings rather than from a national grain market. Perhaps Menilek's conquests were more about taste and spice than territory, and binding the new nation together was more than just politics. Honey was another key ingredient for the liquid side of the festivities. Drinks included honey water as well as fermented honey wine, whose sweet aroma filled the compound's air for days before the event. And there were also the sharp scent of *talla*, a smoky beer fermented from malted and roasted highland barley.

If the genetic raw materials of cooking were of New World or Indian Ocean origin and had come to be grown on Ethiopian farms still at great distance from the court, it was nevertheless the skill and secret formulae of women in mixing the ground red pepper and spices that made particular elite homes and households distinctive. The imperial court was no different: the royal kitchen staff (all women) prepared stews with ground pepper–spice combinations that the palace women specialists mixed according to the king's and queen's personal tastes, no doubt under Taytu's strict supervision.[1] The air on Entoto Mountain that September would have been redolent with garlic, ginger, cumin, smoke from juniper, acacia, and *qosso* wood fires, and that cloying sweetness of fermenting honey wine.[2]

For eight days prior to the feast, the royal servants had gathered huge numbers of fattened cows, oxen, steers, and sheep to select those best suited for grilled meat or stews, and still others for raw meat to be served to the most distinguished guests. The queen's men had to slaughter the livestock and prepare the meat earlier in the week, since Friday, when the feast began, was an Orthodox Christian fasting day and guests could not consume meat until after sunset. The feast began in the early evening on a Friday when guests arrived from distant districts and filed into the tent; the most important persons among them took their assigned seats near the king's and queen's thrones.

The feasting and drinking occupied the whole first day. The chronicler gives us a partial menu of the many dishes prepared and left to marinate overnight: *zegen* (minced beef sautéed in spiced red pepper, well done), *seqseq* (mutton ribs and pieces in pepper stew), *lemlem zegen* (slightly rare beef in spicy sauce), *maraq qelqelu* (mutton ribs in a turmeric-spiced broth), *bozena* (peppered ground pea sauce cooked with bits of meat or jerky). These were the dishes served to the royal favorites, who took seats offered to them by the royal chamberlains. These guests sat at elaborate basket tables where they drank honey wine from special glass flasks and could choose from the servants' trays chunks of raw beef to dip in a thick pepper sauce made with honey wine. The less distinguished guests seated farther from the king sat at wooden benches and drank their smoky barley beer from cowhorn cups; their benches were laid out with woven grass covers, and round injera was set before them. The many other types of dishes these guests dined on are not described in the chronicle, but were no doubt offered to them with decorum and elegance.

The feast continued through Saturday as more guests arrived from outlying districts. By five in the morning on Sunday, the tables were set again by flickering torchlight. The feasting, accompanied by the rhythmic thumping of church drums, continued that whole day until the evening, when the sated guests retired an hour's walk downhill to the *filwoha* (hot mineral springs) to bask in the steamy natural baths there.

On Monday, the fourth day of the feast, Queen Taytu told Menilek that the guests must be tiring of the food. Over his objections, she asked him for five more fattened cows (*sheher*) and proceeded to prepare two more dishes of *emmes* (slightly sautéed meat laced with ginger and foreign spices and cooked in clarified butter), one of beef and one of mutton, which were served to three hundred tables of the most privileged guests.

The feast's sensory repertoire was lost neither on the guests nor on the royal chronicler, who repeatedly emphasizes that the food was the most elaborate that anyone present had ever tasted. It marked the arrival of Shawa as an appropriate seat of political power and ritual elegance. The chronicler, in fact, probably received close scrutiny from the queen herself as he wrote about the event. Under her influence he remarked on both the sensual achievements of the day and on the greater symbolic imagery of the feast as a performance of what anthropologist Clifford Geertz has called the theater-state phenomenon. On that day, the chronicler writes, "the nobility were astonished, remarking how the many new dishes were superior to those of previous days. . . . Emperor Menilek and Wayzero Taytu should not be thanked principally for this feast, for it was a miracle of Our Mother Mary." We have little evidence of St. Mary's cooking skills, but there is persuasive evidence that Empress Taytu was intimately involved in the cooking of the court's most elaborate dishes. The chronicler is also at pains to point out that the audacious Shawans, Menilek and Taytu, had proven their readiness to take the national stage. And in March 1889, the reigning emperor, Yohannes IV, died in battle on the Sudan border, leaving the imperial throne to Menilek and his talented consort.

Taytu's Cookery

One lucid vignette helps make the point about Taytu's understanding of the nuances of cookery and nation. In 1901, fourteen years after Taytu's feast, Nellie Pease, a resident Englishwoman, offered a curious insight into Taytu's views about the authenticity of her national cuisine. Pease admired a *yadoro dabo* (chicken stew bread) that she had enjoyed at lunch while visiting the empress. Taytu enthusiastically recounted for her the intricate method for its preparation:

> "I will tell you how it is made. When the hotly spiced and pep-pered bread [dough] . . . has doubled, and before it is baked, half-boiled eggs are put in the dough; it is then baked as bread loaves. Before the meal the loaves are cut open, the eggs are taken out and the bread is handed around so you can eat it at the same time." . . . I shall try to do this when I get home [to England]. The Queen thought a great deal about this and was amused and pleased. Presently, she said, "But you won't have the spices." I said, "No, but I think I can get them. If not I will take them from Abyssinia." The Queen said . . . "but she won't have the right cooking dish." I said I thought I could manage that too and that I was sorry my house was such a long way off, because I should like to send some to Her Majesty to see how it succeeded. This interested her, as she was sure it would be a failure.[3]

The empress's strong sense of the essential nature of both local experience and equipment notwithstanding, she was probably correct that the subtleties of ingredients, equipment, and method would have made the production of that dish outside of Ethiopia's local ingredients and skill difficult at best.

Stirring the National Dish

The 1887 feast was a prescient historical moment for the modern state of Ethiopia in which food and cooking both played symbolic and material roles. First of all, the consecration of the Church of St. Mary at Entoto marked a point of foundation of the new capital city of Addis Ababa as a spiritual center, but also a permanent economic and political capital. Perhaps as important, the emperor and empress made Addis Ababa into a cultural capital from which a new national political culture was to emerge. Food and cookery were one expression of the attempt to assert a new national identity. Second, the historical moment took place on the eve of the European imperialism in Africa, when Ethiopia's own idea of an empire created from disparate kingdoms was a reaction in many ways to wider European ambitions in Africa and the Nile Valley as manifested at the Berlin conference two years before, when European delegates redrew African colonial borders. The new urban national culture that the emperor and empress envisioned included material cultural expressions that included food and its presentation in public events and in the private households of elite families that aspired to join the new national power elite. Being an Ethiopian in a modern sense was not just an achievement of birth but an agreement to take on common symbols of nationhood: language, dress, and a national cuisine that marked membership. Queen Taytu's role in this process was unmistakable: her attention to the preparation and presentation of food drew on many regional and cultural traditions and served to establish a shared culinary heritage assembled from an empire that defined itself as distinctive vis-à-vis European imperialism and local political struggles for consolidation. This national culture eventually expressed itself in terms of the commercialization of Ethiopian cookery and its expansion into international recognition at the end of the twentieth century.

The Ethiopian cuisine now recognized in restaurants around the world in the early twenty-first century is the product of the same dynamic historical process as Taytu's 1887 feast of Maryam. To a large degree that sensual synergy was similar to the forces that brought together the diverse cultural landscape of Addis Ababa as the urban heart of the empire. And yet still visible in the cuisine is the bygone influence of an empress who had a vision of ways in which food, its cooking, and its presentation could symbolize her vision of a nation.

CHAPTER FOUR

Stirring a National Dish

Ethiopian Cuisine, 1500–2000

IF TAYTU'S feast was a consummation of both a cuisine and a political process, from when and where did the constituent parts of Ethiopia's "classic" cuisine come? Did Taytu in some way really invent it, or were the elements of what is eaten today in Ethiopian restaurants around the world always present in some form? In chapter 7, we will see what those elements were that she drew together. In this chapter, I will describe that iconic cuisine as the end result of historical networks interacting with Ethiopia's farms, soils, markets, and local cultures. Ethiopia's food repertoire now is, after all, a product of the historical landscapes of a entrenched ox-plow cereal-farming system and elite hierarchy that relied historically on a diet of grains, legumes (lentils, peas, chickpeas, beans), root crops, and vegetables—each one an annual crop. The core of the diet had its origins in Ethiopia's highlands and had expanded over at least two millennia, along with the ox-plow farming system, to include a broadening linguistic and ethnic community that shared ideas about food and cooking. This highland diet had its foundations in Ethiopia's endemic crops, such as *teff,* certain varieties of wheat and barley, and *dagussa* (finger millet), as well as complementary crops drawn from a wider world and regional trade, such as peas, chickpeas, lentils, and oil seeds (safflower, linseed, and *nug*).

From a culinary point of view, the diet of Ethiopia's "people of the plow" consisted of particular core elements: fermented teff bread (*injera*) and stews (*wet*) made with a base of shallots (*shinkurt*), dry-fried or sautéed in oil or spiced butter, added late; and some combination of legumes (split or powdered), meat, or vegetables, usually collard greens.[1] Cooking techniques included smoking (for dried meat and milk containers), roasting or grilling of meat or grains on iron griddles, boiling (for grain snacks), braising for meat stews, frying, and baking on ceramic dishes.

The flavors and textures and their sequencing and juxtaposition within a meal are an important element of Ethiopia's cuisine. A simple meal might consist of a single dish—commonly a peppery pea-flour sauce (*shiro*)—or might include a succession of dishes that incorporated roasted meat, elaborate mutton stews, or mutton broth–soaked injera. Consumption is a communal event, with food served to multiple guests gathered around a single *t'ri* (a large, thin metal platter) or *mesob* (shallow, wide basket) that held a stack of large injera (ideally one per person), with a series of dishes placed or ladled in front of each person. This sequencing of savory spice synergies and textures of sauce followed by servings of grilled meat or cooked stew, vegetables, and condiment sauces was fairly rigid at both ritual public settings and in the privacy of a home. In contrast to traditional English cookery, where bland meats appear on a plate alongside spiced elements (chutney, mint sauce, brown sauce, or mustard), the cooking and flavors of Ethiopia's cuisine combined flavor elements within sauces that included either meat or legumes, though on special occasions it also often presented roasted meat with spiced pastes made from red pepper and oil or flax and mustard powder (*awaze* or *siljo*). And unlike Chinese or German foods, which combine sweet and sour, or the European and Middle Eastern concept of sweet (dessert) following savory in a structured meal, Ethiopian meals had virtually no elements of the sweet in the composition and sequence of a meal.

The basic elements of the diet of the highlands and its class implications were in evidence even in ancient times and in images used in the medieval Christian kingdom. The Aksumite empire that dominated the northern highlands in the millennium 500 BCE to 500 CE developed its cereal crops from endemic grasses domesticated as grains, especially teff and finger millet, that suited its local ecology and complemented protein-rich foods like field peas, fava beans, lentils, and chickpeas, crops that farmers rotated with grains. The deep-seated principles of this grain-based diet are evident, for example, in church art that mark scenes with eating (such as the Last Supper or Salome's dance before King Herod's court, as in fig. 4.1), where artists put injera on the table. After all, injera was the staff of life, was it not? The meal as a ritual occasion that included injera as a base was fundamental to Christian cultural and biblical allegory, and such paintings drew part of their significance from showing a meal that included both injera and honey wine in traditional Ethiopian flasks.

FIGURE 4.1 Salome's dance before Herod. Note injera on royal table. *Photo by author*

Heat and Flavor

Beyond the basic grains and protein sources, the highland agro-ecology offered a wide range of elements of flavor—spices, herbs, and especially powdered and powerful capsicum peppers. In fact, we have to struggle a bit to imagine the tastes and smells of Ethiopia's cooking without its range of spices, colors, and pungent combinations of these. These elements, however, were not primordial, but historical elements added to farm repertoires over time, as exotic crops obtained first as precious substances from a sustained long-distance trade with a wider world of the Red Sea and Indian Ocean. We know the points of origin of spices and herbs, though there is no precise record of when or how they arrived at particular places or how women first incorporated them into daily preparations. The image of a spice seller in a rural market (fig. 4.2) shows the spices and herbs that were ubiquitous in even a rural marketplace by the 1970s (and certainly long before then).

By the late fifteenth century, much of Ethiopia's spice repertoire was already in place, except for the peppers that would later arrive from the New World (see chapter 2). The Portuguese Jesuit Manoel de Almeida observed in his residence in Ethiopia the 1630s: "There are many fragrant and medicinal herbs, rue, houseleek, dill, fennel, wild sweet basil, coriander, onions, garlic, and many purgative herbs." In addition to those spices and herbs, de Almeida could have listed grains of paradise or false cardamom (*kewrerima*), fenugreek

FIGURE 4.2 Ethiopian market spice seller, 1974. *Photo by author*

(*abish*), oregano (*t'osin*), ginger (*zinjibel*), turmeric (*ird*), black cumin (*tiqur asmud*), cumin (*qemun*), black pepper (*qundo berbere*), cloves (*qirinfud*), and cinnamon (*qerefa*), spices that had arrived over time from the east via Arab and India trade networks that linked the Red Sea to the Indian Ocean.

The regional geography of the spice trade tells us a good deal about the highland cooking pot's impressive cultural and economic geography. Spices—like cardamom, cloves, black pepper, coriander, and cinnamon— came to the Red Sea and the Horn of Africa via exchange with south Asia, the Maluccan Islands, southeast Asia, and the eastern Mediterranean, respectively, and may have been around in small amounts as early as the early first millennium CE. False cardamom (*kewrerima*), also called "grains of paradise" or malagueta pepper, was neither cardamom nor capsicum pepper, but *Afromomum melegueta,* a pod spice native to West Africa and prized both in Europe as a brewing spice and in the Horn of Africa as a cooking ingredient. But cayenne pepper (*Capsicum frutescens*) and other red peppers that offered fiery flavors and preservative power to stew, meats, and sauces were among the most influential New World plants that arrived in the Ethiopian highlands after the opening of the Atlantic in 1492, along with maize, potatoes, cassava, and other foods. These New World peppers came to define the fundamental flavors and temperature of the cuisine (see chapters 2 and 3).

Salt, a critical additive, is, of course, actually a mineral. It was rare and highly prized on the highlands, where it was present in two forms. One was the *amole,* a salt bar mined from the dried lake salt plains of the Danakil Depression in the northeast. This form served as a dietary supplement but also as a currency in highland trade. The other was *ashabo,* dried granules of sea salt processed from Red Sea coastal salt ponds. Ashabo not only contained sodium chloride, but also carried the taste of its minerals from the soils that surrounded it on the lake beds or drying ponds. Salt was the foundation of long-distance trade, a prized wedding gift, a flavoring for coffee, and a key nutritional resource for sustaining all humans and livestock.[2] Ethiopia's cooks quite properly treat salt as a spice quite distinct from modern iodized granular salt.

Was Ethiopia's food always a marker of class or an elite cuisine? A Portuguese account from the late 1600s describes a surprisingly egalitarian daily highland diet that that had only begun to show signs of emerging class character:

> As they ordinarily sit on the ground, the great nobles on carpets and the rest on mats, their tables are all low and round. They have neither tablecloths nor napkins on them. They wipe their hands on the *apas* [injera] that they eat; the table is full of them in houses where there are plenty. They put food on them, without using plates, if it is raw or roasted meat. If it is a stew of chicken or mutton or their staple fare, which is a kind of thin pap in which they moisten their *apas,* made from the meal of different pulses, such as lentils, chickpeas, linseed, and others peculiar to this country, all of this comes in bowls of black clay. This is the dinner service of poor and rich so that down to our own times nothing better was seen even on the table of the Emperor himself.[3]

FIGURE 4.3
Ethiopian feast, nineteenth century. *Source: Mansfield Parkyns,* Life in Abyssinia, Being Notes Collected during Three Years' Residence in That Country *(1853; repr., London: Frank Cass, 1966)*

That staple fare of the 1630s was a simple dish, s*hiro wet,* common to diets of all economic classes and increasingly popular among urban populations of the twenty-first century: then as now, this was a simple dish of the poor, but much appreciated as well by the affluent. A modern version of the "thin pap" appears in a published recipe for the uninitiated:

Shiro wet (Ethiopian Powdered Split-Pea Sauce)

1½ cups of powdered pulses, including:
    green split peas
    lentils
    broad beans
    chickpeas
red pepper, powdered
garlic, chopped
ginger, chopped
shallots, chopped
rue
basil
oregano
fenugreek
cardamom
cloves
cinnamon
bishop's weed
coriander
salt

Preparation:
    Wash the peas, lentils, beans, and chickpeas; then boil them for 3–5 minutes and drain. Roast them in an oven to dry them and then grind them to a fine powder. Take the ginger, garlic, shallots, and oregano and pound them together until fine. Add the powdered spices together and mix in red pepper. In a frying pan roast the basil, fenugreek, coriander, cloves, cinnamon, salt, and bishop's weed over a low fire. Add to the other spices and grind to a fine powder.
    For the shiro wet, fry the shallots with oil until brown. Add water and let it boil. Sprinkle powdered pea powder a bit at a time, stirring to break down lumps. Add spices and simmer until thick. Serve hot or cold.[4]

This written recipe tells us the basic elements of the dish but misses the point about the cook's practice and the oral nature of cooking knowledge. Compare the stiffly described modern published recipe for the classic pea sauce to the oral version that I transcribed from Derebworq Gabra Hiwot, a woman who learned her cooking in rural Wallo Province in the 1950s and tells us how to make the popular dish. Her choice of spices differs a bit. Even more notable, though, is her sense of choice by the cook who would decide her own preferences, and that of those who will eat the pea stew (shiro). The question was "How do you make shiro?"

Do you mean the shiro flour or the wet? The wet? For example, first, shiro is made with peas or fava beans or chickpeas or whichever you want. With those may it be roasted with, roasted with oil and is roasted with spices to begin. The spices are:

> *kewrerima* [false cardamom or grains of paradise]
> *nech shinkurt* [garlic]
> *tequr azmud* [black cumin]
> *nech azmud* [white cumin]
> *besobla* [basil]
> *tenadam* [rue]

Then *berbere* itself. Salt is added. Then grind it . . . pound it [Derebworq's hand moves up and down]. If you want *qay* [red] you add *berbere* [spiced red pepper powder] and it is pounded. If you want *fisiq* [nonfasting], you add butter, as you please.

For *miten* if you want it thin, it is called *miten* [spiced *shiro* powder] itself, if you want [*wat*] from that you add water. You take the dried split pea/bean and pound it in the mortar with *berbere*. When it is ground [into powder]. First you need one glass of water, like that [she gestures], then two soup spoons of shiro flour, like that [boil it] when it gets thick.

For *shinqurt* (shallots/onions) you use very few for *miten* [shiro powder]. You just put it in with oil and a little water, like that. You take half a *waqit* [handful] like that. If you want more. . . . some people like more onions, so you slice them [*gorad gorad;* she makes a chopping motion] and add them. When it boils, the water decreases, like that. Cooking it, it gets dry and you add water.

Just like that, when it becomes *tuk tuk*, it is done, cooked. It shows oil on top and then it is ready. It says *tik tik*. With peas it becomes thicker

faster, it froths, it rises. For fava beans also it becomes thick faster
and comes up [froths] when you add water. For chickpeas you just
add water it thickens and it is cooked and it is ready. That means you
choose as you want it. The one who is making it decides. Like that.

Q: How much of each thing?

[She cups her hand with fingers extended.] One *weqiyt*, like this. If you
want more you add one *efign* [she cups her two hands together with
fingers extended]. Or less, you use one *terign* [she shows her open
hand]. Or a cup or a soup spoon [she reaches for one on the table].

The simplicity of the preparation of this dish belies the astonishing geography of its ingredients and the complexity of its constituent flavors. Even
more, the oral version includes this cook's use of the senses of sound and
of shape, and adjustments for taste. She uses onomatopoeia (*tuk tuk*) to
suggest the sounds made by the bubbling stew when it reaches its proper
consistency. She uses her hands to indicate amounts and how to stir or to
taste. In other words, to tell you how to make the dish, she has to show you
using sounds and gestures. Written words convey little of the true sense of
how to cook shiro wet sauce. Even a simple dish loses in the translation.

If the daily diet like shiro wet seemed egalitarian to Portuguese observers in
the 1600s, there were forms of food that even in the mid-seventeenth century
marked the privilege of the political elite. Raw beef and its consumption at
large ceremonial gatherings and on military campaigns emphasized both
simplicity of preparation (the soldiers needed only some knives and an ox)
and conspicuous consumption. The Jesuit Manoel de Almeida described
raw meat consumption in the 1630s:

Beef they eat raw, called it Berindô and it is the food they esteem most highly. They put a great deal of salt and pepper on
it, if they have pepper, and the most important people who can
have the gall of the animal that is killed, squeeze it by hitting it
often on the piece in from of them so the meat should soak it up
well; they claim that it gives it a great relish. This is their mustard, though mustard itself is found in the country. They make
another more peculiar dish from the soft matter inside certain
thin entrails with their salt and pepper. It is a dish for princes
and they would not abandon it for any other.[5]

The distinctions of eating that Almeida describes, including the relative scarcity of the New World pepper, were one factor that marked the cuisine of the era. As powdered flavoring, pepper, mixed sparingly with other powdered spices and herbs, became an ingredient available on local farms prepared by local women. By contrast, meat itself was still a marker of social class and wealth.

The latter dish described in the quotation is *dulet*, a dish of roasted mutton tripe, kidneys, and liver usually consumed the same morning as the sheep's slaughter. It is probably as popular today as it was almost four centuries ago.

Raw meat was a component of Taytu's 1887 feast (see chapter 3) and the culinary culture of Menilek's Ethiopia, but took a modest place, rather than dominating the feast, at an occasion in the 1840s described below. Clearly, the egalitarian nature of the diet described for the seventeenth century by

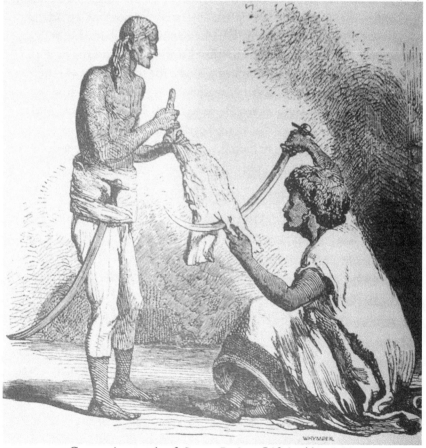

FIGURE 4.4 Consuming raw beef. *Source: Parkyns*, Life in Abyssinia

Almeida had disappeared, replaced by an expression of privilege in both volume of food and elaboration of preparation.

By the mid-nineteenth century, both the elaborate presentation of food and the cuisine itself showed self-conscious elements of social and political hierarchy. Mansfield Parkyns, a three-year resident of the northern Ethiopia's Tigray region in the 1840s, offered to his British readers a description of a feast at the home of a regional chief. The presentation of these foods to guests was a way of marking political privilege and social status: "The company being assembled, the most distinguished personages are requested to be seated, and are placed according to their rank. . . . the *soub-hè* or cooked dishes are brought in by the cook women, each of whom receives a piece of bread dipped in the dish she has carried. . . . They also serve the guests with meat from the dishes . . . they frequently show great favoritism, giving kidneys and tit-bits to one and gristle and bones to another." The next course is the arrival of the raw beef: "While these dishes are generally made of mutton, are on the table, the cow is killed and flayed outside; and immediately on their removal the 'broundo' is brought in. . . . The choicest pieces are carried to the highest tables where are seated the masters of the feast and the most distinguished guests."[6] Of course, the subtle theme that runs through the

FIGURE 4.5 Injera baking, nineteenth century. *Source: Guglielmo Massaia,* I miei trentacinque anni di missione nell'alta Etiopia *(Rome, 1883–95), 4:43*

account is injera, the flat bread made from teff and the ubiquitous foundation of every meal.

Regional Contributions

The landscape of Ethiopian foodways, however, was more than just that of the north or the agricultural highlands that appeared on the tables at Taytu's 1887 feast. Regional variation was another factor that reflected both the local economic base and cultural food preferences. Almeida in the 1630s had noted other ethnic groups' presence and contrasting foodways. Other observers noted that the "Gafates and [Oromo] support themselves entirely on their milk and meat, as the [Oromo] do not sow at all and give milk even to their horses which they make strong with it and barley."[7] Eventually some of these groups assimilated to the dominant political and linguistic culture. By the late 1800s, even the foodways of the Oromo people had changed as that widespread population adjusted their pastoral economy based on cattle to agro-pastoralism, where farming became the dietary and economic base. Cattle were symbolic but not the stuff of the daily diet. A. K. Bulatowicz, an Russian officer who traveled to the south with Menilek's conquering armies, observed the diet of those Oromo people that the emperor sought to incorporate into his empire—especially those who had adopted agriculture and adapted peppered condiments in their cooking, though in some areas they still preferred to use long cowhorn spoons rather than injera to guide food to their mouths:

> The Oromo eat cabbage, cooked *inset* [false banana root], and *durry* [sorghum], beans known as *shumburu* [chickpeas] and lentils. They make it into a type of porridge and eat it with horn spoons. They very rarely eat butter, but use it for their hair. They make *kita,* unfermented pancakes, instead of bread. They also have a type of bread. To prepare it they put the dough on a clay pan and then put another smaller one on top. The fire is underneath the big pan and on top of the small one. This how they produce bread, which is a bit heavy but quite tasty. They like milk and meat, which they eat raw; their food is spicy.[8]

The Oromo group that Bulatowicz saw had a different attitude toward raw meat than earlier Oromo people. English adventurer Nathaniel Pearce reported in the early nineteenth century that while traditional Oromo settled in northern Ethiopia enjoyed feasting on a newly slaughtered ox, they "always broil the meat a little and upbraided the Christians for eating it raw, like dogs."[9]

Other dietary complexes within the new empire were slow to adopt injera; they included those organized around *qocho*, a dense, rubbery bread made from the root corm of *ensete* (*Ensete ventricosum*), or false banana. Bulatowicz also described the food of the people of Kaffa, a southern kingdom whose king had just been forcibly deposed by Menilek and taken to Addis Ababa in golden chains. The Kaffa food scene that Bulatowicz described for the 1880s took place in a kingdom that had just begun to recover from violent, rapacious conquest and depopulation:

> Their food used to consist of meat, milk, and various grains. These days they mainly eat bread made of the tree called kogo [ensete]; only this tree remained after the war. They prepare their bread in the following way. [A] four-year old tree is cut down, its leaves are cut out and the bottom part of the trunk is put in the ground for several months. When it ferments and goes rotten they take it out of the ground and take the bad top part off. They mash the inner soft and fermented part into a paste which they bake on clay pans. This type of bread is not very nutritious, it does not taste good (sour) and it has an unpleasant smell. It is a bit better with the addition of some flour. Their diet is supplemented by various root vegetables that they boil. They also drink a lot of coffee. They drink it several times a day with meals and after. It is brewed in clay pots and they drink it out of cups of horn.[10]

Kaffa is located in the area where coffee originated, from which it spread to the Arab and European worlds. It is not surprising that the Kaffiche diet valued that drink, even in harsh times. Food systems, of course, change with time and under circumstances like war and conquest. Bulatowicz's observations tell us about a time of hardship, before the southern kingdom's shift to a grain-based agriculture and diet in the next decades. Clearly, though, the transition from a pastoral to an agricultural diet was already well underway.

For the Gurage, Walayta, Kaffa, and Gedeo and the cultures of the Gibe area of the southwest, too, qocho was their staple bread, made from the fermented pulp of ensete root corm and eaten with grain and meat dishes, such as the Gurage dish *kitfo*, ground meat sautéed in butter and served with chopped collard greens and farmer's cheese and eaten with a long cowhorn spoon. Many of the domestic workers and laborers in Addis Ababa were Gurage by origin, and through them kitfo became one of the regional dishes that has found its way into the national cuisine.

While the highland cuisines that evolved as part of the annual crop ox-plow grain/pulse complex had common elements (injera, pepper sauces, and shallot-based stews of meat or pulses) it also retained local nuances of style and tradition. Although the imperial court of Gonder, the old seventeenth-century Christian capital, had lost its economic and political base, the cooking of Gonder, as well as its traditions of statecraft, property law, and an elaborated court culture, served in many ways as a model for northern political culture. That court had evolved an elaborate culinary repertoire in elite households and at court that included what they argued to be the best *doro wet* (chicken stew with an egg in a rich crimson-colored, buttered pepper sauce). Other areas had their own signature dishes: Gojjam had its distinctive *senefech* (mustard sauce); Tigray had its *helbet* (whipped fava bean sauce); Gurage food, with its foundation of qocho, specialized in kitfo (sautéed meat in butter and cheese) and chopped sautéed kale/collard greens (*Brassica oleracea*) and eventually also incorporated injera as the basic bread with which to eat those foods. A unique set of local ingredients and local food traditions thus presented a cornucopia of possibilities for feeding Menilek's Ethiopia and its emerging political culture in the late 1800s. Those traditions were the building blocks from which Taytu constructed her national menu and culinary nationhood.

A National Cuisine?

In 1913, twenty-six years after Taytu's definitive feast, Dr. P. Mérab, Emperor Menilek's Georgian French-speaking physician, recorded, for the first time, an exhaustive list of dishes that he considered the national cuisine from his vantage point near the social life of court in Addis Ababa. As the doctor directly responsible for the health of the imperial court, Mérab took a special interest in the elite diet. In his memoir, *Impressions d'Éthiopie,* he noted that Taytu's favorite dish was the wheat bread loaf made with chicken stew (*yadoro dabo*) as a stuffing. The dish was rich with butter and the best pieces of chicken. Mérab especially noted the dish's effect on the queen's health, complaining about her growing girth and calling her a "fat hen," an unsympathetic view, since as her doctor must have known that she was diabetic. Mérab described twenty-one distinct culinary preparations that he reckoned made up the national cuisine of the day. His list shows, perhaps, his close association with the Empress Taytu and Addis Ababa's own composite culinary culture. His French spellings add a touch of the exotic to his list of what he calls "les cordons bleus éthiopiennes":

1. *Le ouôt* [wet], a ragout of mutton or beef or more rarely of chicken, in *berbere* sauce, garlic, and onion. It puts fire in your mouth and obliges you to take a glass of water with every mouthful. The pepper is in such great quantity that it is no longer red, but [the color of] chocolate or wine dregs.

2. *Le tebs* [*tebs*], meat grilled slightly on a grill or cast iron plate; often the taste is raised by a bit of bile; this bile could be from a goat, sheep, or less often of a cow.

3. *Le gomène* [*gomen*/kale], a blanched sauce from the leaves of kale ground with oil; a dish of the young and of abstinence [fasting]. One also finds *le gomène* with butter.

4. *L'infillé* [*infille*/sliced meat dangling on a bone dipped in pepper sauce] is a leg of mutton with forty or so long cuts that give to the leg of mutton the look of an antique whip; cooked 10 or 15 minutes in a pepper sauce, the *infillé* is carried so that the guests can choose the piece that suits them.

5. *L'emmis* [*emmis*], is equally made of pieces of meat drowned in a sauce, cooked and then sprinkled with pepper. Its particularity comes from the fragrance of meat sizzled in fire.

6. *Le chiro* [*shiro*], a sauce with oil, more rarely with butter, pepper, onion, and the flour of legumes (chickpeas, lentils, peas, more rarely beans). . . . It is the everyday food of the poor . . . A meal of *chiro* with *injera* costs less than half a piastre.

7. *L'talba* [*talba*], made of roasted linseed pounded and mixed with bread crumbs and black pepper. There is *talba* for eating and *talba* for drinking. The former is a cake of linseed flour and honey. The *talba* for drinking is one of the principal travel provisions for the town-dwelling class.

8. *Le doulète* [*dulet*/sautéed tripe and kidneys], fricassee of the stomach, liver, kidneys of a sheep or goat mixed or minced. A

delicious dish often served as a hors d'oeuvre. It is called the *Fitawrari* [commander of the army's center] of the dinner, that is to say served before the other dishes.

9. *Le doro-dabbo* [*yadoro dabo*,chicken-stew bread], a chicken-stew stuffing for bread during its cooking; a worthy dish. It is said to be the preferred dish of Empress Taytu.

10. *L'allitcha* [*alicha*], mutton broth with crumbs of bread [injera] and butter with turmeric but without pepper; [chicken] meat and eggs (chicken *allitcha*) are added. It is the favorite dish of Menilek II.

11. *Le samma* [*samma wet*], original dish consisting of nettle leaves and spines (*Urtica simensis)* [cooked in oil]. It is a dish of fasting like *le gomène* and *le chiro*.

12. *Le bouticha* [*kik wet*] resembles *chiro* with the difference that the latter is a true powder while that is not the case with *boutitcha* [i.e., it is made with split peas or beans].

13. *Le mentchet abiche* [*menchet abish*], a dish made with a fine mince, in butter, with onions and strong spices. It is the ordinary dish of the well-to-do families. Menilek is passionate about it. It has the reputation of making one fat since it is agreeable to the point that one eats too much. Its name comes from the grain of the spice *abish* [fenugreek], and the *menchet* is a type of native pot.

14. *Le fit-fit* [*fitfit*], mince of meat and bread [injera]; also made without pepper.

15. *Le doïo*, reminds one of *chiro*, but it is better made and constitutes the daily dish of the soldiers of the chiefs. There is between a little and a lot of butter.

16. *Le seldjo* [*siljo*], fava bean flour cooked in water with mustard and many other ingredients [spices], except *berbere;* after cooking the paste is put in a pot and stored in a corner of the house and is only eaten after eight days. The flavor is very strong and the odor is more so. It rises in the nose like pure mustard.

17. *Le bozana* [*bozena*] is *chiro*, with the addition of dried powdered meat. This powder carries a taste of preserved meat like sausage or ham; when *bozena* is put on a bit of fire one adds butter and condiments. The dish is much loved by the populace.

18. *L'elbet* [*ilbet*] is also a complex dish made with the flour of fava, lentils, etc. with *nug* [*Guizotia abyssinica*] oil. It is strongly whipped and beaten like an egg cream; it can be saved for one month, though the foam does not appear as when it was fresh.

19. *Le yassa-ouôt* [*yassa wet*] is a fried fish with onions [shallots], oil and various ingredients that set off the sauce. The expression means a fish dish.

20. *Ouatala*, a sort of ham made of zebu beef fat that is the hump [of a cow] that reaches about 5 kilograms and used for this purpose: it is cut into lanyards and salted and spiced to taste and then hung in the back of the house where there is acrid smoke. At the end of some days the fat takes on the taste of smoked ham. It is eaten as breakfast to start the work day with *talla* [millet beer] or coffee.

21. *Le mar-dabbo* [*yamar dabo*], honey bread, a honey cake, a trifle. Abyssinians have other cakes and sweets between honey with barley flour, linseed grains, and other oil seeds. One of the best known is *chamiet*, which is drunk with delicacy, especially for sickness. Another cake, *tchikko* [*ch'uko*], is eaten and presents the look of an undercooked paste of barley flour and butter. It is different than *chamiet* in that the honey is replaced by butter. Large grains of salt are plentiful to the point that they irritate and break the teeth. The locals love *tchikko*.[11]

Mérab's list reveals an emergent national cuisine and elaborates sensual details of the dishes and ingredients that had featured prominently at Taytu's 1887 feast. His list is credible because of his long residence in the capital and his medical interest in diet and nutrition. While his exhaustive description shows some awareness of economic and social class, it is somewhat ignorant or dismissive of the nature of the daily diet of rural folk and the strong influence of Christian fasts, the days when devout Christians and rural folk consumed only pulses, grains, and oils. Mérab's list also shows a decided bias toward an urban diet. It excludes the considerations of rural poverty and class relations, and also ignores food as a part of the emerging commercialization of hospitality in the early twentieth century (see below).

Commercializing Hospitality and the National Dish, 1620–2005

Mérab's list shows us a glimpse of the cooking traditions of an elite class, the food of the home—even a royal home. But where does the restaurant as a site for presentation of the national cuisine arise? That cuisine, which had evolved as a part of imperial and elite feasting occasions, emerged over the course of the twentieth century during profound economic changes and the growing commercialization of hospitality. Such hospitality, however, was not always for sale. On the highlands, historically lodging and food were not for sale but came as a function of political generosity for privileged guests or cultural obligations to the stranger. Menilek's chronicler had noted the obligation of hospitality toward strangers: "The stranger/ guest who is invited receives a fattened ox for his supper."[12] On the reality of local hospitality in the 1620s, Jerónimo Lobo wrote: "There are no inns anywhere in the empire, but a person can always find shelter in villages no matter where he goes. . . . Whenever one arrives after three o'clock in the afternoon there is an obligation for them to give him a house, a cot on which to sleep, and food to eat appropriate to the person's stage in life, and he may be given a cow for his servants' supper in addition to bread, wine, and also cooked food."[13]

Lobo's experience, however, was that of the valued foreign guest. For most exhausted strangers, a cow was probably only a distant hope. In the mid-nineteenth century, Johan Krapf noted similar norms of hospitality: "In general it is customary for a traveler to sit down on the ground in public places where the villagers can see you, and if anyone will receive you, he will come and call you. Should you wait, however, for a considerable time without having been called, you may then attempt to ask for lodging in a house you choose; and if you are sent away, it is best to go to a church."[14] While there was an expectation of food and a place to sleep for rural travelers, it did not always happen. In contrast to Krapf's somewhat optimistic statement, Parkyns in Tigray at about the same time found little succor when he arrived in a village with his entourage:

> Meanwhile we had nothing to eat, either for ourselves or our
> servants. We had been obliged to send a servant round the camp

crying "Who has got bread for money?"—offering at the same
time an exorbitant price; but even by this means we procured
not a tenth of the quantity necessary for our party. . . . But although our circumstances were well known, no one, excepting
a lady named Senedou, offered us even a bit of bread. We had
given her a little essence of cloves and she in return sent us five
cakes [injera] and a dish of meat stewed in pepper and butter.[15]

Like Parkyns, travelers in Shawa in the nineteenth century often found
that food along the road was not available for purchase. Meals were not for
sale, and local folk and officials made provisions available only to those with
written orders from the king or local governor.[16]

Inns, hotels, and restaurants seem to have been a twentieth-century
consequence of urbanization in the capital and along the spiderweb of
all-weather roads that eventually radiated out from the capital. In 1907,
Empress Taytu herself opened Ethiopia's first hotel, a building that served
food, provided hot water for guests, and offered a public sitting room. In
1913, Mérab noted that, like the new railroad town of Dire Dawa in the east,
Addis Ababa sported a rapidly growing number of *tedjeries* (tej houses) and
lodgings that offered meals, beds, foot washing, drink, and "pleasures of the
flesh." He also noted that such establishments served a particular clientele,
"men without families, unemployed young men, the trader, the traveler, the
peasant who has come to the city on business, domestic servants, soldiers,
filchers, idlers, and escaped slaves."[17] By the time of his writing, there were
over a hundred of these houses in the capital.

Mérab also noted the introduction of European ideas about hospitality,
indicating "ten or twelve" inns that catered to European clients, run for
the most part by Greeks, a group of mercantile expatriates who had also
introduced other amenities of urban life, such as distilled alcohol (*araki*),
wheat breads, and pastries. The capital's only restaurant was a Greek-
owned establishment in the city center with an optimistic French name
(La Confiance). Fan Dunkley, an English diplomat's wife who arrived at
Addis Ababa by train in the early 1930s, recalled the travelers' fare en route:
"Railway lunch is available at three wayside buffets, but as the cooking is
Greek, oily, and with plenty of garlic, we preferred to take our own hampers
of cold chicken, tinned fruit, etc."[18] During the Italian period (1936–41), the
Fascist government established a number of well-appointed tourist hotels
in key administrative centers like Bishoftu, Jimma, and Dessie. The hotels

FIGURE 4.6 La Confiance Restaurant, Addis Ababa, c. 1925. *Source: Fasil Giorghis and Denis Gérard*, Addis Ababa 1886–1941: The City and Its Architectural Heritage *(Addis Ababa: Shama Books, 2007), 105*

served Italian fare, but admitted Europeans only and had little effect on the country's national cuisine or the economic culture of hospitality.[19]

In the period after the Italian occupation, the growing national road network and transport infrastructure included small hotels and *bunnabet* (literally, coffeehouses) that popped up along the railway line from Djibouti and then along overland travel routes and in regional capitals. In these new towns and bus stopovers, single males—teachers or salaried government workers—took food contracts to provide themselves with meals from single or divorced women who had opened hotels in the towns themselves or ran teahouses on the roadside. The food for sale in these settings was simple fare, but was predominately highland cuisine: injera and a single dish of meat (*t'ibs* or *qay wet*) or legume stews for fasting days. It was functional but neither elaborate nor especially well prepared—not up to the standards of mother's cooking. Cooking required time and a selection of ingredients not always available to roadside establishments. The buses and trucks that plied the road networks provided a steady clientele of travelers and cash resources. Drivers and bus passengers were temporary customers, but collectively provided a steady stream of evening and midday diners. The bars and small-town hotels that began to appear along the road networks in the empire adapted and disseminated the tastes and ingredients of the central highlands as the emerging standard of public, commercialized food. Even in the far reaches of the empire, travelers came to expect injera, rather than local dishes, as roadside fare.

The young men who came to these small road settlements (including teachers and young Peace Corps volunteers like me) often shared the common fate of eating in small coffeehouses where the quality of food varied. Only the largest towns had shops with food ingredients in them. When I arrived in 1973 in a small town of two thousand residents, the only canned food available was a single can of sardines (which I bought and consumed in the first week). Residents of the town ate at home with their families. Those who sought more variety had to take culinary refuge in larger towns where hotels served pasta and more elaborately prepared mutton stews with injera.

Addis Ababa's growth as the administrative and commercial capital in the 1960s and 1970s brought increasing numbers of salaried government officials and staff, a well-heeled international community, and a newly emerging educated Ethiopian middle class. While many preferred the privacy of home-cooked food, everyday meat consumption and regional variations on the highland diets appeared there as well. Foreign restaurants, such as the venerable Castelli's, Omar Kayam, the Creamery, Oroscopos Pizzeria, Enrico's Pastries, Bole Mini, and the new Hilton Hotel, established food outside the home as a phenomenon of the urban bourgeoisie, many of whom were Ethiopian. Until the 1970s, however, none of these establishments served "national" food, which remained a specialty of the private home or public events.

At the lower end of the economic scale, teachers, office workers, and service-sector employees—predominantly male—needed daily meals prepared by women. The new professional class established contracts with small bars or private houses for their daily meals of injera and wet. Qay wet (red pepper stew) of either mutton or beef was the usual fare, or shiro wet (pepper sauce from legume powder) or *misir wet* (lentil stew) on fasting days. But injera was the sine qua non.[20] Young women who were divorced or attempting to escape the drudgery of rural life served as workers or cooks, serving the needs and desires of male guests and diners.

Injera underwent its own commercialization in public restaurants and urban households. White teff injera was the preferred type for elite households that held their own agricultural land in areas on the outskirts of the capital, like Ada or Becho. Most folks, however, used the darker injera, which was *sergegna*, literally a "marriage" of white and red teff, or the "black" teff injera, or flour that mixed teff and finger millet (or maize after the

FIGURE 4.7. Neighborhood butcher shop, Addis Ababa, 2008. *Photo by author*

1980s), the lowest on the scale. Beginning in the 1970s, urban dwellers often abandoned the collective meal from the *t'ri* (metal platter) and *masob* (woven basket table) in favor of the genteel use of individual plates and injera rolled up and resembling ace bandages.

Raw meat might appear at feasts in private homes or at some public occasions, but the delicacy did not suit the urban milieu, where commercial butcher shops in neighborhoods at the city's edge (Dukam, Gulele, Ayer Tena, Qotebe) were increasingly the source of meat (especially beef) for urban pots and griddles. Raw-meat consumers preferred the warmth of the flesh fresh from slaughter, not easily available from a commercial butcher. Although some neighbors, religious associations, and family groups slaughtered animals collectively for special occasions like opulent weddings at international hotels, daily urban life made it easier to buy beef by the kilo from a commercial butcher.

Those teachers, students, and functionaries who came to the capital and to towns from the south, west, and east through the postwar decades spoke different languages and had different foodways but in short order conformed to a new urban culture oriented to the Amharic language, the public culture of the Shawan imperial court of Haile Selassie, and a cuisine that was dynamic but nonetheless rooted in the norms set down during Addis Ababa's formation.

Why some dishes or foods appeared as part of a normal urban diet and some did not is a difficult question. Some regional non-Abyssinian ethnic dishes, but only a few, received a place at the national table, including kitfo, the Gurage chopped-meat dish (often served raw like steak tartare or lightly sautéed), which became a regular menu item or a specialty of certain restaurants (many said that the restaurant at the Shell petrol station behind the venerable Ras Hotel served the best in Addis), though it increasingly appeared with injera rather than with qocho (ensete bread), and horn spoons served as utensils for eating the raw or lightly cooked meat and for spooning it onto the injera. Diners used forks (and spoons) for eating spaghetti. Food preparations from Ethiopia's Islamic communities in the east, southwest, and north were not included (coffee was an exception; see below). Muslims from Wallo, Gojjam, and Gonder tended to eat dishes similar to those of their Christian neighbors, although the different Muslim and Christian traditions for blessing the slaughter of animals meant that they did not eat one another's meat. On Christian fasting days Muslims and Christians often ate at the same restaurants since only vegetarian foods were involved. And not all regional foods from the north made it to Shawa. *Metata* was a Gonder dish made from cheese fermented for forty days during the pre-Easter fast and used to break the fast. Its ripe aroma made it an acquired taste, and it never reached Addis Ababa's national table.[21]

Snacks and town-based breakfast fare were also an exception. *Ch'uko*, a preparation made from barley flour, butter, and honey and mentioned by Mérab, was probably adopted by the multiethnic Shawans from Oromo kitchens, but it was a snack, not a main dish. Bakeries sprouted around the city, providing wheat bread and rolls served with spiced-infused tea (*shayna dabo*), which became a breakfast staple but, again, were more a morning snack than a meal. *Ful*, a delicious paste made from fava beans, diced shallots, cheese, and oil and eaten with freshly baked bread, appeared as a breakfast food in road towns and a few teashops around Muslim neighborhoods, but has never attained the routine presence that it enjoys in neighboring Sudan, Somalia, or parts of Eritrea. One finds the flavorful mashed bean dish ful most commonly at bus stations or markets where Muslim shops dominate.

By the early 1960s, the first of the restaurants serving Ethiopian cuisine appeared, designating injera and wat as *Yabahal megeb* (national food). First, the small hotels in the Mercato and Piazza commercial areas offered elaborate menus that included classical meat and fasting dishes, all served with injera. These hotels often catered to regional clienteles from northern areas of Tigray, Eritrea, Gonder, or Gojjam but tended to feature similar fare with injera, with the notable addition of kitfo, served properly in a clay dish and swimming in spiced butter. The Addis Ababa Restaurant in the Qidus Giyorgis neighborhood was among the first such specialized restaurants that made a conscious effort to reproduce the elaborated cuisine of a wealthy private home as well as to decorate its dining room with specific cultural objects to offer the ambience of such a home.[22] Other restaurants followed suit, including the Karamara, located in the upscale Bole district near the airport and housed in the woven wicker buildings of the Dorze people (though it served exclusively the Abyssinian national cuisine) and featuring Amhara/Tigrayan musical performances.

Revolutionary Fare

The commercialization of Ethiopia's national cuisine stalled abruptly when the 1974 revolution and its socialist experiment abruptly nationalized urban housing, imposed grain price controls, and forced entrepreneurship underground. In the Derg era (1974–91), rationing of foodstuffs and rising prices for grains (especially teff) suppressed both public and private hospitality. Although few restaurants with national food risked opening, members of the *ancien régime* and urban middle class sought to support themselves and save their housing property from confiscation by using their villas in Addis Ababa and provincial towns as "speakeasy" restaurants, called *zigubegn* (literally "close me in"). Zigubegn establishments blended the accepting of payment for food with the ritual and ambiance of the private home. Though they did not have printed menus as many formal restaurants had, these restaurants often served a high quality of food, combining classic highland cuisine with innovations like multiple grades of injera and slight variations on traditional dishes. In other cases, former salaried functionaries converted private homes into formal upscale dining spots. Zigubegn establishments usually had no signs and relied on word of mouth, but their customers gave them informal names (such as EDU) that implied clandestine allegiances to antisocialist elements.[23] Others, such as the Banatu Restaurant (near Olympia intersection on the Bole Road), catered notoriously to functionaries of the military government, but also served well-prepared national food.

The Derg period was a time of austerity for both the national and household economies, but it was also a period of clever adaptation. Few new dishes emerged nationally, though maize quietly became the country's most produced crop (see below). One innovation in food and its presentation was the increasing practice of serving individual plates at the table, with injera offered in rolled-up strips rather than shared on a common platter in layers enjoyed communally. Some have argued that this was a modern touch, but others noticed that it saved injera during austere times. While this practice had begun before the 1974 revolution, it became more common during those hard times and was part of a general trend toward middle-class values in urban areas.

Maize: No Room at the Inn

Perhaps the most perplexing exclusion of all from Ethiopian national cuisine is not related to religion, ethnicity, or availability. Since its introduction via Arab Red Sea trade in the sixteenth century, maize served in the northern ox-plow system as a garden crop eaten at the green, milky stage and rarely as a main crop. Over the course of the twentieth century it replaced sorghum in lower-lying areas, and the high yields of improved varieties encouraged farmers to sow it instead of wheat, teff, and barley. But it has

FIGURE 4.8
Roasting maize
in Bahir Dar,
Ethiopia, 2003.
Photo by author

FIGURE 4.9 Modern maize snack, newspaper ad, Ethiopia, 2003. *Photo by author*

never made an appearance in the national cuisine. It appears only on the margins of elite diets as a roasted snack in the late summer, or as a porridge in some societies on the periphery (in the Omo Valley, along the Sudan border, along the Kenya border). And at times it is used for making a type of injera (which falls apart annoyingly) or as a cheap additive to wheat-bread dough in commercial bakeries.

Probably the best explanation for maize's powerful place in the field but failure to be invited to table is that it now occupies a culinary niche once held by finger millet (dagussa), which in the historical food repertoire was always used as an additive, but never as a discernible food. Dagussa in some areas might be added to injera to moderate its cost. But its favored use was as the base for alcohol in the form of *katikala* (white lightning) or *talla* (household-brewed beer). Maize increasingly came to serve in all of those roles, and thus has had to enter the diet by the back door in the form of alcohol.

Cuisinal Creativity at the Core: *Tegabino Shiro*

In contrast to the pattern of market conformity evident in diaspora restaurants (see chapter 7), the recent economic expansion in Ethiopia's domestic economy and arrival of private overseas remittance capital has brought innovation in Ethiopia itself, the cuisine's historical cradle. Part of the change has brought Ethiopian "national" cuisine to the restaurants of the major hotels in the capital—the Hilton, Ghion, Sheraton, and Simen—and now many more upscale restaurants that advertise their culinary erudition in the "national dish" to both the Ethiopian middle class and international communities. Recently, the domestic attribute of *baltena* (a term meaning adeptness at cooking or household work) has spread from the private home to public restaurant settings or to prepackaged cooking ingredients.

Shops in urban neighborhoods now sell prepackaged berbere, shiro powder, Maggi bouillon cubes (the signs say, "It tastes like chicken and it will make you chew your fingers"), and cracked grain for breakfast porridge.

FIGURE 4.10
Maggi bouillon cube ad, Ethiopia: "Tastes Like Chicken." *Photo by author*

These convenience foods are the result of pressures on city-dwellers' time, but also offer an air of modernity that appeals to many cooks.

What is most remarkable, however, is the nature of the menu items at these new commercial food establishments. Rather than just expanding their menus with new dishes, as in the diaspora case, restaurateurs have reached back into the popular rustic roots of rural staple foods in the same way in which Italian gourmands elevated and "dignified" polenta from a peasant staple to an accompaniment to refined nouvelle national cuisine in Venice's best trattoria.

The best examples for Ethiopia are two simple dishes of basic ingredients that have rural peasant roots but that are now standard fare in the best restaurants: *qwanta frerfrer* and *tegabino shiro*. Qwanta frerfrer is a dish of dried meat (beef, mutton, or goat) and soaked injera scraps elevated from its original status of a leftover dish served for breakfast to one that appears prominently on menus at the finest national restaurants in Addis Ababa or Washington DC. Qwanta appeared on Mérab's 1913 list, praised by the Docteur for its smoky quality, which he ironically noted was like a good *jambon* (smoked ham). He was not far wrong.

Tegabino (or tegamino) shiro is, however, the very best case and the hero of this story for local creativity and a nostalgic culinary stretch back to agrarian cultural roots. This dish is a sauce made from heavily spiced legume—chickpea, field pea, or fava bean—flour, oil (or butter), and water brought bubbling ("tuk tuk") to the table in a miniature clay pot or shallow (often dented) aluminum pan. Its true aficionados usually consume it with a dark or sergegna injera. The spices are complex and powerful, but the dish is easy to prepare and cooks can make it from prepared powder in a matter of minutes.

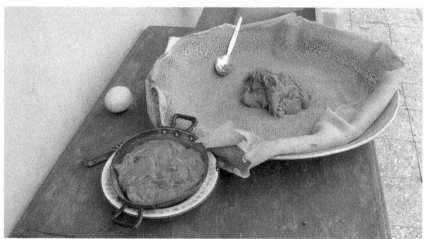

FIGURE 4.11 *Tegabino shiro* in a roadside hotel, 2005. *Photo by author*

It is a very popular restaurant dish since it can serve as a main meal on fasting days (when made with oil) or as *fisiq* (nonfasting food) made with spiced clarified butter and as *bozena* (with bits of dried meat). It can be a meal in itself (with injera) or part of a mixed sampler plate (*beyanetu*).

Tegabino's is a Horatio Alger story of a successful rise from plebeian roots. As explained to me by a owner of a small roadside hotel in Gojjam, tegabino's humble origins were in the Eritrean Red Sea port of Assab, where local coffeeshops prepared road food for long-haul truck drivers in a hurry. The quickest way to feed them was to have spiced legume powder at the ready and to use the shallow aluminum pan—called by the Italian name *tegame* or *tegamino* (the small version)—to cook on demand when hungry drivers pulled off the road at all hours. Even though the Assab's trade stopped after the 1998 Eritrean-Ethiopian war, the quick but tasty tegamino shiro had become a staple of the bars and teahouses along Ethiopia's far-flung road networks, slowly changing its name to the now more common adaptation *tegabino*. As it made its way from the roadside to the new cafés in Addis Ababa and smaller towns, the dish also moved upscale from the often dented and rough tegamino pans to rustic but elegant black

FIGURE 4.12 *Tegabino bozena* (with dried meat), Addis Ababa, 2005. *Photo by author*

clay pots made especially for the purpose and suggesting both authenticity and elegance in presentation.[24] Tegabino's low price and rustic authenticity make it among the most popular restaurant dishes.

OUR ANALYSIS of cuisine can illustrate bursts of creativity, cultural introspection, conformity, or a bold assertion of independence. For Ethiopia one of those moments was the 1887 feast of Maryam (chapter 3), a politically confident moment at the eve of a new assertion of empire. The feast was an assemblage of foods and ingredients that demonstrated the grasp of the kingdom and its base in an ox-plow agricultural ecology that could include grains, legumes, honey, spices, and meats from different regions and agro-ecologies.

The cuisine assembled by the Empress Taytu, however, specifically excluded the foods of regional Islamic cultures—rice, samosa, ful, raw goat (*bakal* or *kibbee*). Although these foods have recently emerged in urban diets as Islam has become more visible in national culture, this has occurred more in Ethiopia itself than in the diaspora. The foodways of pastoralism (blood, camel milk/meat) have never moved outside of the rural cultural base in Ethiopia or anywhere else in Africa, just as elsewhere in the world only Scotland's haggis or perhaps a dish from Mongolia seems to have managed that leap to a place in a national/nationalist cuisine.

Although Ethiopia's iconic cuisine also excluded maize, it did incorporate other foods from around the wider empire (particularly Gurage dishes like kitfo and *katanya*, layers of injera spread with pepper paste). Coffee ceremoniously offered as a capstone to a special meal, however, was an exception to the latter rule, even though it carried strong Islamic and pre-Christian associations with mischievous spirits. Its adoption took place rapidly when Menilek and the Egyptian Orthodox patriarch Abuna Matewos in the 1890s reconfigured its ritual symbols to conform to Christian practice. Even in the postimperial era, Ethiopia's national identity in the *Ghebbi* (Menilek's old palace and now the residence of the head of state) and in the restaurants of the diaspora pays homage to the national cuisine.

The process of inclusion in and exclusion of parts of Ethiopian cookery as its national cuisine was a consensus of high-profile cultural mavens like Empress Taytu) as well as elite consumers who chose to move public presentations at a public feast into restaurants, private homes, and ritual celebrations, a process that continued over the formation of Ethiopia's national cultural identity in the twentieth century.

PART THREE

Africa's Cooking

Some Common Ground of Culture and of Cuisine

Africa's culinary history is resplendent with local nuances dictated by the ecology of ingredients and cultural traditions. Ethiopia's case shows a movement toward a national cuisine that is not obvious in the rest of the continent. Yet there are also broader patterns of cooking and signature foods that connect regions. Chapter 5 describes cooking ideas and practices in West Africa, where languages and political histories of trade and empire provided similarity across the region. Two signature dishes help guide us though what might otherwise seem a confusing local diversity.

Chapter 6 argues for two quite different influences in cooking cultures in eastern and southern Africa. One is the overwhelming dominance of maize porridge as a common culinary theme, from the South African veld to the Kenyan highlands. The other appears in the Atlantic and Indian ocean rims, where the circulation of people and of ingredients for the pot created a cosmopolitan menu from Mombasa to Mozambique, from Cape Town to Luanda. The mix in local women's kitchens showed local practice but added the flavors of cooking from Portugal, India, Indonesia, and the nearby ocean culinary ecologies.

CHAPTER FIVE

A West African Culinary Grammar

IN WEST AFRICA, in contrast to Ethiopia, there is no single political force over its history but rather a wide range of political influences (including colonialism) and a set of ecologies and overlapping cultural traditions that guided its cooking history. There are, however, common themes, and Nigerian novelist Chinua Achebe gives us a creative view of the culture of food and cooking:

> After kola nuts had been presented and eaten, the people of the sky set before their guests the most delectable dishes Tortoise has ever seen or dreamt of. The soup was brought out hot from the fire and in the very pot in which it had been cooked. It was full of meat and fish. Tortoise began to sniff aloud. There was pounded yam and also yam pottage cooked with palm oil and fresh fish. There were also pots of palm wine. When everything had been set before the guests, one of the people of the sky came forward and tasted a little from each pot. He then invited the birds to eat. But Tortoise jumped to his feet and asked: "For whom have you prepared this feast?" "For all of you," replied the man.[1]

West Africa's geography sets the table, so to speak, for the depth, complexities, and deep-seated connections between its cooking traditions. It is nevertheless surprising that in otherwise quite distinct West African political cultures and aesthetic traditions, West Africa's language families, so diverse in some ways, share fundamental elements of a common cuisine—dishes like groundnut soup, Jollof rice, and starchy staples like *fufu* (pounded yam, cassava, or plantain). These culinary preparations may appear mummified as formal recipes in modern cookery books, but the recipes, after all, are only Platonic shadows of women's accumulated oral knowledge that plays itself out daily in kitchens and pots. Rather than being unchanging artifacts, these West African culinary traditions are deeply historical and fluid, reflecting active bodies of local history, ecology, and cultural exchange across time and across a broad region.

West African Cuisine: A Geographical Thesis

This chapter argues that, despite their wide range, West African traditions of cooking are more alike than they are different. Moreover, their similarities parallel the ecologies that underlie the region's history. More than any other region of Africa—and of Europe, for that matter—West African cooking shows historical innovation, regional coherence, and a complexity of composition. These common traits are inventions of human design, yet they also reflect the overlapping of physical ecology that binds coastlines, forest areas, savanna, desert, and the transition zones between them. A small herring-like fish caught by a Ga fisherman off the coast at Accra, Ghana, might appear in a stew that night. It might also end up smoked by a woman and traded inland, where it might flavor a light palm oil soup in Kumasi a week later. A shea nut collected by a young girl at the edge of the sahel in Mali near Dogon country might end up as shea butter and travel down the Niger River to Timbuctu, where a wife will cook it with baobab leaves for her husband's dinner, eaten with boiled millet and goat meat. Making sense of the types of cooking across such a vast mix of peoples and ecologies makes the culinary historian's task a tough one. But rewarding.

As with the case of Ethiopia in the previous chapters, the approach here is to present a historical baseline of cookery and to explore the historical record for its core principles, culinary textures, and directions of evolution. The focus of my argument is the Kwa language and cultural area, which spans the coast from Saint Louis (in Senegal) to Ghana to the Bight of Biafra and into Cameroon; it reaches from the coast and across the forest to the edge of the savanna's forest mosaic, bordering the dry Sahel zone. It includes the languages of the Yoruba, Ibo, Akan, and Ga. To Kwaland we must also add a few others from West Africa's cultural mix—Hausa and Berber from the Afro-Asiatic family, and West Atlantic language groups like Wolof, Pulaar, and Mande, each with its own iconic food culture.

My approach seeks to explain that culinary landscape as part of a dynamic and historical diffusion of ideas and cookery that spans virtually all of West Africa. There are, in fact, two main culture areas: a large zone of diffusion from the Mali empire—the Mande peoples—associated with the savanna zone, and the Akan culture zone, based in the forest area of what is now central Ghana.

Culinary Consequences of the Mali Empire, 1250–1500

The foundations of foodways in West Africa reflect its broad, and local, historical movements, which included edible morsels carried in trans-Saharan caravans and seeds exchanged by women in village compounds along the way. The key ingredients for cookery that percolated around the region included the starchy staples described in chapter 2 as well as the oils, vegetables, and meats offered by the local ecology of savanna and the edge of West Africa's Upper Guinea forest. Among the oils used for cooking or adding flavor and color, West Africans might use deep-red-colored palm oil (in the forest zone), peanut oil (in the savanna), or shea nut butter (in the forest mosaic zone). Pastoral peoples like the Fulani or Tuareg in drier areas where livestock herding rather than agriculture predominated would rely on butter, or on oils from the marketplace. Political systems that flowered along the fertile trade networks between these areas might have distinct ethnic and linguistic foundations (Soninke, Mandinka, Songhay, Kanuri), but they had expanded across ecological and ethnic boundaries that encouraged the sharing of culinary arts and its daily practice. Women learned cooking from one another just as adjacent groups learned one another's languages, mixing and inventing new words and ideas about cooking.

The Mali empire was the most extensive and polyglot of these multiethnic states. From 1250 to 1485, Mali spread its cultural and economic heritage from the desert's edge, along the Niger Valley, and into forest areas to the south and what the narrator of the great Mande epic, *Sundiata*, calls the "twelve doors of Mali." The repertoire of foods, ingredients, and ideas about cookery that took root with its expanding political kingdom remained vibrant long after the political empire itself had withered. With that legacy and the historical memory of Mali's cultural diaspora spread a sense of culinary identity that historian Natalie Mettler describes as "iconic," with sauces, ingredients, and culinary aromas that appear even in *Sundiata*. Mettler reminds us that in that story Sundiata's enemies use the smell of a certain sauce spice called *datu* to lure his family into capture. It was the aromatic nostalgia for a favorite food that was their downfall.[2]

In the late eighteenth century, the English traveler Mungo Park, who followed the course of the Niger Valley from the west, described a marvelous mix of the old and new in the range of food ingredients he saw in use near the Gambia River, then part of Mali's far-flung cultural diaspora:

> The grains which are chiefly cultivated are Indian corn, (*zea mays*); two kinds of *holcus spicatus*, called by the natives *soono* and *sanio* [a local millet-like grain]; *holcus niger*, and *holcus bicolor* [types of sorghum]. . . . These, together with rice, are raised in considerable quantities; besides which, the inhabitants, in the vicinity of the towns and villages, have gardens which produce onions, calavances [chickpeas], yams, cassvi, ground-nuts, pompions [pumpkins], gourds, water-melons, and some other esculent plants.[3]

Despite this impressive repertoire of foods, Mungo Park's snapshot of the upper Niger Valley still reveals only a small piece of a larger culinary landscape. His modest listing includes foods of African innovation like sorghum, fonio, yam, and watermelons; foods from the New World like groundnuts, cassava, and squash; and foods of Mediterranean origin like onions and chickpeas. These each reflected long-standing patterns of exchange that contributed to the West African cook's broth. Mungo Park's observations also reveal that techniques of preparation and consumer tastes traversed much of the area of the Niger River and its cultural tributaries and showed the influence of cultural contacts from across the Sahara.

The preparation of couscous (a steamed grain product) in the eighteenth-century Niger Valley, for example, suggests a broader thesis argued in this chapter, namely the presence of a West African regional cuisine that has (and had) distinctive local variations, but a remarkable stability over time. Park's term "corn" can refer to any type of grain, in this case probably sorghum rather than the wheat used in the North African version:

> In preparing their corn for food, the natives use a large wooden mortar called a *paloon*, in which they bruise the seed until it parts with the outer covering, or husk, which is then separated from the clean corn, by exposing it to the wind; nearly in the same manner as wheat is cleared from the chaff in England. The corn thus freed from the husk is returned to the mortar, and beaten into meal; which is dressed variously in different countries; but the most common preparation of it among the nations

of the Gambia, is a sort of pudding, which they call *kouskous*. It is made by first moistening the flour with water, and then stirring and shaking it about in a large calabash, or gourd, till it adheres together in small granules, resembling sago. It is then put into an earthen pot, whose bottom is perforated with a number of small holes; and this pot being placed upon another, the two vessels are luted together, either with a paste of meal and water, or with cows' dung, and placed upon the fire. In the lower vessel is commonly some animal food and water, the steam or vapour of which ascends through the perforations in the bottom of the upper vessel, and softens and prepares the *kouskous*, which is very much esteemed throughout the countries that I visited. I am informed, that the same manner of preparing flour, is very generally used on the Barbary coast, and that the dish so prepared, is there called by the same name. It is therefore probable, that the Negroes borrowed the practice from the Moors.[4]

For West Africans in the savanna, steamed couscous resembled the rice that was a familiar staple popular along the West African coast and in the inland Niger Delta.

The methods and the materials that Park described showed both local invention and a substantial interaction with trans-Saharan culinary culture. The couscous he observed in the 1790s probably was only a small part of a full array of preparations of porridges and grain-flour-based dishes served both to elite travelers and in everyday village settings in the savanna's grain-based culinary region under the influence of Mali. From the empire's economic networks the cooking included not only couscous and rice, but also the flavor of groundnut stew described below.

If the Mali empire's rise and decline between the mid-1300s and 1500s was visible across much of West Africa, the decline in the savanna's trans-Saharan trade fortunes in the sixteenth and seventeenth centuries was part of global changes that accompanied the rise of the Atlantic world. The economic impact of the Atlantic trade also included the Columbian Exchange of food crops (see chapter 2) as well as the more complex and tragic dynamics of the movement, through the Atlantic slave trade, of Africa's captive labor, human knowledge, and food ideas into the New World. Food and cuisine provided the base for West Africa's modern culinary tradition as well as the diasporan cuisines of the New World.

Forest Fare: Akan, the Gold Coast and Beyond

On the African side of the Atlantic economy, a series of new states in Kwaland (Dahomey, Benin, Oyo, Asante) and ethnic identities grew in the Atlantic era and expanded their regional influence across adjacent ecological and cultural zones, especially in the 1600s and 1700s. This was a period of profound political and economic change that moved West Africa's center of gravity from the savanna to the emerging coastal kingdoms and trade centers. The cultural remnants of the Mali trade diaspora left cultural and religious enclaves of "Djula" (a Mande word meaning "traders") in the royal capitals and trade entrepôts of the new states and at key points along the West African coast. The Djula were Mandinka people from Mali who served as trade entrepreneurs, blacksmiths, and clerics. Cultural crosscurrents also traveled along Africa's Atlantic coastal rim from Saint Louis (in Senegal) to the Gold Coast to Douala in Cameroon, further stirring the mix of cultural exchange and creativity in foods.[5] These influences were the founding ingredients of West Africa's linguistic and culinary grammars.

The exchange of ingredients, aesthetic choices, and cooking techniques took sensual form in what people ate. The carriers of information on local food culture were often European travelers who moved along the coast seeking to make their fortune from trading with the Afro-Portuguese settlements and new kingdoms farther inland. Food was only occasionally the object of their attention, but the brief flashes of written descriptions of the foods they encountered show us how cooking techniques moved and changed, even if travelers often expressed their dismay or disapproval over local fare.

But there is also evidence that some visitors came to appreciate the culinary products of local cooks and local ingredients. Around 1700, Dutch trader Wilem Bosman described the cooking he found on the Gold Coast. His rudimentary description of the local meals probably masks the complex mix of ingredients, the flavors, and the techniques: "But for an extraordinary Dish, they take Fish, a handful of Corn, as much Dough, and some Palm-Oyl, which they boil together in Water; and this they call *Mallaget;* and is, I can assure you, a Lordly Entertainment amongst them; and to speak the truth, 'tis no very disagreeable Food."[6] From such historical accounts we can infer a fuller range of ingredients, methods of preparing them, and aesthetics of taste. Bosman was a trader and probably no sort of cook himself, but at least he enjoyed the final result, produced no doubt by the women of the houses that he occupied on his way. The Gold Coast has some of the most detailed descriptions from coastal towns, such as Accra, where the local Ga people lived with a small settlement of Danish, Swedish, and Dutch settler/traders. Bosman also described the diet of the Gold Coast's poor in stark terms, suggesting elements of the "sober" life of the common folk at a time before the full impact of the Atlantic trade: "Their common Food is a Pot full of Millet boiled to the consistence of Bread, or instead of that Jambs [yams] and Potatoes; over which they pour a little Palm-Oyl, with a few boiled herbs, to which they add a stinking Fish. This they esteem a nice Dish; for 'tis but seldome they can get the Fish and Herbs: As for Oxen, Sheep, Hens, or other Flesh, they only buy that for Holy-days."[7]

Modern historian Ray Kea summarizes European observations of local foods, more broadly arguing that there was, in fact, a more varied diet in the 1660s on the Gold Coast. He refers especially to *kenkey*, which was maize meal steamed tamale-like in the maize husks: "Many commoners in the coastal towns subsisted on fish, fowl, cereals (in the form of *kenkey* or some other 'bread'), palm oil, yams, fruits, vegetables of different kinds and palm wine. Poor commoners consumed yams or *kenkey*, palm oil, fish, and a few vegetables."[8] The class elements of diet were apparently quite evident, as were the effects of both seasonal fluctuation and inflation over time. Other European observers offered calculations that a day laborer's yearly income of 288 *dambas* would buy a daily meal of fish (including kenkey, palm oil, salt, pepper, and some vegetables) over the course of one year. A year's supply of grain (in this case maize) for an adult cost between 46 to 183 dambas of gold in an era when an annual cash income for a day laborer was 288 dambas.[9]

The early 1600s were clearly a transitional moment in the foundations of foods that made up West Africa's diet. Pieter de Marees' drawing from circa 1600 shows clearly the mix of new crops available to West African cooks, and his description of Gold Coast breadmaking offers a snapshot of a time when millet and maize coexisted as staple grains in the local diet:

> Over night they steepe this Millia with a little Mais in faire water, and in the morning after they have washt, and made themselves readie, they take the Millia and lay it upon a stone, as Painters doe when they grind their colours, then they take another stone about a foot long, and with their hands grinds the Millia as small as they can, till in a manner it be dough, and then it sheweth like baked Buckway Cakes, they temper their dough with fresh water and Salt, and then make Rowles thereof as

bigge as two fists, and that they lay upon a warm harth, whereon it baketh a little, and this is the bread which they use.[10]

We can imagine as well that since maize was becoming a key ingredient on the coast in this period, so were ingredients that fundamentally changed the flavor and texture of West African's diets: red pepper, peanuts, locust beans (carob), eggplant, and tomatoes. A number of indigenous African crops and ones brought from elsewhere in the world appeared in coastal gardens maintained near European trade forts. At the English fort at Cape Coast castle in 1727, the traveler William Smith saw a garden plot some eight miles in circumference that contained "every Thing that grows within the Torrid Zone," including oranges, lemons, limes, citrons, "and many sorts of European salads." Others visiting French, Danish, or Portuguese outposts reported seeing chickpeas, eggplants, onions, garlic, shallots, cucumbers, cabbages, leafy vegetables, and chives.[11] The workers in these coastal fort gardens were no doubt local Africans who had their own farms in the area. No doubt they had lent some of their own seeds or borrowed a few from their European settlers. West African cooks (and farmers) had a huge variety from which to choose.

Staples and flavors in West African cooking that emerged along the coast and among inland trading partners showed both overall consistency and the ingenuity of local cooks. Yet early accounts from outsiders (almost all male Europeans) offer little sense yet of an elaboration of cuisine. They note the relative scarcity of onions, garlic, and ginger, three important ingredients of more recent West African cookery. The Dutch trader Bosman described the foods and diets of different parts of the West African coast and how they compared to the Gold Coast. For the area to the east, which he called the "Slave Coast" (Dahomey and the Bight of Benin), Bosman noted the West African pattern of steaming "bread" and other items made from ingredients found commonly along the West African coast:

> There is not one oven in this whole Country, by reason the Negroes never use them, but always boil their bread.
>
> Potatoes are what they commonly Eat instead of Bread with all sorts of Victuals, and here is such abundant Plenty of them, that I believe the whole Coast does not produce a like Number.
>
> Here are also Jammes [yams], but neither, in such Plenty nor so Good as on the *Gold*-Coast, nor are they much esteemed here.

Here are several sorts of small Beans in very great Plenty, amongst which is one species, of which our People make Oyl-Cakes, which are as light as ours in *Holland;* and those who are used to them, like their Tast well enough. They are called here *Acraes.* Onions and Ginger grow here, tho' in but small Quantities, especially of the former. All the other Fruits of the Earth which the *Gold*-Coast produceth grow here also. . . .

Here are great numbers of Palm-Trees the whole Country over, but the wine is drawn off and Drank by very few here: For they Cultivate them only in order to draw Oyl from them.[12]

Here Bosman missed the fact that palm oil and palm wine come from different types of palm trees and different parts of the plant. Palm oil comes from the fruit (nuts) of the oil palm, and palm wine comes from cutting a palm tree itself to yield the milky sap.

Bosman also compared the Gold Coast fare to the foods and ingredients of the inland kingdom of Fida (Dahomey) and the politically sophisticated and ritually elaborate kingdom of Benin in southwestern Nigeria:

The inhabitants of this Country, if possessed of any Riches, Eat and Drink very well; that is the say, of the best. The common Diet of the Rich is Beef, Mutton or Chickens, and Jammes [yam] for their Bread, which after they have boiled, they beat very fine, in order to make Cakes [*fufu*] of it.

The meaner Sort content themselves with smoak'd or dry'd Fish; which, if salted, is very like what we in *Europe* call Raf and Reekel. Their bread is also Jammes, Banana's and Beans; they Drink Water and *Pardon*-Wine, which is none of the best. The Richer Sort drink Water and Brandy, when they can get it. . . .

The River upwards is not well stor'd with Fish; all that they eat here coming from a place called Boca de la Mare, or the Mouth of the Sea, where they are dry'd and smoak'd; but most of it not being salted tasts very ill and stinks abominably.

The Fruits of the Earth are, first, Corn, or great *Milho* [sorghum]; for they have none of the small Sort [millet]. The large *Milho* [maize] is here cheap, but they do not esteem it; wherefore but little is sow'd which yet yields a prodigious quantity of Grain, and grows very luxuriantly. . . .

>Here are not many Potatoes, but a prodigious abundant Plenty of Jammes; which is also their most ready Diet. They eat them with all manner of Edibles instead of Bread; wherefore they are very careful that this Fruit be planted and gathered in its proper Season.
>
>Here are two sorts of Beans, both [of] which are very like Horse-Beans [fava].
>
>I never saw any Rice here, nor do I believe that any grows in *Benin,* tho' the morassy Land near the River seems very proper for it.[13]

During this period of the slave trade, food and diet were also a grisly part of the Atlantic world's impact. Europeans sometimes commented on the foods offered to slaves in coastal castles or stocked on ships for the long middle passage. Bosman noted that an English ship captain, after filing his ship full of slaves, he went to the "Portuguese Island [São Tomé], where he stored himself with Provisions for his Goods." We do not know the precise cargo of provisions, but for crossing the Atlantic one eighteenth-century rations list for captives' weekly diet includes the following: "Sunday—pork, beans, porridge, tobacco; Monday—beans, porridge, tobacco, brandy; Tuesday— beans, porridge, tobacco; Wednesday—beans, porridge, brandy; Thursday— pork, beans, porridge, brandy; Friday—beans, porridge, tobacco; Saturday— *millie* (twice), brandy."[14] This list indicates a post-Columbian diet of boiled grain meal (porridge) of available grains (millet, sorghum, or cassava), maize (*millie*) in some form, beans (possibly fava, pigeon peas, cowpeas, or locust beans), alcohol, and tobacco. The pork may have been dried victuals carried from Europe or perhaps bush meat (wild boar, cane rat, or grasscutter rodent). While this diet may seem monotonous to a modern palate, its balance of nutrients suggests that health of the captives mattered to the captors, at least in an economic sense if not a humane one. The list, however, is only a plan of what the slaves would receive, and may not indicate the grim realities of their sustenance on their perilous sojourn across the Atlantic world. Once in the tropical ecology of the New World, Africans had to make their own way in collecting medicines and foraging for local foods, adapting to new plants, whose leaves, roots, and fruits would often have seemed familiar equivalents to those from their home diets in Africa.[15]

Bosman's brief comments on the "Grain Coast" (the Windward Coast, from Sierra Leone to Ivory Coast) in the last decade of the seventeenth century show parts of the West African foods and the shortage of live-stock in the tsetse zone, where sleeping sickness took a heavy toll on domestic livestock:

> The Product of this Land consists of a small Quantity of great Milhio [sorghum], Jammes, Potatoes, and abundance of Rice. The Arboriferous Fruits here, as well as on the *Gold-Coast*, are Paquovers [papayas], Banana's, Anana's [pineapples], etc.
>
> They are not well stored with Cattle; for they have neither Kine nor Hogs, and but a few Sheep; also not many Chicken, but they are good.[16]

Descriptions of food by male European observers, whatever their depth of experience or language skills, offer a vague list of ingredients, but little sense that a cuisine had evolved in the early years of West Africa's Atlantic-era kingdoms and their hinterlands. Just as the sophistication of political and economic systems evolved in the eighteenth and nineteenth centuries, so, likely, did the aesthetics and means of cooking—a product of expanding trade networks, elite class formation, and cultural borrowing. The emergence of elite cultures in the Kwa region (e.g., kingdoms like Asante and Aja/Dahomey) and at the Bight of Benin that resulted from the economic expansion of the Atlantic rim very likely was the stimulus for complex cuisine as well (a situation that took place also in England and France in a similar period).[17]

Africa's Mutually Intelligible Cuisine: A Culinary Template

West Africa from Senegal to Cameroon is a coherent language region where cultures, politics, and religions overlap. Creole and pidgin languages allow communications between trade partners and men and women of different language groups. Its culinary palette demonstrates many common elements that show centuries of interactions across ecologies of trade and common ideas about cooking, including starchy staples from particular ecologies on the political margins of the old Mali empire and bush meat from forest zones, as well as dried "stink fish" and powdered shrimp from the coastal fishing communities. Moreover, the range of ingredients available demonstrates the trade that moved commodities from hinterlands to the core areas as well as the communities of culinary knowledge that offered a full array of techniques for boiling, frying, grinding, drying, and steaming complex bodies of flavor and texture in stews and one-pot meals.

FIGURE 5.1 An Asante feast with palm wine, c. 1820. *Source: T. Edward Bowdich, Mission from Cape Coast Castle to Ashantee, ed. W. E. F. Ward (London: Frank Cass, 1966)*

Figure 5.1 shows the ritual significance of palm wine and the feast in Asante public life. There are, regretfully, only a few glimpses in the historical record to testify to the subtleties of the food preparations that preceded colonial rule.[18] For the Akan region of West Africa's Gold Coast we have to wait until 1931, when the anthropologist and physician Margaret Field published a valuable pamphlet, "General Survey of Gold Coast Food."[19] Field worked slightly earlier than Audrey Richards, though in West Africa rather than Richards's Central African site. Field came to her study of foods from an interest in the science of nutrition, a field only poorly understood by colonial anthropologists. Like Richards, she was a pioneer in appreciating the nature of women's work and knowledge. Hers is the first published survey of African food and cooking, though obviously it drew on a long-standing and deep body of oral knowledge among women of common households as well as royal courts in West Africa. So, like Dr. Mérab's list of Ethiopian dishes, this menu is a historical document of a certain moment in Gold Coast culinary history.

Field's systematic description of Gold Coast cuisine catalogues forty-three distinctive preparations, which she divides into six categories: starchy foods, stews, protein foods other than meat or fish, fish, fruits, and oil seeds and nut foods. Her survey is a benchmark that primarily reflects the everyday cuisine of the compounds and streets of Gold Coast's southern areas. What she observed and described in 1931 was, in essence, a snapshot of the historical cuisine of the forest/savanna/coastal political and cultural ecology of West Africa. Variations of the culinary palette found in the cultures of Benin (Dahomey), Togo, Côte d'Ivoire, Sierra Leone, Senegal, and especially southwestern Nigeria show local innovation and adaptation, as well as personal preferences, but share the nuances of the culinary community evident in Gold Coast at its prewar, midcolonial period. Britain had formally colonized Gold Coast thirty-five years earlier, and independence as Ghana was still a quarter century away.

Though recorded by a European observer, Field's list clearly reflects historical layering, generational experience and bodies of oral communication accumulated over time. The menu of dishes is a walk through the southern Gold Coast's kitchens. Many of these dishes are obviously urbanized versions of rustic preparations. Her survey includes the following dishes and preparations, for which she offers the Twi (Akan language) name and adds the equivalent in the Ga and Ewe languages also spoken in the Gold Coast. The range of ingredients as well as the powerful role of maize is remarkable. To clarify some of her references, I have added the dishes' key staple and/or a descriptive name in this summary.

FERMENTED STARCHY FOODS

Kpokpoi (maize)

Fermented maize dough dried by lining a basin with it and rubbing it into a powder with the finger tips. The dough is then steamed in layers in a double-boiler.

Kenkey (maize)

Maize is soaked in water for three days and then stone ground and put in a pot covered with plantain leaves to ferment, then ground again. The mixture is then rolled and encased in plantain leaves (or maize husks) and steamed/boiled for some hours.

Banku (maize)

Maize kernels are sprouted, ground, and set aside for three days. The fermented dough is then spread in a basin and dried. The thin dough is cooked either by mixing with water and salt and stirred in an iron pot. Banku is then eaten lukewarm with stew or soup.

Ensenehu (maize)

Maize kernels are washed and dehulled by beating gently with a pestle. Dehulled grains are ground into white meal and stored for three days in a bowl. Dough is then covered in dry maize leaves (husks) and boiled for an hour. It is eaten with stew.

Abete (maize)

Maize is roasted brown and then ground and cooked as with *ensenehu*. It is often eaten with *nkontomire* or palm-nut soup.

Akasa (maize)

Soured maize dough is mixed with water to a smooth paste and then rubbed through a sieve into a pot and boiled for an hour into a thick gruel. Sugar is often added at the end and served as the chief invalid food.

Otoo (maize)

Much the same as *akasa*, but eaten with lumps intact.

Abolo (maize)

Soured maize dough is mixed with wheat flour and water and fermented for several hours. Lumps are then put on "*aboloba*" leaves and baked in the oven.

Atweme (wheat)

Wheat dough fermented with palm wine and rolled thinly and fried in deep fat till crisp and brown. It appears either as thin strips or flat cakes.

Bodobodo (wheat)

A sweet wheat bread where the flour is mixed with palm wine and baked in a hemispherical wood-fired oven.

Gari (cassava)

Peeled and grated cassava stored in a cloth sack and then pressed between two boards and fermented for three days. It is then sifted and dried in a hot pan for storage as flour. When needed it is then sprinkled into boiling water and cooked into a thick paste.

UNFERMENTED STARCHY FOODS

Ablemamu (maize)

Dry maize is heated in an iron pot until brown and then finely stone ground and sifted. It is then stirred in a pot until it thickens as a kind of porridge

Aprapransa (maize)

Fish (sometimes with beans) cooked in a light palm-nut soup and then removed and broken into flakes and mixed with *ablemamu* (above) and cooked into a paste.

Tue (maize)

Dried corn pounded and mixed with water, strained through a cloth and then cooked with water in an iron pot into a soft paste. Sugar and salt are added.

Mpampa (maize and plantain)

Roasted maize is ground and mixed with water into a paste. Ripe plantains are boiled, pounded and mixed with the maize and some pepper.

Klaklo (maize and plantain)

A fried dough confection of ground roasted maize and pounded plantain that is fried in palm oil or palm kernel oil sold prepared in the marketplace.

Mankontwew (cocoyam)

Cocoyams (taro) peeled, cut up, and boiled in water. They are then mashed and cooked again with salt and palm oil added. Eaten either hot or cold.

Oto (cocoyam)

Prepared as for *mankontwew*, except with the addition of chopped onions, mashed pepper, and mashed stink fish with palm oil mixed in until the whole mass is a stiff brownish-yellow paste.

Ayaba (plantain)

Ripe plantains are peeled and cut lengthways and put in salted water. The sliced plantain are then deep fried in oil.

Ntebrefua (plantain)

Unripe plantain are boiled and then mashed with boiled ground peppers and palm oil.

Tartari (plantain and rice)

Ripe plantain are pounded in a wooden mortar and rice is ground to a fine flour. The two are mixed with chopped onions, salt and pepper into a paste and allowed to stand for three hours. The paste is then formed into small cakes and fried in palm oil until brown.

Santum kyewe (sweet potato)

Deep-fried pieces of sweet potato

Dundu (cocoyam)

Deep-fried pieces of cocoyam (taro)

Kokonte (cassava)

Cassava that is cut into small cubes, sun-dried, then fried in palm oil and pounded in a mortar into a fine powder for storage. To serve it is boiled in a pot into a dough, rolled into balls and served cold with soup.

Tapioca (cassava)

Cassava prepared similar to *gari* (above), but not fermented. The fiber is separated out of the grated cassava in a cloth and the caked starch is dry fried into irregular granules.

Fufu (yam, cassava, sweet potato, plantain and/or banana)

The root or banana is boiled and pounded in a mortar until the floury mass forms a moist, gluey lump about one kilo in weight. It is eaten with soup.

Fula (rice)

Rice is soaked overnight and then pounded in a *fufu* mortar. The powder is then cooked in a little boiling water and mixed with pepper, ginger, and various crushed seeds. The mass is then rolled into balls, rolled in rice flour. When required as food the balls are then crumbled into water or milk as a drink.

Asianku (plantain)

Unripe sun-dried plantain are pounded and the powder sifted and cooked in a little water. The cooked paste is mixed with mashed ripe bananas and pepper before serving.

STEWS AND SOUPS[20]

Nkakra (Fish and Vegetable Stew)

Lumps of fish or meat are boiled for an hour in water without seasoning. Then salt, pepper, onions, and tomatoes are added, then okra and garden eggs (small eggplant). Vegetables are then fished out, mashed and returned to the stew for two more hours. Mixture is served with *fufu* or *kenkey*.

Nmewonu (Palm Nut Soup)

Palm nuts boiled in water until soft and then pounded in a mortar. The pounded mass is then mixed again with water to separate the oil from the fiber. Into the oil and water is put meat and/or dried fish, salt, pepper, and onions and other vegetables; the whole is boiled until the vegetables are soft, then removed, mashed and returned to the soup. A layer of red oil floats on top of the soup.

Nkatie wonu (Groundnut Soup)

The groundnut husks are removed by mixing with sand and ashes roasting in a small iron pot. The nuts are then stoneground into an oily dough. Meat or fish, onions and other vegetables are boiled until soft and then the groundnut paste is stirred in and boiled again for some hours. To this soup are added hard-boiled eggs and the soup is served with fufu or boiled rice.

Mpotompoto (Yam Stew)

Skinned and sliced yams are boiled; peppers, sliced onions, and tomatoes are added. Fresh and stink [smoked] fish are boned and added. When soft the peppers and tomatoes are removed, mashed and returned to the pot. When cooked the yam is removed, mashed together with palm oil. The rest of the soup is then poured over this lump in a basin.

Okrama fro (Okra Soup)

Similar to Nkakra (above) but the okra and garden eggs are not mashed. The meat and fish are often cooked separately and then mixed with the sliced onions whole cooked okra and whole garden eggs and then cooked more.

Nkontomire (Cocoyam Leaf Soup)

Tender leaves of the cocoyam or cassava plant are boiled until soft and mashed. Sliced onions, tomatoes, fresh fish and stink fish are fried in palm oil. The mashed leaves are then added to this and the whole reheated.

Ampesi (Garden Egg Stew)

Sliced yams are boiled together with garden eggs and any sort of edible greens. Onions and tomatoes and fish or meat are fried in oil and then the boiled garden eggs are separated from the yams and after mashing are added to the frying mass and the whole fried together. The mixture is eaten with yams.

BEAN FOODS

Edwu Twew (Beans in Fish Sauce)

Beans are boiled and rubbed through a sieve. Ground peppers, chopped onions, and "stink fish" are fried lightly in palm oil and then the bean mixture is added and cooked for an hour of so. The dish is served with rice, *kenkey,* yam or other starchy base.

Emo Na Ada (Rice and Beans)

Equal amounts of rice and beans are put with water on the fire separately. Onions, tomatoes, and peppers are cut up and fried in a pot with oil for some minutes. A little water is added together with the cooked beans and the whole is cooked for about ten minutes. The rice is mashed, rolled into balls and served with the rest of the mixture poured over it.

Aprapranza (Bean Stew)

Any kind of beans, usually "Togoland" beans, are thrown into boiling water. When soft, some boiled peppers, tomatoes, onions, and salt are put in. Then palm oil is added and the whole is cooked for a very long time.

Akara (Fried Bean Balls)

A bean meal is made by roasting Togoland beans and grinding and sifting them into a meal. This meal is wetted, made into a dough and allowed to stand several days. It is then made into small balls about the size of doughnuts and deep fried in palm oil. [Field says that she saw these in the Nswam market, but the seller claimed they had no name. Akara is the Yoruba (Nigeria) name.]

A student of cooking cultures might use this list to compile an impressive tally of ingredients, or to survey techniques (boiling, steaming, frying, roasting). And what could one also speculate about the evidence of trade and cultural exchange implied in these preparations?

Field's comprehensive compendium of food preparations from 1931 reflects a stage of maturity of the Asante cultural empire that existed beneath the political umbrella of Britain's Gold Coast colonial rule. The empire combined the then 250-year-old Asante hegemony over the ecologies of forest, forest mosaic, and coastal regions and adjacent tributary cultures like the Fante, Ewe, and Ga people.

The food habits and daily sustenance in the Gold Coast area that Field describes for the 1930s appear far more sophisticated than the earlier accounts from European observers indicate, though they show a similar repertoire of methods and ingredients. Field's list gives us a good idea of the complexity of types of dishes, but little of how women made them or taught them to the next generation. Most of that complexity was probably present much earlier on, but likely it was hidden from outside male observers or they just failed to mention it. For them it might have been unremarkable, but for the modern culinary observer it is fascinating to witness.

West Africa's culinary history was a product of layers of economic change, movements of people (especially into urban sites), and enlargement of the scale of trade. Perhaps the most profound influence was the onset of European colonialism, when Britain, France, Portugal, Belgium, and Germany, after the 1884–85 Berlin Conference, launched their "scramble for Africa." Unlike eastern and southern Africa, however, West Africa was never home to colonies of European settlers who sought to build what Alfred Crosby has called "NeoEuropes."[21] By contrast, colonial rule in West Africa accelerated contact with a global economy, but, with the possible exception of the French colonial enclaves at Dakar and Abijian, no West African colony had a large resident European population or an infusion of Asian or south Asian migrants, though communities of Lebanese, Greeks, and Syrians eventually became part of West Africa's urban life. Cities and towns grew and became ethnically diverse and economically vibrant, accelerating the development of a cuisine that blended several ethnic culinary traditions and fostered innovation. Rural cookery came to the city to join the traditions of the African political elite and a middle class that grew in economic success. At least one of the effects of the colonial presence, however, was the rise of the number of male servants given responsibility for European households' food preparation. The professionalization of cooks helped spur the emergence of formalized dishes that became a colonial cuisine.

Through the second half of the twentieth century, food culture continued to evolve in burgeoning urban areas of the colonial Gold Coast and, after 1957, the newly independent Ghana. These new cultural settings revolved around women's economic independence, public and private space, and the continent's most complex mix of starchy staples and stews. Historian Claire Robertson's detailed and intriguing 1978 study of Ga market women in Accra, Ghana, gives us further insights into the emerging culture of food. Her survey of women's economic activity indicates that the most popular trade among women was, in fact, the sale of prepared food. Ghana was unique in Africa in that women selling ready-to-eat food on the street predated colonial rule and probably predated the modern fast food phenomenon in America, Europe, and parts of Africa.[22] She identifies six distinct categories that women contributed to a modern Ghana's public cuisine:

1. Makers of kenkey (steamed, fermented maize dough)
2. Proprietors of "chop bars," small stalls serving various kinds of food. Stews offered could include palmnut, groundnut, or light soup offered with fufu, kenkey, rice, gari, or yam
3. Makers of porridge (called *akasa, kpokponsu,* or *koko*) sold on the street as breakfast or lunch to children
4. Sellers of fried snacks of plantain, doughnuts, and pancakes
5. Sellers of baked foods and breads (a modern adaptation using ovens)
6. Sellers of homemade maize wine

The public presentation of food in West Africa to urban commercial markets appears from the historical record to mark a long-standing phenomenon and a marked contrast to culinary traditions in eastern and southern Africa and to Ethiopia, where cooks never prepared food for public sale and people never consumed it in public. In modern Kumasi (capital of the former Asante kingdom), residents commonly purchase both their morning and noontime meals from commercial vendors, usually women in market stalls. Those meals include the full range of starchy staples (rice, gari, boiled yam, kenkey, plantain) as well as stews with fish, beans, and meat, whose various ethnic origins reflect the cultural and linguistic mélange of urban life.[23] Urban food markets, thus, have historically been points of public culinary diffusion (see the case of Jollof rice, below), innovation, and eventually private appropriation of new foods into the home.

In the case of southern Ghana, it seems that the public-private distinctions of culinary practice (in other words, cooking) have given food and its preparation the deep social significance of status that underlies most cuisines globally. Cooking in southern Ghanaian society (this applies to Asante, and presumably many others) is still a fundamentally private act with connotations for marriage and/or sexual liaison. Anthropologist Gracia Clark notes that in the Twi language the same verb (*di*) connotes both eating and sex, and forms the basis for joking relationships and sexual innuendo. A man's providing of regular "chop" money to a woman to prepare his food marks the beginning of a marriage or formal courtship. For Asante, the evening meal is, ideally, a private, household event at which the labor-intensive fufu is the ideal accompaniment to stews. Thus, a wife's dissatisfaction in a marriage may manifest itself first in persistent and studied "carelessness" in her cooking. Moreover, for single males or travelers the consumption of an evening meal outside the home often implies a more nuanced social/sexual relationship in the offing.[24]

The social and economic distinctions in this town-based culinary complexity were already evident in the political hierarchy of the Kwa-language-area kingdoms or chiefships, including the Asante empire, that dominated the Gold Coast area in the eighteenth and nineteenth centuries. Town diets stand in sharp contrast to the food systems of the small-scale societies peripheral to that political system. Jack Goody's study of the LoDagaa of northwest Ghana's savanna, for example, suggests that as recently as the late 1950s there was little social or economic differentiation by types of cuisine; rather, it was by the amount of food available to chief and commoners and to men and women. Cooking for the LoDagaa, as in Asante, was the exclusive domain of women who had the knowledge (*nooro be nooro*, "working their wonders") for the process of what Goody calls "applying heat to the raw products in order to turn them into a meal, the process of cooking."[25] In the LoDagaa savanna zone, unlike in the Akan area, cooks boiled or steamed virtually all of the food, though they sometimes smoked fish and meat for preservation, and men roasted ears of maize as a snack. Frying was generally restricted to the preparation of snacks made for sale in the market, following the town example. The elaboration of domestic cooking that appears in Field's list of dishes—boiling, steaming, frying, mashing, fermenting, and so on—does not appear in those societies that were outside the core Akan areas near the cities of Kumasi or Accra. Goody tells us that "among the LoDagaa, that dish [the basic diet] is the same from day to day—porridge made from guinea-corn or millet, and accompanied by a soup. . . . If there is little variation day by day, there is necessarily little variation in weekly diet, with no special days for special foods, except for meat on festivals."[26] What Goody described stands in sharp contrast to urban, elite cooking that had become a social art of great sophistication in the south of Ghana and among urban societies of the West African coast.

If LoDagaa's position on Ghana's political and geographic periphery limited its participation in the Kwa/Akan culinary hegemony, other culture areas of West Africa showed a Kwa-like flowering in the art of cooking. Cooking in West Africa's forest zones showed great variety in both ingredients and method. One of these areas was the Yoruba/Edo region in southwest Nigeria, where a series of city states and kingdoms (e.g., Oyo, Benin, Ife, Ibadan) incorporated elite political leadership and trade influence that included trade with the coast's marine foods and contact with savanna ecologies to the north. The cuisine of the eastern Kwa language region (southern Nigeria to Cameroon), like that of the Kwa region to the west (Ghana, Côte d'Ivoire), shows remarkable continuity of ingredients, flavors, and cooking techniques within the region, just as languages shared common words, grammatical structures, or phonetic tones. Key dishes offered in common between the two regions might differ somewhat in emphasis and secondary ingredients, but overall show fundamental similarity in taste, social meaning, and cooking techniques. These dishes include groundnut soup, *egusi* stew, palaver stew, and palm nut stew. Distinctive ingredients that show clearly their cooking's straddling of forest, forest mosaic, savanna, and coastal ecologies include forest snails, dried powdered shrimp, bushmeat, garden eggs (small eggplant), and palm oil. This distinctiveness also includes preferences among available starchy staples. Pounded yam is the consummate starch in Kwa cuisine, kenkey in Ga (Accra) cookery, rice in Senegalese and Malian cuisine, and *amala*, gari (cassava), and rice in much Yoruba and southern Nigerian cooking. Local aficionados would, of course, debate their personal preferences with great fervor between ethnic regions, amongst villages and urban neighborhoods, and within households. Senegalese from the port city of St. Louis are so dedicated to rice as their favorite staple food that the Wolof people have given them the nickname "Danga lekk ceeb" ("you eat rice").

Common Ground across the West African Culinary Landscape: Groundnut Stew and Jollof Rice

The geography of food in West Africa includes a number of dishes that are mutually intelligible across language and culture groups, marking an interaction of both taste and texture and the ecology of ingredients. What the following recipe calls groundnut soup would also answer to names like peanut butter stew (Liberia), *mafé* (Senegal/Mali), *taushe* (northern Nigeria), *nkatie wonu* (Ga), *azi detsi* (Ewe), *gyada* (Nigeria Hausa), *gujiya* (Niger Hausa). There are also local versions in Côte d'Ivoire, Sierra Leone, and Togo. Its primary ingredients are groundnut paste, assorted meats (chicken or fish), tomatoes, ginger, and onion. Its variations by taste, texture, and local tradition include the cook's option to add locust bean (carob), sweet potatoes, cabbage, spinach, or carrots; spices and herbs could include some combination of ginger, ground red pepper, pumpkin leaves, *zogale*, okra, sorrel, or most any type of edible greens available locally.[27] Its starchy accompaniment would most likely be the local or personal favorite (fufu in Kumasi, rice in Dakar, gari in Lagos). In West Africa from Ghana to the Bight of Benin fufu would be the usual choice, but it would be rice in Senegal, Mali, and most any part of the old Mali empire.

Taushe (Groundnut Soup, Nigerian Style)

Ingredients:
500 kg assorted parts of meat (washed)
1 medium smoked fish
225 g stockfish (salt cod)
225 g bush meat
500 g roasted groundnuts
1 pt stock or water
100 g ground crayfish
25 g *iru* (locust bean)
2 medium tomatoes
100 g ground pepper
1 onion
3 large peppers
salt to taste

Place the washed meats in a large pot, add a drop of water or stock, season with salt and ground pepper, and boil for 30 minutes or until tender. Add the smoked fish and stockfish, cook for another 10 minutes. Add the rest of the stock. Bring to the boil and add the ground fresh tomatoes, onions, pepper, iru, and groundnut. Cook for 20 minutes until the soup thickens. Sprinkle in ground crayfish and stir. Simmer for another 10 minutes. Check seasoning and serve hot with boiled rice.[28]

What does this recipe reveal about West African histories of trade and cultural exchange? The recipe, above, more properly called a culinary text, appeared in London in the late twentieth century. It suggests much about the history of West African cuisine, its structural elements, it agro-ecological foundations, and its geographic specificity. The historical origins of *mafé*, or Senegalese groundnut stew, are obscure, though there are a fair number of clues to its historical geography. Senegalese usually accept its origins as a Malian dish called *tigh-dege-na* (Bambara/Mandinka), and one could argue that its ingredients are a dead giveaway that the cook has been trained in a savanna ecology. Its characteristic ingredient, groundnut paste, is a New World, post-Columbian foodstuff that became a mainstay across the African savanna belt from Senegal to Niger and also in places like the northeast Congo. Second, groundnuts filled an agricultural niche in the savanna ecology of the Niger, Gambia, and Senegal river valleys since farmers can rotate them with grains to balance soil fertility. The meats, poultry, and fish the stew may incorporate reflect local choices, including forest-based bush meat, beef, lamb, or chicken, or guinea fowl (the best choice, in my opinion). In Senegal the choice is usually meat or poultry, while elsewhere it may also include fish. The fish choices include traditional smoked herring (stink fish) or imported stockfish (Norwegian salt cod) or whatever is available. Above all, the presence of a primordial groundnut stew consumed across West Africa suggests movement across a north-south ecological axis that married savanna ingredients with coastal trade and a local cook's favorite ingredients.

A second dish that marks the connections in West Africa's culinary geography is a ubiquitous dish called Jollof rice. Jollof rice is unusual in that it is a heavy single-pot dish that combines a starchy staple (rice) with meats, seasonings, and stew ingredients. Jollof rice appears prominently in most West African cuisines, such as Wolof (Senegal), Sierra Leone, Ghana, and Nigeria. Ironically, it is not called Jollof rice in Senegal (home of the historical Jollof empire), where that country's elaborate version is called *thiebou dienn* (or phonetically *cheeb u jen*) and where it incorporates smoked or fresh fish. *Cheeb u yapp* is the same rice dish made with meat. This recipe from a Sierra Leone woman's cookbook shows a considerable number of additives of New World ingredients, including tomato paste, mushrooms, stock cubes, and cilantro leaves.

Jollof Rice

500 g lean beef or chicken
Salt and ground white pepper to taste
Vegetable oil for frying
1 l stock or water with 3 crushed stock cubes
3 large onions, finely chopped
4 cloves garlic, peeled and finely chopped
2–3 chilies finely chopped
4 large tomatoes, blanched, peeled, and blended or mashed

45 g tomato paste

250 g each of assorted chopped vegetables, e.g., carrots, green beans, mushrooms, and capsicum (sweet or bell peppers)

500 g long-grain rice

Lettuce, parsley, or fresh coriander (cilantro) and hard-boiled eggs to garnish

Cut meat or chicken into 5 cm cubes or small pieces and season with salt and pepper. Cover and allow to stand for 1–2 hours.

Heat oil in frying pan and fry the meat or chicken pieces until brown. Remove the meat from oil and add to the stock in a large, heavy-based saucepan. Simmer on low heat until meat begins to soften, then remove from heat.

Drain excess oil from frying pan, leaving enough oil to fry onions, garlic, and chilies (hot peppers) until golden. Add tomatoes, tomato paste, half the combined vegetables, and 250 ml of stock from the meat mixture. Stir well, adjust seasoning, and simmer on low heat for 5–7 minutes. Add this vegetable sauce to the meat mixture in the saucepan and simmer gently. Finally, stir in the uncooked long-grain rice. Adjust the seasoning again, cover, and simmer slowly on low heat for about 15 minutes.

Arrange the remaining vegetables on top of the rice and continue to simmer until the rice absorbs all of the stock, softens, and cooks, and the meat is tender.[29]

Jollof rice, or versions of the recipe recounted above, has a wide geography that ranges from Senegambia to Nigeria with substantial local household variations; it is often called *riz au gras* in Francophone areas. As a rice-based dish, it has achieved popularity in urban cultures throughout the region, even in yam-, cassava-, and plantain-loving subcultures. Its protein ingredient can be poultry, beef, or—in New World versions—ham. A commercially canned Nigerian version now available through the Internet (Oluomu brand) contains smoked fish.

Jollof rice's point of origin and its most authentic form are points of substantial debate. The online *Congo Cookbook* dismisses what it calls a common claim that it is a Nigerian dish, arguing that it had its origins among the Wolof cooks of Senegal and Gambia, but that it has now spread to the New World under the names of red rice and Spanish rice. Ad copy for the Nigerian canned version offers "Jolloff rice" as "originally from Sierra

Leone but now [a] popular dish throughout the West African subregion."[30] Fran Osseo-Asare, a published authority on West African food, tells us that Jollof is "commonly called the 'national dish' of the Wolof people of Senegal."[31] That particular argument may well derive from the presence of a mid-sixteenth-century Senegambian Jollof kingdom, and is plausible given the importance of rice in the upper Niger Valley. Yet how would such an adaptive cultural artifact move from Senegal south and west as far as Nigeria, a highly unlikely path not evident in other linguistic, historical, or political patterns? Specialists may never agree.

That dish's prevalence in urban settings throughout West Africa suggests a further compelling hypothesis: that Jollof rice was a food introduced throughout West Africa by a quite familiar cultural dispersion left over from the old Mali empire. West Africa's Djula people (see above), found in almost all West African commercial centers, were a trade diaspora, remnants of the far-flung commercial influence of the old Mali empire who established cultural enclaves in areas as widely dispersed as the variations of Jollof rice itself. These cultural diasporas spread Islam as well as particular skills, such as blacksmithing, small-scale marketing, and rice agronomy. Thus, like the movement of groundnut stew (soup) from the agro-ecology of the savanna, which first adopted peanuts from the New World, Jollof rice also appears to have diffused as part of a regional cultural and economic diaspora that soon manifested itself in local cooking cultures. The cooks appropriated new ingredients from local women acting as both innovators and tasters.

THE ESSENTIAL character of West African cookery appears in a parable in Achebe's novel *Things Fall Apart*, quoted at the beginning of this chapter. There the animals of the forest organized a meal composed of its classic elements: a one-pot dish, meat and fish commingled; yam; and palm wine, the popular local drink. The primary evidence for the common heritage of West African cooking/cuisine derives not from the formal historical record of European observers, colonial records, or Arabic-language text, but from the living transcripts of daily cooking. Cooks practiced in chop bars, shared ideas in intimate small talk between women, and eventually adapted written versions that have appeared in modern recipe books, on the Internet, and in all of the versions reflecting cultural currents and the historical ecology of a given region. The dishes themselves suggest their origins, influences, and deeper histories via their ingredients, their methods of preparation, and their place alongside other foods in a meal. The movement of ideas about cooking and the use of imported ingredients show clearly the avenues north to south across vegetation or climate zones as well as west to east across common ecologies.

Across the West African region, the cuisines appear as local and creative variations on a theme, with particular characteristics that stand apart from cooking elsewhere in Africa and elsewhere in the world. Distinct approaches to the Kwa culinary tradition include many items mentioned in the *Things Fall Apart* meal:

1. The mixing of fish and meat in a single dish, a phenomenon evident in New Orleans jambalaya

2. The pounding of yam, cassava, and plantain to make fufu, an action that releases starches from the starch sac and creates a characteristic glutinous texture for a West African meal's starchy accompaniment[32]

3. The use of powdered shellfish (crayfish or shrimp) or powdered locust bean (carob) as a flavoring and thickening agent in savory dishes

4. The steaming of wrapped starch flour to form "breads"

5. The use of particular vegetables, such as okra, cassava, collard greens, and various plant leaves, often mashed and then added to stew

6. The use of oils such as palm, peanut, and shea butter both as cooking lubricants and for color and flavor

Perhaps most distinctive of all of West Africa's common cuisinal characteristics is the clear and enthusiastic adaptation of culinary possibilities of the Atlantic world, bringing new ingredients such as maize, cassava, cocoyam, certain beans, and capsicum peppers from the New World into a marriage with African ingredients such as malagueta pepper, okra, black-eyed peas (cowpeas), and garden eggs (small eggplants). Most importantly, the cookery of West Africa was never static; its variety and its enrichment appear to have grown alongside the nation building and economic change that came with the circulation of an Atlantic stew that began in the fifteenth century, and it has continued to grow vigorously into the twenty-first century. That it also appeared full blown and in parts in the New World Caribbean, Creole, Brazilian, and southern cuisines of North America is a testimony to its dynamism and adaptability (see chapter 7).

CHAPTER SIX

History and Cookery in the Maize Belt and Africa's Maritime World

LET'S SAY I am a meandering traveler who decides to take a sort of Cape-to-Cairo trip up north from South Africa to the African Great Lakes through the inland heart of southern and eastern Africa. Along the way I stop at local farms, roadside chop houses, friends' kitchens, and small-town restaurants. Eventually I get a strange and growing sense of déjà vu, finding that the daily fare I am offered in each place I stop is a surprisingly similar preparation of a roughly milled maize flour boiled into a stiff porridge, but presented by my hosts under a bewildering variety of names. In the highveld of South Africa or Lesotho it is called *mealie pap* or *papa*. In Venda country near the Limpopo River it is *mutuku*. Across the border in Zimbabwe it is *sadza;* just to the east in Malawi it is *nsima* or *nshima*, as it is in Zambia to the north and west. North again into Congo near Kisangani it is *bidia* or *moteke*. In Tanzania, Kenya, and eastern Uganda it is *ugali*, while in Kongo in the west it is *nfundi*, and in Mozambique it is *xima* or *upswa*. Although consumers of this food in each location would undoubtedly call their national type—or their mother's version—distinctive, it's all the same stuff. It's the same basic food that a Venetian would call *polenta*, a Serbian would call *mamalinga*, or an Alabaman would mistakenly call *hominy grits* (see chapter 2).

A dietary map of Africa at the end of the twentieth century shows the geography of maize—and maize porridge—as the central staple of Africa's culinary landscape (see map 2.1). Given the ubiquitous nature of maize as a farm crop and as a percentage of calories in national diets, it is remarkable

FIGURE 6.1 Cooking *sadza*, Zimbabwe, 2006. *Photo by author*

that it almost never appears in the published literature of cooking. In Jessica Harris's fine and otherwise extensive volume *The African Cookbook*, maize appears only three times, and then only in the form of South African *samp* (similar to the corn mush of the southern United States, or the Hispanic version, *pozole*). Fran Osseo-Assare's more academic and comprehensive work *Food Culture in Sub-Saharan Africa* offers only a single recipe for maize, Congolese *bidia* (a Chiluba term that also means "food"), though she reminds us that maize sometimes appears in the Central African form of *fufu*. Laurens van der Post's glossy 1970 book *African Cooking* in the Time-Life series calls maize "Indian corn" and offers only two recipes that use it, one of them a "green mealie" (i.e., fresh maize kernels) bread served at a white Afrikaner *braai* (barbecue).[1] More recently, Ethio-Swedish chef Marcus Samuelsson's book envisions a new African cuisine that is the basis for his Manhattan restaurant, but maize plays only a minor role.[2] One would never know from the literature that maize is Africa's most produced food crop and that Africans in places like Malawi, Zambia, Lesotho, Zimbabwe, and Kenya eat a higher percentage of maize in their diets than do any people in the world.[3] Over half of all calories (54 percent) in Malawi come from maize.

If maize has flown under the modern cookbook radar as unworthy of mention by international cooks, it was nonetheless highly visible in African farmers' fields and in their pot of basic daily food. Perhaps a more representative account of maize porridge's domination of Africa's daily dietary reality and the imagination of Central and southern Africa appears in the book *Mozambique Flavours*, an honest compilation of recipes collected from European women living in Maputo, Mozambique's capital. Their account recognizes poverty as an all-too-common ingredient of cooking creativity: "When times are difficult and food or money is lacking, especially in the dry season, people will eat *xima* [maize porridge] without a sauce. Instead a small piece of dried fish will be cut off and roasted over the fire. As it is cooking, people sit close to the fire and eat the *xima* as the scent of the fish wafts by. This, it is said, makes the *xima* more appetizing and makes people feel more full."[4]

The agrarian revolution that made maize porridge a staple in eastern and southern Africa and a good slice of Central Africa began in the sixteenth century when maize arrived in Africa from the New World but had its true apotheosis in African cooking pots in only in the past half century. From the perspective of the early twenty-first century we have to try hard to imagine the pots of those regions of Africa without maize (or cassava, Asian rice, or plantain, other exotic starchy staples). Yet, eastern and southern Africa's passion for maize as the staff of life was a twentieth-century phenomenon. The staples of these regions prior to the Columbian Circulation were to a large degree Africa's own types of millets and sorghum or small pockets of West African rice that suited dry regions or lives organized around the daily and seasonal needs of herds of cattle, camels, sheep, or goats.

Unlike the West Africans who had a choice between yams, indigenous rice, and locally adapted grains (sorghum, millet, or *fonio*), eastern and southern African cooks relied on boiled grain or grain-based porridge as the base for their daily meals. As men went off to the cities and mines after the 1880s, women shifted their farm management to grow the labor-saving maize, and, taking what they knew about porridge, began stirring the new maize flour into their pots of boiling water, stirring vigorously as always until it reached the stubborn thickness that they sought. The change to maize as the primary diet choice took place as well in the mine hostels where mine owners fed their black African workers the cheapest food possible—maize porridge. It took only a few decades for maize to become the food of choice.[5]

Maize came to South Africa as part of the political struggle, wrenching economic change, and urbanization that would result in the 1948–1993 era of apartheid. As men migrated off farms to the mines and cities and women served as domestic servant or stayed to manage small farms, maize as food dominated their daily lives and, rather surprisingly, changed its color from yellow to white.[6] These processes were about food, but they also emerged as part and parcel of the South African government's policy of racial separation, which consciously separated black from white and created quite separate traditions of cooking and cuisine. It also influenced over the twentieth century the wider political and social lives of the southern African region, increasing dependence on maize as a daily food.

Maize also flourished elsewhere in southern Africa. Although in areas like Malawi many people consider that maize had always been their staple food, historical records show that the transition was a slow and subtle one. The few detailed accounts we have of maize in southern Africa before the twentieth century describe quite simple fare with little elaboration of preparation or admixtures of flavor. In 1840, the French missionary Thomas Arbousset, accompanied by the Basotho chief Moshoeshoe and his son, visited the chief of an isolated village tucked into the Maluti Mountains of Lesotho and South Africa. We get from this account a glimpse (or taste) of the local cooks' offering to hungry travelers, one of whom was a local king: "The good man offered us some sweet reeds; then his wives arrived to roast some corn cobs; from time to time they also brought us a kind of moist bread or *bohobe*, made from half ripe Indian corn, from Turkish corn, and pumpkin. All this ground and boiled together without salt is not, it is true, very appetizing; but what does one not eat when one is hungry?"[7]

The bland half-ripe maize served to the guest and described in other accounts of the period was undoubtedly the green milky stage of the older flint maize type then available in a land where both salt and spices of any sort were precious and rare. Like the moist bread, maize was relatively new and only complemented sorghum (the preferred staple) and squash as a vegetable rather than being the grain staple it later would become. Maize porridge by 1840 was not yet the dominant food that it would become a century later in Lesotho and elsewhere.

In most accounts we learn little of women's ideas about cooking or their daily struggles to vary the components of the meals they concocted. Occasionally, however, we find an acute observer who describes the methods that a young cook would have learned from accumulated experience among women as kin and as neighbors. As we have seen, anthropologist Audrey Richards was just such an observer, who for the first time in Central Africa described in a systematic way the cookery of the Bemba of northeast Zambia (called Northern Rhodesia in her day). Richards's description of the Bemba kitchen in 1938 offers us a glimpse of regional cooking when the politics of colonialism and preapartheid South Africa were emerging as the drivers of African diet. After all, daily lives and daily meals did go on, and cooking provided the sounds and daily rhythms of women's pestles, work songs, and eyes squinting from cooking smoke as the pots boiled and women felt the sting of their bubbling porridge as it thickened.

Richards recorded her own observations of Bemba women's practice of cooking millet porridge, the staple of their daily bowls just before the tidal wave of maize inundated the local scene. She describes both the grain preparation and the consistency of the final product, which resembled the later maize porridge. Her description gives us a sense of the daily rhythm of food preparation, but also of the language of cooking:

> The preparation of porridge (*ukunayo bwali*) is obviously the most important task of the Bemba cook. Porridge is the essential element of any meal, and the time taken to cook it determines the whole routine of eating, and indirectly the tribal practices of hospitality.
>
> To make the porridge, grain is threshed separately each day. The work is exhausting, and it is very rare for a housewife to grind a two days' supply. The millet heads must first be pounded (*ukutwa*) to free the fine grains from the stalks. The Bemba use high wooden mortars (*amabende,* sing: *libende*) from 2 to 3 feet

high, in which they stamp the millet with stout poles about 3 feet long. Sometimes the woman stands to pound her grain, stamping rhythmically up and down with hands placed wide apart on the pestle. Sometimes she sits on a stool grasping the mortar with her legs. Another method is to pound the grain in a hollow in the ground. Two women then sit opposite each other with legs apart and pound alternately, singing to keep time. Each holds a flail with one hand, and with a quick movement of the other sweeps fresh heads of millet into the hole in the ground. This last method is probably less efficient, but it is more companionable and preferred by young people. The pounding is exhausting work. The women's bodies steam in the sun and the village resounds with the regular thud of the flails.

The grain has now to be sifted from the chaff (*ukuela*). Winnowing consists in sending the grain swirling with a circular motion of the big open basket (*ulupe*) which sends the chaff to the surface where it can be scooped off while the grain remains beneath. It is then pounded for a few moments again (*ukusokola*) and then winnowed again (*ukupunga*). The chaff is emptied on the garden beds around the village and to this the natives attribute the greater fertility of this land. . . .

It now remains to grind the flour (*ukupela*). Against the wall of the veranda of each house is a small circular platform, about 9 inches from the ground, worn into a smooth grove with much grinding. In front of this the woman kneels, and on it she places the handful of grain which she grinds beneath a small stone. This task is reckoned very hard work and the women sing to lighten their labour. The rhythmic to-and-fro of the grinding stone, and the notes of the song, falling flatter and flatter, are the common sounds in a village in the late afternoon.

The flour so produced is of a coarse quality, and careful housewives sometimes grind it fresh before making the thin gruel (*umusunga*) with which a small baby is fed. Some species of millet are distinguished as being easier to grind than others, and the flour is graded according to whiteness, Kaffir-corn [sorghum] flour being the lightest.

To cook the porridge, the flour is merely tipped from the basket into water boiling in a big *inongo*. The process of gauging the right proportion of flour to water is apparently gained by experience and no woman could give me a clear account of her reasons for measuring out what she did. To stir the porridge one of the big flat spoons (*miko*), about 2 1/2 feet high, is first dipped in hot water, and then plunged into the seething mass of porridge. It must be held with two hands, the left at the top and the right near the blade, so that the heavy mass of porridge is moved with the whole weight of the body. This is arduous work and the interior of the porridge is sometimes hardly cooked, especially when a young girl cooks for large numbers. The process is complete in two or three minutes and great lumps of *ubwali*, now brown and smooth and solid, are scraped off the *miko* into eating baskets. Here they are patted smooth with the stirrer into balls like plum puddings (*ukumeta*), a point on which the housewife prides herself.[8]

In the 1930s, and before, making millet porridge was a daily task. For other areas that adapted the root crop cassava as a daily staple, the sequence and rhythm was a result of the character of cassava, which required several days of soaking in a river or stream, then chopping and drying. Woman then pounded the dried cassava into a flour, completing a four-to-six-day cycle of cooking. For neighboring Bisa women, this routine required advance planning that Bemba women who prepared their millet porridge were pleased to avoid.[9]

Bemba country in what is now northeast Zambia was, in fact, rather slow to adopt maize as its primary staple compared to other areas of Central Africa. Richards in the 1930s caught a society in transition from an agricultural and fishing economy to a modern economy of labor migration and new diets. Zambia's first president, Kenneth Kaunda, recalled to me a childhood of the early 1930s in which multicolored boiled or roasted ears of fresh maize were a garden snacking food and millet was still the staple. By the end of World War II, however, maize porridge, under its various local names, dominated the culinary landscape of almost all of eastern and southern Africa, including Bemba country. This is true even as modern recipes designed to celebrate the dignity of the traditional diet of the region recall the simplicity of ingredients and scarcity of both salt and spices. A modern published recipe from just over the South African border captures the simplicity:

Mutuku (Venda Sour Porridge with Bran)

250 g yellow mealie meal (coarse ground maize)
500 g fine white mealie meal
700 ml water

Mix the yellow mealie meal, white mealie meal, and water, and leave to
ferment for 2 days. Bring this mixture to the boil and cook for 10–20
minutes. Simmer for 10 minutes and serve with meat and vegetables.[10]

Though the use of yellow maize meal in the recipe is unusual, this particular formula nonetheless conveys a strong sense of rustic practice. In 2005 I stood in the queue at a Johannesburg Pick n Pay supermarket. The woman in front of me had a one-kilo plastic package of millet flour. When I asked her about it, she responded that her family liked it, though she always kept a fifty-kilo sack of maize at hand for everyday meals. Ironically, maize is now the everyday and the historic millet is the exotic treat.

The Relish: Cookery in the Maize Belt

Language about food preparations differs somewhat by region. While in West Africa and in Ethiopia the terms for "dishes" or "stews" are translated as such (or more directly as *wet* or *zigine* for Ethiopia and Eritrea), in the maize belt the vegetable and meat preparations that accompany the main starchy staple take the name "relishes" both in translation and by common usage locally. As Audrey Richards observed in the 1930s, the techniques of preparation of these dishes to accompany porridge largely excluded frying in oil, baking, or roasting (except over an open fire). Boiling in a pot was the usual practice in Bembaland and in much of the maize belt. Central African cooking uses almost no spices. Salt, the primary seasoning, was a long-distance trade item in most agro-ecologies away from the coast, and therefore scarce, perhaps even more scarce than in highland Ethiopia or in the forest/savanna ecology of West Africa.

While maize porridge had become the core of the daily meal and was what most people thought of as "food," meat, in the form of beef, goat, mutton, and poultry, was a small but treasured part of the cooked diet in eastern and southern Africa. In some areas, like Bemba, local freshwater fish—dried or fresh-caught—were more common; the neighbors of Bemba living in Luapula district nicknamed them "eaters of fish." In other areas near forest or less-populated zones, such as in Congo, use of roasted game meat was distinctive in the diet, though not always in elaborated cookery. In Central Africa leafy vegetables like kale, cassava leaves, or local spinaches were, and are, the foundation of relishes to accompany the porridge; meat and fish were treasured, tasty additives and not the foundation of the meal.

The art of cooking in the area that became the maize-belt in the twentieth century included the preparation of cooked vegetables and green leafy stews (relishes) that accompanied the starchy, stiff porridges of millet, sorghum, cassava, and, later, maize. Sometimes special treats like a peanut/groundnut paste would enliven the relish. When compared to the cuisine of Ethiopia or West Africa, those sauces reflected a surprisingly narrow geography of ingredients and methods of cookery. Audrey Richards's Bemba study sets out patterns that seem to have broad application. Her anthropologist's description offers a unique snapshot of an era on the cusp of globalization:

> The kitchen equipment of the [Bemba] native woman only permits her to boil or stew, and the different dishes used as relish, which she distinguishes with separate names, usually have the same composition but are stewed for a shorter or longer time, or with the addition of more or less water. *Ukuipika,* the word for "stew", is, in fact, the general term used for cooking. The chief methods used are the following:
>
> I. *Stewing (ukuipika).* By this method the food is placed in cold water in an open earthenware vessel and left to simmer from three to six hours over the fire, with additional water added if necessary. Meat and fish are stewed till the flesh falls apart from the bone and a rich gravy (*umuto*), considered a great delicacy, has been formed. Green vegetables are also stewed, fresh peas and beans to form the dish known as *imifoba,* and also the green leaf relish, whether the wild spinaches or the cultivated plants such as cassava, leaves, bean, cow-pea, pumpkin, &c., leaves which form the very common Bemba dish known as *umusalu.* Gourds of different kinds are also boiled in water until they are soft, and sweet potatoes cooked similarly with broad leaves put to cover the pot so as to prevent evaporation. Maize cobs are also most commonly boiled (*kunwenena*).
>
> Dried foods such as beans and peas are usually stewed four or five hours over a low fire until a sort of puree or paste is formed

(*mintipu*), or the same dish may be dried still harder and patted to form a solid cake known as *citata*, which is an unpopular kind of food only prepared in the hunger months when it is eaten in the absence of porridge.

2. *Stewing with ground-nut sauce (ukusashila)*. The art of good cooking among the Bemba is to have sufficient ground-nut sauce (*ntwilo*) to add to other relishes to make them palatable. To make the sauce the nuts are pounded into shreds in a mortar (*ukutwila*) and these shreds constantly taken out in the hand and squeezed into a small bowl of water, so that the white oil from the nuts makes a milky fluid. The residue is then returned to the mortar and pounded again until the last drop of oil is extracted and a thickish cream results. The *ntwilo* is then ready for use. It is poured on to any cooked relish, and the whole stewed up again for a short time with the addition of salt. *Ntwilo* is thought to make meat or fish stews specially nice, and to be appetizing with stewed spinaches, locusts, or caterpillars, but with the tasteless dried leaf relishes and mushrooms it is considered almost essential. Hence the insistence of the Bemba cultivator that he must grow at least one patch of ground-nuts every season, although in practice he rarely succeeds in producing sufficient to last through the year.

3. *Roasting (ukuoca) or dry cooking (ukusalula)*. The Bemba have no real method of baking or roasting, but they occasionally cook foods in the ashes of open fires, and prepare sweet potatoes, maize cobs, or meat skewered on sticks in this way when on a journey. Another method of cooking is to put the food on an open potsherd over the fire with just sufficient water to prevent scorching (*ukusalula nkwangwa*). It is one of the few quick ways of preparing a relish. Fat meat is sometimes cooked in this manner, fresh green legume pods, ground-beans, ground-nuts, or dried spinaches softened with a little potash salt (*ifishikisa*). But this latter dish is used only as a last resource. Natives say it is so dry and hard "You eat it and it goes crack, crack, crack in your mouth" (*mulelya muleti kwa kwa kwa!*).

4. *Seasoning*. It is interesting that salt, that scarce commodity, is only used for the most tasteless foods, i.e. spinaches, dried potatoes, or mushrooms (*fyafubulula*), the wild orchid (*cikanda*),

and the dried cakes made of legumes (*citata*). It is also used to bring out the flavour of the ground-nut sauce. It is invariably added after cooking. The use of a potash salt (*ifishikisa*) made from the bark of certain trees, to soften dried spinaches, is an interesting adaptation to the environment.[11]

There appears to have been considerable continuity over time, as well as distance. Historian John Thornton offers a glimpse of cookery and meals in the kingdom of the Kongo in the seventeenth century. Kongo was directly west of Bembaland, but set closer to the Atlantic seaboard and in a more forested landscape:

> Cooking was done in earthenware pots, and meals consisted of three parts, typically served on three plates. The first was boiled grain, usually corn, which was dried, then pounded, and the flour mixed into boiling water to make *nfundi*, the "daily bread" that the Kongolese asked God to give them each day when they said the Lord's prayer. The nfundi was cooked quite stiff, and most people rolled it into bite-size balls to eat it. The second plate contained *mwamba*, which was a stew made up of meat if it was available, or fish and numerous vegetable supplements, in a base of palm oil. Balls of nfundi, dimpled with the thumb to make a small cup, were dipped into the mwamba. In the third plate were vegetables, most commonly *wandu*, probably pigeon peas, which are still called Congo beans in the West Indies today. Fruit was eaten separately and the whole was washed down with water or palm wine drunk from cups made from gourds.[12]

The seasons of the natural world also provided opportunities to vary the diet (see chapter 1). One of the distinctive features of Central African foodways is the range of insects appreciated as a seasonal source of snacks and relishes. The *Malawi Cookbook,* assembled by a group of English housewives but offering an ecumenical/cosmopolitan list of cookery and ingredients, features a list of edible insects and their preparations:

Ana a Njuchi (Bee larvae)

> Method: Remove the nests from the tree and boil them. Take out the larvae from the comb and dry them. Fry with a little salt, and dry again if desired. Serve as a relish or as an appetiser.

Bwamnoni (Large Green Bush Crickets)

These swarm at street lights, especially in April to May. They are migratory, and differ from locusts and true grasshoppers in having very long antennae.

Method: Remove the wings and the horned part of the legs. Boil them in water for 5 minutes and then dry in the sun. Winnow off any remaining wings if necessary. Fry in a pan with a little salt and a little fat if liked. Serve as a relish.

Dziwala (Grasshoppers) *Ancanthacris ruficornis*

These large grasshoppers are mostly found in the late dry season though a few are seen throughout the year.

Method: Remove the wings and the horned part of the legs. Boil them in water for 5 minutes and then dry in the sun. Winnow off any remaining wings and fry them in a pan with a little salt. They may also be fried with a little fat. Serve as a relish. If frying with fat, a little chopped onion, chopped tomato and/or groundnut flour may be added to the pan.

Dzombe (Red Locust) *Nomadacris septemfasciata*

This locust is most numerous around Lake Chilwa but also occurs on the grasslands of Zomba plateau and Mulanje Mountain. It is see throughout the dry season, and swarms in the latter half.

Method: As for Dziwala (Grasshoppers) above.

Inswa or Mbulika (Flying Ants) large termites of the genus *Macrotermes*

Inswa are most conspicuous in the early rainy season and are common throughout the country.

Method 1: heat a pan and fry the ants dry. Remove from the pan, dry in the sun and winnow them to remove the wings. Pick over carefully to remove any stones. Heat the pan with or without a little fat, add the flying ants and a little dry salt and fry until done. Serve with nsima or as an appetizer.

Method 2: Wash the flying ants in water and leave to drain for a short while. Add salt and fry them without oil, stirring all of the time, until the wings are burnt. Remove them from the heat and keep them in a warm place for about 5 minutes to dry completely. They may be fried again in oil if desired.

Variation: If oil is used, add a little chopped onion and chopped tomatoes to the pan. Groundnut flour may also be added.

Mafullufute (Black Flying Ants) *Carebara vidua*

These occur mainly in the rainy season and can be distinguished from the common sausage fly by their almost spherical abdomens.

Method: Fry the flying ants with a little salt, but no fat. Serve hot or cold or as a relish.

Mofa, Pphalabungu, Kawichi, Mbwabwa, Katondo (Green Caterpillars)

These caterpillars appear in March and feed on grass. They are common in Central Region.

Method: Remove the stomach and intestines and then wash the caterpillars. Boil for 5 minutes in some water and dry in the sun. Heat a frying pan and fry the caterpillars with a little salt and oil. Serve as a relish.

Variation: Add one chopped tomato, one chopped onion, and a little groundnut oil to the pan. Note: After sun drying, the caterpillars may be stored for up to three months.

Nkhululu (Sand Cricket) *Brachytrypes mimbarnaceus*

Method: After digging up the crickets, remove the wings if any, the stomach and intestines (most important) and wash them. Heat a frying pan and fry the crickets with a little salt and a little fat if liked. If fat is used, chopped onions may also be added. Allow the crickets to dry and serve as a relish.

Nkhunguni (Large Green Shield Bug) *Nezara robusta*

These are found in great numbers from May to July, especially in Mwanza District.

Method: As for Dziwala (Grasshoppers) above.

Nkhungu (Lake Fly) a tiny fly of the family Chaoboridae Chaobora edulis

These occur only on the Lake and swarm once a month at the time of the new moon. They form huge clouds over the lake which are visible many miles away. Lake fly are extremely nutritious, being high in protein and calcium and containing six times as much iron as ox liver.

Method:

1 cake dried lake fly	1 cup groundnuts, fried and pounded
1 tomato chopped	a little oil
1 onion, chopped	salt

Nsensya (Shield Bug) *phaerocoris*

Method: Wash them and fry with a little salt until brown. Serve as a relish.

Njenje (Cicada) *Monomotapa*

These large cicadas are most conspicuous in the early rainy season

Method: Remove the wings and fry with a little oil and salt. Serve as a relish.[13]

The potpourri of ingredients and cooking methods described by Richards for southern Africa in 1938 also appears in a more recent book, Bomme Basemzansi's *South African Indigenous Foods,* a collection of recipes from South African women from five rural communities. Here the compiler's goal is authenticity, with recipes written in a basic form, reflecting core elements rather than the flair that might have been added by women (as mothers, wives, and in-laws) as creative cooks in their own households.

Three examples of cooked dishes from KwaZulu-Natal (South Africa), Venda (South Africa/Mozambique), and Kenya (Kikuyu/Central Province) illustrate the paucity of spice ingredients but the presence of New World starch bases (maize, potatoes, peanuts) and the use of local vegetable greens. The emphasis appears to be on what ingredients could be grown or collected locally, rather than the regional trade items like spices, dried proteins (fish, meat jerky, shellfish powder), and grains that West Africans, Ethiopians, or ancient Egyptians obtained from wider networks of trade and exchange across ecologies. Here are five basic maize belt concoctions from four different regions of eastern and southern Africa.

From KwaZulu-Natal, three women offer a standard everyday relish:

Imfino yezintanga (Pumpkin Leaves and Peanuts)

400 ml water or milk
200 g pumpkin leaves, rinsed and shredded
150 g peanuts, crushed
Add salt to taste

Bring water or milk to the boil. Add the leaves, reduce the heat and simmer until cooked. Be careful not to overcook the leaves. Add the crushed peanuts and salt to taste. Simmer for 15 minutes and serve hot.[14]

In this preparation from Venda in Limpopo Province (South Africa) peanuts appear again, this time with a different type of local protein:

Masonja/Dhovi (Mopane Worms and Ground Peanuts, Venda, South Africa)

250 ml mopani worms
125 g peanuts, ground
2.5 ml salt
750 ml water

Soak mopani worms in hot water for 7 minutes. Wash twice with warm water. Bring water to boil, add mopani worms and salt, cook for 10 minutes or until water has been absorbed. Add peanuts, simmer for 5 minutes and serve.[15]

For the classic Kikuyu preparation *Irio*, food writer Jessica Harris adds elements of the modern kitchen and supermarket, namely fresh or frozen sweet corn, kidney beans from the New World, and spinach (rather than local beans).

Irio (Kenya)

1/4 liter fresh corn kernels
1/4 liter cooked kidney beans
4 medium potatoes in 1/2 inch cubes
500 g spinach
salt and black pepper

Place all of the ingredients in a large stockpot with water. Bring to a boil over low heat and cook until tender. Drain and serve hot. Each diner mashes the ingredients together before eating.[16]

Harris notes that this stew and a similar one (*abrow ne ase*) from Ghana are similar to American succotash (a fresh corn-and-bean casserole), which may include the indigenous African black-eyed peas instead of the New World lima beans.[17]

A fourth recipe, this time from the Xhosa-speaking Eastern Cape, emphasizes the local knowledge of wild greens, maize meal, and margarine, an element of industrial modernity purchased from the local Pick n Pay supermarket (South Africa's biggest chain). Here spring onions (scallions) are a late addition to the mix, suggesting they are an ingredient for flavor that differs from the local wild greens.

Umfino (Wild Vegetables)

80 g *ihlaba* (wild spinach), chopped
80 g *umsobo* (wild vegetables), chopped
80 g *unqophose* (wild vegetables), chopped
80 g *mbikicane* (wild vegetables), chopped
900 ml water
310 g mealie meal
1 bunch of spring onions, chopped
60 ml butter or margarine
Add salt to taste

Mix the wild vegetables and wash in cold, salted water. Drain and add the vegetables to saucepan with 500 ml of salted water. Simmer for 20 minutes. Add the mealie meal, spring onions, and butter and the rest of the boiled water. Add salt to taste. Mix well and simmer for another 20–25 minutes. Stir occasionally until well done. Serve hot.[18]

Although the nuances of the preparation are lost in putting it in written form, the dish seems quite similar to the Bemba forms from the 1930s.

Based on both historical encounters rendered into written form and recipes that convey the structures of women's oral craft, particular patterns emerge from the cookery of this broad swath of Africa's culinary geography. Unlike the dishes of the West African Kwa cuisine or Ethiopian *wet*, the maize belt's relishes contain almost no spices, though they occasionally contain chopped fresh chilies and a few wild herbs.[19] As a flavoring, salt appears in modern recipes, but was certainly rare and used sparingly in the older accounts, even as late as the 1930s. Ash made from particular tree barks was the most common substitute for kitchen salt and spices. And unlike West Africa, which featured a wide variety of textured starchy staples—fufu, gari, boiled yam, fried plantain, indigenous rice—or powdered shellfish as flavoring and thickener, the maize belt relied more uniformly on thick porridge from grain staples (millet, sorghum, maize) or cassava. Adding peanuts to relishes for taste and texture appears to have been a widespread practice, though not at every meal. All in all, the list of ingredients used in the African maize belt was consummately local, a feature that distinguished it from Ethiopia, West Africa, and the Nile Valley and stands in marked contrast to the dishes that appeared on Africa's coasts and eventually along the road networks that added contacts with maritime tastes.

Africa's Culinary Oceana: Mombasa to Cape Town, Luanda, and Back

The overland Cape-to-Cairo sojourn suggested at the opening of this chapter offered a leitmotif of maize porridge and bland, unsalted vegetable relishes with a minimum of spices and herbs. If perhaps our traveler chose instead to head south via a sailing voyage using a wooden-hulled dhow hugging the coast from Mogadishu to Lamu to Dar es Salaam, to Maputo, and thence to Durban, to Cape Town, and to Luanda on Angola's Atlantic seaboard, he would witness a maritime culinary tour de force that includes the marine ecology of coastal fisheries with hulls reeking of shark oil, or the diesel fumes of the ocean trade with both Atlantic and Indian Ocean networks. This culinary flow would move along with the seasonal monsoon winds— north from June to December and south from January to May. Visible along the way would be the movement of coastal peoples on small vessels hugging the shores but carrying with them Somali, Arab, Swahili, Portuguese, Indian, and Malay ideas about cooking and knowledge about the cornucopia of ingredients available locally and in the cargo holds of their small sailing vessels, the dhows that persisted as the primary means of local transport.

The cooking of maritime and coastal Africa was as much a sociological phenomenon as a cultural one. If the traders were largely male, their cooks, companions, and sexual partners were most often local women, who were usually the domestic managers and cooks who appropriated tastes and ingredients into new mixes that both pleased male bosses or husbands and expanded their palates.

On the large, regional scale two historical processes formed the basis for Africa's maritime cuisine. The first was the evolution of an Indian Ocean trade network that rode the seasonal winds from south Asia and the Persian Gulf and along the East African coast. Beginning in the ninth century, coastal towns began appearing in sheltering inlets and natural harbors on the East African coast. This process was part of the emergence of a Swahili urban culture that extended from southern Somalia to Mozambique, but established trade north into the Red Sea and Persian Gulf, and from port towns like Mombasa and Kilwa along the caravan routes to the Great Lakes, to Great Zimbabwe, and to the South African highveld. With the spread of Islam and marriage lineages that tied Banyam merchants from India and trading families from Oman also came the high-value, low-bulk trade goods like cloves, cinnamon, cardamom, coriander, black pepper, curry leaf, coconut, and ginger. Some of these goods, like Asian rice, sugar cane, coconut, and ginger, took root locally, while others ingredients became a mainstay of trade, finding themselves in the cooking pots of the African coastal populations. Eventually, when New World capsicum peppers circulated into the Indian Ocean world and flavored its cookery, East African coastal dishes came to resemble the curries, lamb kebabs, samosa, daal (lentil stews), and tandoori of South Asia and the Gulf. The arrival of Indian and Chinese railway workers, Indian sugar field workers in the nineteenth-century Natal, and Indian shopkeepers in the early twentieth century in East Africa flavored the foods of ports, railroad towns, and markets of Africa's windows on the Indian Ocean world.

Africa's maritime world offered a cosmopolitan, open, and eclectic menu for residents or for sailors who carried ideas, nostalgic hungers for homeland comfort food, and exotic foodstuffs with them. Groups came for different reasons to African's oceanic coastal world. Some (Malays) come as forced/indentured labor from the Dutch Indies. Others (Indians, Chinese) came to earn a wage living as workers on East African or South African railways, or as household servants. Others came from Madagascar or Mozambique as slaves captured in inland wars and sold to European traders who brought them to African port cities. In contrast to the spice-challenged maize belt, the regions along the Indian Ocean and south Atlantic coasts demonstrated a remarkably broad acceptance of ingredients, ideas, and sensual synergies in cookery from the Atlantic and Indian Ocean basins. Both African culinary communities show the genius to adapt and absorb, though the gastronomic results show a great contrast in aroma, tastes, and peppered heat.

A fine demonstration of the blend of small farm livestock and the global larder of spices is the following recipe from the kitchen of Waheeda Khan, an Asian Kenyan whose father came to British East Africa from Afghanistan to work on the railway in the early 1900s. Waheeda's kitchen collection of ingredients reflected the historical influences of Kenya's colonial culture and her personal links to the Indian Ocean as well as the railroad's penetration of the highlands along the way to Lake Victoria. Her repertoire included turmeric, ground red pepper, whole cumin, ground cumin, fresh coriander, salt, and the south Asian blend of garam masala.[20] The spicy goat stew found in her home would also be likely to appear in a Kisumu home (on Lake Victoria), in Nakuru (on the central highlands) or in a Dar es Salaam beachfront hotel. Given global trade in recent times, the French beans and Irish potato ingredients are not out of place in her cosmopolitan kitchen:

Spicy Goat Stew (Curried Goat)

1 large onion (chopped)
vegetable oil
2 cloves crushed garlic
1 teaspoon crushed fresh ginger
3 large tomatoes, chopped
1 teaspoon cayenne pepper
1 teaspoon garam masala
1 teaspoon salt
2 medium Irish potatoes, cubed
½ cup sliced French green beans
1–2 pounds cubes goat meat
3 cups water
1 tablespoon chopped fresh coriander (cilantro)

Sauté the onion until crisp. Add the garlic, ginger, and tomatoes and cook until it forms a thick paste. Add the spices, salt, meat, and water. Cover and cook until the meat is tender. Add the potatoes and green beans; cook until tender. Cook uncovered and add the chopped cilantro before serving. Serve with rice, ugali, or chapati.

It would be a challenge to any geographer to plot the precise culinary and geographic origins of this dish and its ingredients. Yet the taste and aroma of her goat curry would not strike a diner as exotic in any African port city. The role of ports, mercantile towns, and oceanic diaspora populations was fundamental: Mogadishu, Malindi, Lamu, Mombasa, Dar es Salaam, Maputo, Durban, Cape Town, and Luanda occupy an arc swinging from northeast, southwest back to northwest along Africa's mercantile coastlines. These were each ports of entry and ports of exchange for long-distance trade in spices, enterprising consumers, human taste preferences, the commercialization of hospitality (hotels, hostels, and restaurants), seeds for local planting, and styles of cooking.

Maputo (formerly called Lourenço Marques) and coastal Mozambique were part of this mix in a mélange of oceanic and local ingredients. One cookbook published in the 1990s listed the basic ingredients of a typical Maputo cook house cabinet: "Cassava flour; peeled and sifted peanuts and cashew nuts; beans, matapa and nhangana (the leaves of cassava and beans respectively) which, outside of Mozambique, can be substituted by cabbage or squash leaves; and fresh grated coconut which is kept on hand in the refrigerator for when coconut milk is needed."[21] This list, however, gives rather short shrift to the full range of fresh market ingredients that appear in national cookbooks for those maritime cuisines in historical contact with Africa's port cities and caravan networks. To this list we should add, from local markets, prawns, crab, clams, calamari (squid), rock lobsters, tuna, snapper, coconuts, sweet bananas, dried cod, cow peas, papaya, pineapple, mango, and cashew nuts.

Malayan indentured servants brought to Cape Town from the Dutch East Indies in the late 1600s and 1700s served on the docks of that port city, and Malay women took on work as domestic servants in kitchens of Cape Dutch families. After several generations of experience with ingredients such as fresh local ocean fish (e.g., snoek and kingklip), imported dried or salted fish, and mutton from frontier flocks, the Malay-influenced Cape dishes combined Indian Ocean curry spices, New World chilies, and a white custard that a French chef might call a béchamel sauce. The maritime world of the two ocean systems that met at the Cape of Good Hope resulted in the following dish, which sometimes uses salt cod (the imported "stockfish" found commonly in Nigerian dishes) from cold North Atlantic waters. Though the fish complements the Malay spice combinations, the dish bears a Dutch-Afrikaans name.

Gesmoorde vis (Fish and Potatoes with Tomato Sauce)

1 pound white fish
3 medium boiling potatoes
4 medium ripe tomatoes
3 tablespoons vegetable oil
3 small onions, peeled and sliced into thin rings
2 tablespoons chopped fresh chilies
1 teaspoon finely chopped garlic
1 tablespoon light-brown sugar
1 lemon sliced into wedges (for garnish)
Parsley sprigs (for garnish)

One day ahead of time, place the salt cod in a glass or enamel bowl. Cover it with cold water and soak for 12 hours, changing the water every 3 to 4 hours. Drain the cod and rinse it under cold running water. Cut it into 1 inch square pieces.

Cook the potatoes in salted water under just tender. Drain and peel the potatoes, and cut them into 1 inch cubes.

Place the tomatoes in a pan of boiling water for ten seconds and then plunge them into cold water. Remove the loosened skins and slice them into 1/8 inch rounds.

In a heavy skillet, heat the oil and brown the onions until soft and golden (8–10 minutes). Add the tomatoes, 1 tablespoon of the chilies, the garlic, sugar, and cook uncovered until most of the liquid has evaporated. Add the cod and potatoes, reduce the heat to low, and cover tightly. Simmer for 20–25 minutes or until fish flakes easily.

Serve with hot rice and chutney or lime pickle.[22]

The final touch here of sweet chutney and the astringent lime pickle truly reveals the culinary geography of the Cape as a meeting point of two oceanic cuisines.

A defining dish that classically combines the history of Malay cookery, the South African livestock frontier, and the Cape's cultural mélange is *bobotie*, a baked pie dish that combines minced lamb or beef (originally game meat), eggs, lemon, lemon leaves, butter, onion, garlic, turmeric, a little soaked wheat bread, and curry powder. Like the classic Greek dish moussaka, bobotie consists of sautéed meat, onions, and spices covered with a beaten egg mixture (béchamel) that forms a golden custard crust when baked. The dish, developed by generations of Malay women cooks in the Cape's elite white households, became a mainstay of Cape Town and frontier game cookery in agricultural settlements like Stellenbosch, now one of the world's great producers of red estate wines. Bobotie served with a bottle of a local red-wine blend of Cabernet Sauvignon, Shiraz, and Merlot grapes aged in American oak barrels is a magnificent culinary occasion.

The second scene of Africa's maritime adventures took place along the Atlantic side. Contemporaneous with the cultural mélange forming at the Cape of Good Hope was a Portuguese effort to draw together a colonial network of coastal entrepôts at Luanda (in Angola), and at Lourenço Marques (later Maputo) in Mozambique that linked the Atlantic world to African cultures in Africa and in a Brazilian diaspora with strong African influences. Over time, these maritime culturals evolved colonial class systems that mixed new materials from the circulation of local tastes and Atlantic networks of ingredients, especially New World capsicum pepper and spices from the eastern Mediterranean. The South African writer Laurens van der Post described two such preparations from port cities in Lusophone Africa during a culinary tour in the late 1960s:

Açorda Soup (Luanda, Angola)

A combination of cooked shrimp, eggs, tomatoes, and bread, seasoned with fresh coriander, red pepper, and garlic. The shrimp were browned in oil and garlic and simmered in a stock made with the shells of shrimp and the heads of fish. Then the stock was strained and the liquid joined with the other ingredients; the eggs were poached in this soup and served with another sprinkling of coriander, surrounded by hot cooked shrimp.[23]

This version of what many might call a Portuguese bread soup with prawns was as much at home in Luanda as in Lisbon. Another adaptation outside of New World influence came in the form of a particular taste, the *peri-peri* sauce that spread via coastal trade networks and cosmopolitan cuisines. It is a distinctive adaptation of Africa's capsicum pepper in its southern African version.

> Every Mozambican cook has her own way of preparing a *piripiri* sauce. One housewife of Lourenço Marques [Maputo] begins by sieving lemon juice, warming it in a pan, and adding red,

freshly picked chilies. The mixture is simmered on a low fire for exactly five minutes, then the peppers are removed, salted and pounded to a smooth paste. This pulp is returned to the pan with the original lemon juice and simmered for a while longer. This sauce can be eaten over steak, mutton, fowl, fish and shell-fish, preferably with rice of some kind.[24]

This flavoring was distinctive in that it was both a condiment served alongside meats and an ingredient for stews. It appealed to a coastal immigration community that had already adapted to the spice synergies of the Indian Ocean along the Swahili coast. A recent adaptation of peri-peri chicken appears in Jessica Harris's *African Cookbook:*

Galinha Piri Piri (Mozambique)

3 cloves garlic, minced
1 bay leaf
3 ml hot paprika
3 minced bird chilies
¼ liter coconut milk
1 chicken, cut up
8 ml lemon juice
15 ml butter
20 ml olive oil

Mix the garlic, bay leaf, paprika, and chilies together with a large bowl to form a thick paste and slowly add the coconut milk, stirring all along. Score the skin of the chicken pieces. Place the chicken in the marinade, cover with plastic, and refrigerate for 12 hours, turning occasionally.

Remove the chicken from the marinade and reserve the liquid. Add the lemon juice, the butter and olive oil to the marinade and bring to a boil over medium heat. Reserve some marinade as a dipping sauce. Use the mixture to baste the chicken. Grill the chicken over medium coals or under broiler, using the marinade as a basting sauce.[25]

In this case Harris treats peri-peri as a marinade rather than as a cooked stew ingredient comparable to the peanut sauces of Central and West Africa. In either case, the pungency of the mashed chilies and garlic offers a sharp contrast to the virtual absence of spices and flavorings in rural cooking in the maize belt. If the coastal exuberance of flavors found in the Cape, the Swahili coast, and the ports of Lusophone Africa was a reflection of trade and the emergence of cosmopolitan maritime culture along the oceanic rims, the foods prepared in rural areas emphasized the high cost of spices and preference for bulk over flavor.

PART FOUR

Africa's Global Menu

Chapter 7 explores the deep traditions that African women brought to the New World and that then circulated between the peoples of an Atlantic economic culture. That circulation included certain foods, but especially the wiles of the kitchen in eras of slavery, emancipation, and culinary adaptation. The chapter opens questions about the culinary history of African America, the Caribbean, Brazil, and the mélange of North America that is Louisiana Creole cooking.

CHAPTER SEVEN

Diaspora Cookery

Africa, Circulation, and the New World Pot

IN MAY of 2006 I walked a mile eastward from the Harvard University campus along Cambridge Street and into East Cambridge, a neighborhood known a decade ago for its Portuguese shops, restaurants, and groceries. Nowadays, however, that Cambridge Street stroll reveals an eclectic mix of grocery store fronts in the green, yellow, and black of the Jamaican flag or the green, blue, and yellow of the Brazilian flag. Along the way, grocers display at their doorways colorful bins of green plantain, black-and-yellow yams, long, thin, reddish cassava. Shelves within those doors offer sacks of long-grain African-style rice from Guatemala, plastic bags of grated cassava from Brazil, packages of pounded yam from Nigeria, and maize flour from Haiti; there are bright red bottles of Ghanaian palm oil (*dendê*, in Brazilian Portuguese) and packets of Jamaican jerk spices. The package labels boast their products' manufacture in Brazil, Nigeria, Ghana, Haiti, Jamaica, Guatemala—all places in the Western Hemisphere that have absorbed African ideas and ingredients into their national food cultures.

Interspersed among the new upscale pubs now spreading eastward along Cambridge Street are also local storefront restaurants whose menus offer fried yucca (cassava) and dishes that they describe as from Bahia (northeast Brazil), the Caribbean, and "Dixie." Though the tastes, textures, and ingredients of the dishes on offer in the restaurants and the foodstuffs for sale in the groceries have a flavor sharply reminiscent of fare from a Nigerian or Angolan street food kiosk, the ethnic and national identities claimed by the proprietors are Brazilian, Haitian, Dominican, or the more generic ethnic

FIGURE 7.1 Bahia *feijão tropeira* (beans and grated cassava). *Photo by author*

"Caribbean." The African undercurrent, however, is unmistakable, and only barely beneath the surface. Even the venerable Casa Portugal restaurant has a menu item "Angolan chicken," hinting at the deeper historical influence at play in the foods on offer and the complex ancestry of the proprietors.

Food as a historical topic quite clearly reveals the subtle and sensual side of the cultural, economic, and biological encounters of the African-Atlantic world. This chapter examines examples of the circulation of African transcripts of cooking that exist in the forms of practice and, increasingly, as formal written texts (recipes and cookbooks). These sights and smells of this lively street scene from urban America suggest the overlapping and layering of global cuisines and a mélange of ideas about cooking, dining, and eating. If the origins of many of the raw foodstuffs were originally in the New World, their appearance on the tables and shelves of Cambridge Street shows the effects of generations of cooking heritage of the Atlantic world, the transfer and recirculation of seeds and cuttings, as well as the circulation of African influence.

The demographic history of the Atlantic world tells us much about the encounter of ideas about food and the culinary geography of that region that binds Africa and the Americas. While the New World diaspora Africans, whether African Americans, Afro-Brazilians, or Caribbean peoples, shared much in the struggle within and against slavery, they had diverging centers of gravity and cultural landscapes. For example, between 1609 and 1808 the original thirteen colonies of the United States received less than 5 percent of the total Africans who arrived in the New World (about 500,000 of the 12,000,000 total) in the slave trade in those years. Moreover, by 1810 over 90 percent of the U.S. black population had been born in the United States, as compared to only 50 percent native-born New World persons of African descent in the Caribbean and Latin America.[1] North America's black population was unique in the New World in that it reproduced itself culturally and demographically from fairly early on in the Atlantic experience. Thus, peoples of African descent in North America evolved a distinctive native-born culture and culinary experience at a time when Caribbean and Latin American populations had more consistent contact with new African-born arrivals and cultural flows of religion, language, and food preparation from the African side of the Atlantic rim.[2] Low fertility rates in the Caribbean meant that the colonies there continuously required and received new captives to sustain their agricultural labor force: 83 percent of all new African arrivals between 1650 and 1780 came to the West Indies. Similar conditions applied in Brazil. Africa's diaspora cultures of food and cookery therefore diverged from one another and in the extent of their direct contact with African cookery.

It should be noted that the percentage of women in the human trade from Africa changed over time. Did the greater numbers of women, the repositories of cooking knowledge, in later years and in certain places intensify African cooking influences and transfer of knowledge that reinvigorated both styles and ingredients in cooking?

The outlawing of the slave trade in North America and the British colonies (Jamaica in particular) in 1808 and 1807, respectively, and in the French colonies reduced new African populations to a trickle in those places. But during the second peak of the slave trade in the 1840s the new wave of forced African migration brought Africans to places (Brazil and Cuba) from places (southwest Nigeria and Dahomey/Benin) where political conflict generated captives for sale to New World slave economies that were still thriving. The new infusions of West African cultures in large numbers, especially via women, brought generations of experience and ideas about the preparation of food from African culinary practice, which had adapted to include the numerous New World crops imported there, to the original home of staples like cassava, cocoyam, maize, and capsicum peppers. The Atlantic system, again, was in fact far less a simple exchange than a circulation of both ideas and material goods. The results formed the foundation of signature dishes that have become symbols of identity and culinary traditions in North America as well as the Caribbean Rim, and whose principles and practices were familiar to African cooks as well. Cuban *ajiaco*, Caribbean rice and beans, and New Orleans jambalaya were all part of this swirl of influence and culinary creativity.

New World African-Influenced Cookeries

New World culinary cultures formed in the era of the slave trade in ways that indicate their particular ecological setting, historical engagements with Native American peoples, and the individual regions' colonial experience. The New World's mix of colonialisms was even more diverse than Africa's. Colonial powers in the Caribbean, Latin America, and North America included France, Britain, Spain, the Netherlands, and Portugal—and later the United States—and the list of cultures includes a huge variety of African cultures that enlivened the mix. The islands and mainland colonies developed signature "national" dishes, and styles of cooking, even as they shared common concepts of cookery.[3] Local preferences in flavors of dishes and in starchy staples varied in accordance with the sequence, cultural content, and local ecologies but expressed clearly the Atlantic circulation of peoples, language, and ingredients. Language adaptations between European, local, and African influences included Haitian Creole, Guyanese Dutch, Cuban Spanish, Jamaican Patois, and the lilt of local dialects of West Indian English that have influenced music, poetry, and theater. Pan-Atlantic expressions of cookery also presented several discernible cuisines, five of which I will analyze here, including recipes that illustrate and document their core ideas and history:

African American

> "I've got something good for you," he said, placing a glass of water before me. "How about the special?"
> "What's the special?"
> "Pork chops, grits, one egg, hot biscuits and coffee!" He leaned over the counter with a look that seemed to say, There, that ought to excite you, boy. Could everyone see that I was southern? (Ralph Ellison, *Invisible Man* [1947], 147)

Ralph Ellison's nameless protagonist's encounter with the diner in post–Harlem Renaissance New York makes oblique reference not only to the Great Migration of African Americans to northern cities in the interwar years, but also to the movement of southern foods associated with poverty, sharecropper agriculture, and a past of slavery. Pork chops, grits, and biscuits were, in fact, the high end of what in the late 1960s came to be celebrated as "soul food," and included what poet Amiri Baraka listed as including "chitterlings and neckbones but also maws, knuckles, pork chops, fatback, fried porgies, potlikker, turnips, kale, watermelon, black-eyed peas, grits, gravy, hoppin' john, hushpuppies, hoecake, buttermilk biscuits, pancakes, dumplings, okra, and . . . bean pies . . . as well as fried chicken, barbecue, sweet potato pies, and mustard and collard greens."[4] It was from these foods so emblematic of the American South that Ellison's southern migrant hero wished to dissociate himself as he made his way in Manhattan. Yet it was also these foods that became the core of a culinary identity in the late 1960s, as it emerged in a new generation of cookbooks, in newspaper articles, and in an American public culture that had come to celebrate black cultural identity rather than assimilation.

The list of elements that make up the arsenal of soul food shows two characteristics. First, many of the items have an African origin, including collard greens, okra, watermelon, and black-eyed peas (cowpeas). Of the New World foods, maize for grits, hushpuppies, and hoecakes and several types of beans and sweet potatoes appear in forms that resemble African cookery of those foods and probably reflect an Atlantic world circulation of culinary practice.[5] Was "soul food" African cooking or did it reflect an accommodation to the experience of struggle in America?

The second characteristic of the foods in the soul food menu is the surprising degree of regional variation, showing the distinctive experience of African Americans and their greater historical distance from African arrivals than people of the Caribbean and Latin America. For example, according to data from surveys of African American households in the late nineteenth century, prior to the Great Migration of the 1910s and 1920s, sharecropping families in Tuskegee County, Alabama, based meals on salt pork and bacon eaten with cornbread baked on a griddle. Those with gardens also had collard greens, turnips, or other vegetables boiled with pork fat. Eggs were part of the spring diet but not winter fare. Tuskegee cooks also made "cracklin bread" by frying fat until brittle, crushing it into cornmeal with water, soda, and salt, and then baking it.

Black Americans in Franklin Country, Virginia, however, ate what the principal of the Hampton Institute (the famous historically black university located nearby) called "hog and hominy." While Franklin County farmers also rented land rather than owning it, their cooking showed a much richer base in proteins than that of the sharecroppers of Tuskegee. In addition to eating better cuts of meat like pork shoulder and boiled ham, Franklin County's African American residents lived close to the Great Dismal Swamp and Chesapeake Bay, from which they obtained salted herring and fresh fish, which they ate with "ash cake," unrefined cornmeal mixed with brackish swamp water and baked directly in hot ashes. Cabbage, mustard greens, and sweet potatoes baked or boiled in fat also found their way into local meals and later literary imaginations.[6]

Notably, African American cooking and diets reflected substantial differences from other New World diets in the amounts of pork products and maize-based breads. While there was regional variability along a continuum from the rice-based diets of the Carolinas to the old South and Texas, where maize breads and porridges were the staple, there was also continuity in core side dishes. Collard greens (*Brassica oleracea*) was one of those dishes. A member of the kale/cabbage family, collards had their distant origin in the Mediterranean world, but probably came to the New World directly from Africa. Collards are rich in vitamin A as well as potassium, calcium, and iron. A South Carolina Geechee influence is evident in these recipes passed on by writer and chef Vertamae Smart-Grosvenor, one from her grandmother and one from jazz musician and playwright Archie Shepp:

Collard Greens

To Clean Greens

First pick the greens. That is, separate each leaf from the stalk. Pick out the yellow or discolored or weird-looking leaves and remove the tough stems. Take each leaf and shake it for bugs. Then wash the leaves three times or until there is no more grit. Then you fold each leaf in half and then roll them up as for a jelly roll, then with a knife or scissors you cut them up. . . . Always cook greens in enough water to cover. Some people add a little vinegar to the pot likker. Cornbread with pot likker is delicious.

Collard Greens à la Shepp

Have the meat boiling when you clean the greens. Then put the cleaned and cut-up greens in when the meat is just about done. Add salt, pepper, a bit of hot sauce and a bit of sugar. Cook on high heat for 15 minutes, stirring often. Turn off and let cook, stirring often while it is cooling. . . . and don't get mushy.[7]

The Great Migration that brought African Americans from the southern United States to northern industrial cities established the foundations of a culinary identity that would emerge in the 1960s as "soul food." African American cookery, featuring dishes such as greens, maize meal, beans, and cuts of pork, has much in common with southern U.S. cooking overall. Yet Amiri Baraka's idea that soul food comes from the identity of the consumer rather than from the dishes themselves carries considerable weight. You are what you eat and you eat what you are.

Creole (Louisiana)

Arguably the most cosmopolitan culture in the North American quarter of the Atlantic world is that of the Gulf Coast at New Orleans and Louisiana's Mississippi Delta. At the mouth of the Mississippi was the last point of entry of captive Africans in North America, where they met well-settled African Americans. With a cultural mix that also included Spanish, French-Canadian, Native American, and Caribbean cultural infusions, the port city of New Orleans resembled cosmopolitan spots like Luanda (Angola), Lourenço Marques (Mozambique), Dakar (Senegal), Salvador (Bahia, Brazil), and Cape Town and Durban (South Africa), where subtropical ecologies and the creolization of cooking and tastes ran parallel to fascinating transformations of language, music, and popular culture. Cooking ingredients were often local fresh items—crawfish, shrimp, chopped peppers, tomatoes—as well as additions drawn from the larger Atlantic world, such as long-grain rice, dried and powdered capsicum (e.g., cayenne), okra, and beans.

Jambalaya, a signature dish from Louisiana Creole cooking, strongly evokes Creole, Cajun, and West African roots and the Caribbean pot. Many origins have been suggested for the name; most likely the name and the dish itself derive from *jambon* (ham in French) and *à la ya-ya* (a generic West African reference to rice). Jambalaya is a dish typical of the West African *dafa* ("cook everything") one-pot dish (see chapter 5's opening quotation from Chinua Achebe's *Things Fall Apart*). Like Jollof rice (see chapter 5), jambalaya's long-grain African-style rice is cooked with and absorbs juices from meats, fish, and vegetables. Moreover, in the distinct West African cooking style, meat, fish, and shellfish commingle in the same pot. Readers and cooks should be able to discern in this recipe key elements of West African/Atlantic cooking as well as the adaptation of new ingredients:

Jambalaya (Creole)

1 lb meat (chicken, ham, wild game, andouille sausage)
½ lb shrimp
½ lb crawfish
sliced onion
red bell pepper
1 cup tomato sauce
salt (pinch)
sugar (pinch)
paprika
garlic
cayenne pepper
black pepper
vegetable oil
2 cups long-grain rice
green onions
chicken or meat stock

Add oil to pot at high heat, then add chicken and meat to brown it well on all sides. Add sausage, onions, peppers, and spices. Sauté for 5 minutes, then add the shrimp, crawfish, and tomato sauce. Add broth and rice while stirring. Bring to boil and then cover. Simmer on low fire for 20 minutes. Turn off fire and let rest for 5 minutes. Add green onions.[8]

"Creole" refers to the language and culture (including traditions of cookery) of peoples thrown together by circumstance into a common physical environment and social structure formed by race, ethnicity, and, in Louisiana, the riverain, wetland ecology of the bayou. The andouille sausage in this jambalaya recipe ultimately came from the French Normandy and Brittany migrants to Nova Scotia who were forcibly removed in 1755 from British Canada to French Louisiana. The sausage approximated the texture of the original "bush meat" in Creole jambalaya, forest and bayou critters such as oysters, duck, turtle, venison, or wild boar, which complemented the crawfish and shrimp of the freshwater/saltwater mix peculiar to the Mississippi Delta. But the signature dish of Creole culinary culture might equally be gumbo, a stew made of okra and bits of meat and poultry or shellfish, served as a soup or with rice.

Brazil (Bahia)

Northeast Brazil's Bahia area shows directly the Atlantic circulations of people, economies of labor, and political ideas across a vast New World landscape. Bahia was among the world's most recent recipients of African forced migration, during the last burst of the illegal trading from Nigeria's Bight of Benin region (Yoruba areas of southwestern Nigeria) in the 1840s and 1850s. The African captives brought with them first-person memories of Ifa divination, the cosmology of Santeria and Candomblé religious ritual, and a culinary tradition that knew well the use of cassava, palm oil, and pepper sauces. *Moqueca* is a Bahian-style dish, adapted from native Brazilian peoples, that African cooks and households over time translated from steaming in banana leaves and cooked over charcoal.

Moqueca (Fish Stew with Coconut Milk)

2 lb white fish (with skin)
Juice of 2 limes
½ cup coconut milk
2 tsp vegetable oil
½ tsp salt
1 chopped onion
1 clove garlic, minced
3 tsp parsley
2 tsp tomato paste
1 tsp pepper sauce
2 tsp palm oil
1 cup water

Place fish in bowl with lime juice and marinate for 15 minutes. Heat oil in pan and add onions and garlic. Sauté until translucent. Add marinated fish, tomato paste, and water. Simmer for 10 minutes until fish flakes. Mix in coconut milk, pepper sauce, parsley, and simmer for 5 minutes. Serve with white long-grain rice.[9]

FIGURE 7.2 Brazilian *moqueca de peixe*. *Photo by author*

At the table with a *moqueca* would likely appear typical signs of the Atlantic-African world: side dishes of oily fried plantain, crisp fried cassava, chopped collard greens, *feijão tropeiro* (beans and grated cassava), and long-grain rice. Like Creole jambalaya and Louisiana gumbos, moqueca is a one-pot stew, which is now made in a distinctive local clay pot—much like the pot used for Ethiopian *tegabino shiro* mentioned in chapter 4.

Cuba/Haiti/Caribbean

Caribbean cooking, like Caribbean rum making, differs in subtle ways among Anglophone, Francophone, and Spanish-speaking islands and coasts. These differences result from the cultural admixture of European settlers and those of African descent, the cultural/demographic balance, and the more recent evolution of national identities. The Cuban national dish *ajiaco* is a chicken stew that nationalist anthropologist Fernando Ortiz has claimed as a symbol of Cuba's national identity, including its African cultural component. Authentic versions of this dish vary, but include cassava (yucca), maize, and lime. The Cuban type bears only a partial resemblance to the *ajaico Bogotana* of Colombia, served with local potatoes and a indigenous oregano-like herb (*guazca*). This dish has deep historical roots that reflect the Caribbean but also broader connections with what we might call Atlantic cookery. In the 1500s a Spanish settler described the local dish, which included classic New World elements that later came to be West and Central African staples: "They have this dish which is a union of fresh meats cut up in small pieces that stew with diverse root vegetables that are stimulated by means of a caustic pepper called 'aji-aji,' that they give color with a seed called 'vija' that grows plentiful. This is their main dish, by way of saying their only dish."[10]

Ajiaco Criollo (Cuban Creole Stew)

¼ pound tasajo (salt-dried beef) desalted
3½ quarts water
½ pound flank steak (cut into 2-inch chunks)
1 pound beef short ribs (chopped into 1-inch slices)
1 bay leaf
1 medium-size *malanga amarilla* (yellow taro), peeled and quartered
1 medium-sized *yuca*, peeled and cut into 2-inch rounds
1 large green plantain, peeled and cut into 2-inch rounds
1 large white sweet potato
1 large white *malanga* (taro), peeled and quartered
1 tropical *ñame* (yam), peeled and quartered
1 large ripe plantain, peeled and cut into six rounds
1 cup peeled and seeded *calabaza* (squash)
2 large ears of corn, husked and cut into 2 inch rounds

In a large stockpot over medium-high heat, combine the dried beef and water, bring to a boil, and simmer covered 1 hour. Add the steak, ribs, and bay leaf; reduce the heat to low and cook for another hour, skimming off any scum that comes to the surface.

Over low heat, add the vegetables in 5-minute intervals, then add the corn and cook an additional 10–15 minutes. Serve hot.

Sometimes the synergies of taste and the cooks' intuition reveal historical connections more clearly than formal historical documents. This recipe is virtually identical to a recipe for "iyako" given as a "ritual recipe" for the initiation of Orisha priests in southwestern Nigeria, including the use of yams, salted beef, cassava (yucca), and sliced ears of corn.[11]

The spicy goat curries, jerk chicken, and beans and rice of Jamaica resemble Haitian stews more than they do the Cuban and Puerto Rican root crops used in common dishes. Rice and beans, however, are a common standard and reveal much about regional and global histories. The rice-and-black-bean dish *congri* also goes by the name of *Cristianos y Moros* (Christians and Moors), a tongue-in-cheek reference to the mixed grains of white rice and black beans and the historical conflicts of Europeans and Africans on the Iberian Peninsula and in the Mediterranean—the world of Shakespeare's *Othello*.

Congri or Cristianos y Moros (Cuban Style)

1 lb dried black beans
1 lb long-grain white rice
1 large onion
4 cloves garlic
1 medium hot pepper
3 Tbsp vegetable oil
1 Tbsp salt
½ tsp oregano
¼ tsp cumin
½ tsp paprika
1 bay leaf
2 Tbsp olive oil

Simmer the beans in water until they are well softened (about 1 hour). In another pot put 3 tablespoons of oil with the rice and stir until the rice has been well coated with oil. Then add the garlic, pepper, onion, cumin, oregano, salt, paprika, and 2½ cups water and simmer for 15 or 20 minutes until the rice is dried. Cook it covered on a slow fire. If the rice is still firm, add some hot bean water until the rice is completely tender. When the rice is done, add one or two ladles of beans, without liquid, so that which is added does not cause the beans to lose their shape.[12]

Note that in this Cuban recipe the cook prepares the rice in the Spanish style, coating it in oil, not the African/New World style. Cuban cooking's affinity for West African rice styles is attested by the special reverence given *respa*, the crispy caramelized residue that children nibble from the edges of the rice pan.

Africa's Second Wave

Africa's engagement with the New World has now taken on a new form. Since the 1970s, the number of Africans migrating to the New World—the United States and Canada in particular—has surpassed the total number of Africans who arrived in North America during the era of the slave trade. The new

FIGURE 7.3 Roha
Ethiopian restaurant,
Washington, DC.
Photo by author

immigrants are far more broadly based in their geographic origins and economic background in Africa and in their opportunities for economic entrepreneurship than earlier groups. While Africans from the era of the slave trade were mainly from the mouth of the Congo and West Africa in general, the new generation of African immigrants in the twentieth century added large coherent communities from Ethiopia, Eritrea, Kenya, Sudan, Zambia, Somalia, and Egypt.

Many of Africa's migrants to America in the late twentieth century are well-educated and trained professionals or political refugees settled as ethnic communities in particular locations (Somalis in Columbus, Ohio, and Portland, Maine; Oromo in Minneapolis; Nigerians in Houston). Only Ethiopia/Eritrea, however, has emerged as the bearer of a national cuisine as an identifiable part of North American restaurant culture (as opposed to foods served in African homes). This may be, in part, because Ethiopia had already defined and elaborated its own emblematic cuisine in a process described in chapters 3 and 4, a cuisine that could be exported during the middle-class and elite exodus of the late 1970s and 1980s.

Ethiopian Cuisine in the Diaspora: Accommodation and Conformity

Public hospitality and creativity in Ethiopian food had a true efflorescence in the liberal economic policies that began in the post-Derg period (1991–2005).

FIGURE 7.4 Dukem restaurant sign, Addis Ababa. *Photo by author*

Ethiopia's 1974 revolution and the military government, political dislocations, and outright persecutions that followed created a large and economically successful diaspora in Europe and the North America whose monetary remittances have created a dynamic flow of private capital in the post-1991 period.

This flow of capital remittances and the relocation of Ethiopians—often cultural elites—has had important effects on the creativity and expansion of an international Ethiopian cuisine in Europe and North America, but also in Ethiopia itself. In the post-1974 era Ethiopian restaurants have become a ubiquitous part of cosmopolitan urban landscapes in Washington, London, Chicago, Los Angeles, Rome, Atlanta, Boston, and countless other cities. Even in smaller cities like New Brunswick, New Jersey, and New Haven, Connecticut, the cuisine of Ethiopia (or Eritrea in New Haven) appears along with the panoply of other ethnic restaurants known by the dining public. Washington DC's historically African American Adams Morgan neighborhood, for example, has a changing array of restaurants and names that project both cuisine and political orientation toward the *ancien régime,* the current government, or the independence of Eritrea. The names give away the politics of the owner and the clientele—Fasika (Christian), Addis Ababa (centrist), Red Sea (Eritrean)—or an attempt to be neutral—Dukem (a town south of Addis Ababa)—though not much difference in the menu items offered. Their menus all show fundamental orientation toward the classical dishes detailed in Mérab's 1913 list: *doro wet, qay wet, misir wet, yabeg t'ibs,* and so on, all served on top of an attempt at *injera* that, to a purist palate, only approximates the Ethiopian teff version.[13]

Pressures for market conformity have, however, brought changes to the menus of Ethiopian restaurants. Some of these, like fasting food from the Orthodox Christian fast renamed as "vegetarian," are market-savvy innovations. Others suggest transgressions against the basic rules of the historical cuisine in the structures of taste, meaning, and processing of food. The following are cases in point:

- Dessert as a menu item (sweetness following savory violates a basic tenet of what constitutes a meal in Ethiopia; sweetness is for snacks, not part of meal structure)
- Raw foods (green leafy salads/tomatoes) are found nowhere in the structure of a traditional meal, save raw beef. Lettuce and tomato salads are recent additions both in Addis Ababa and in expatriate dining spots outside Ethiopia.
- Fasting food (indicating a religious practice/belief) has been transmogrified as vegetarian (either practiced as a healthy alternative or as a gesture to the new civil religion of veganism or vegetarianism).
- Use of North American eragrostis ("love grass" or annual bunch grass) instead of teff (*Eragrostis abyssinica*) and self-rising flour to make injera has added heaviness and sacrificed the texture and flexibility of the basic staple bread as found in Ethiopia.

Exposure to the international market has brought change to Ethiopian cuisine as presented to American and European customers. Most menus now include green salads, tomatoes, shrimp, and even boneless chicken (all anathema in traditional highland fare). In an ultimate accommodation to North American structures of taste, Chicago's Ras Dashen restaurant offers a dessert of *injera* bread pudding topped with blueberries and vanilla ice cream.[14]

Other attempts at culinary market conformity have included offering a wrap sandwich (using a wheat-flour tortilla) using the synergies of spices to convey the deeper structure of flavor in Ethiopian cuisine. Makeda, a restaurant in New Brunswick, New Jersey, organizes its hip menu to include wraps "inspired" by African flavors. Their "Addis Ababa" wrap offers a wrapped tortilla of "Ethiopian beans and *corn* [my italics] with tomatoes and collard greens, drizzled with chili butter."[15]

No similar exodus took place for emblematic culinary cultures like Yoruba (Nigeria), southern Ghana, Senegal, or Angola. For North Africa and Egypt (as also with Lebanese and Syrian) those foodways blended seamlessly into French culinary culture in both Paris and eventually in other world capitals as well. Nevertheless, a process of adaptation to new audiences has begun, even more slowly compared to other Central Asian and Asian cookery (Korean, Thai, Japanese, even Afghan). Those cuisines have reached the stage beyond the storefront eatery that caters primarily to immigrant communities themselves, and appear now in culinary magazines, commanding prices that support an haute cuisine clientele. African restaurateurs, for their part, have begun to adapt to a common sequencing of tastes and presentation for upscale consumer markets (i.e., appetizer courses, salad, dessert) that would have been anathema to the home culture's consumers. The restaurant in New Brunswick, New Jersey, mentioned above has taken up an Ethiopian/ Eritrean identity and produced high-quality food, adapting its menu to a cosmopolitan audience in a university town. It has converted Ethiopia's tradition of austere seasonal fasting (no meat or dairy products) to two menu columns, one for meat and one for vegetarian, that can be mixed and matched. Salad greens appear in the vegetarian column along with beans and lentil dishes and the Muslim breakfast dish *ful* (fool).

A more pointed illustration of the adaptation to the commercialization of African tastes is this same restaurant's Africa-Inspired Wraps, a concession to the Mexican burrito/Lebanese falafel sandwich roll-ups that seeks to capture the synergies of taste and ingredients that it implicitly argues are somehow distinctly "African."

EXPERIENCE MAKEDA'S AFRICA-INSPIRED WRAPS [MAKEDA RESTAURANT, NEW BRUNSWICK, NJ]

Cote d'Ivoire
Sautéed chicken with coconut ginger mayonnaise in a spinach wrap

Kumassi Special
Grilled chicken with jalapeño butter and sweet onion marmalade

Kilimanjaro
Grilled lamb with mango chutney drizzled with chili oil

Casablanca
Sauteed lamb strips with curried couscous in an apricot barbecue sauce

Lagos Jumping
   Sliced filet mignon with roasted tomatoes and jalapeño pepper butter, drizzled with a balsamic reduction sauce—mild or hot

Seychelles
   Ginger beef with vegetable stew, seasoned with cumin

Mombassa
   Sauteed shrimp and crabmeat with a lemon-mustard sauce encased in a spinach wrap

Cape Town
   Curried vegetable stew encased in a spinach wrap

Addis Ababa
   Ethiopian beans and corn with tomatoes and collard greens, drizzled with chili butter

The Nile
   Fried eggplant with cucumbers, yogurt, and peanuts, drizzled with curry oil.

Some of the combinations of flavors and ingredients (Ethiopian corn, Egyptian curry oil, Lagos filet mignon) appear fanciful. Mombasa, the coastal Kenyan hometown of Muslim Swahili, might be shocked to find the inclusion of crab and shrimp in its namesake sandwich. The combinations of flavors, textures, and ingredients, however, have begun to reframe African cookery in a global context. The most visible example of this effect may be Ethio-Swedish chef Marcus Samuelsson's New York restaurant Merkato 55 and his popular book *The Soul of a New Cuisine,* which is the result of his personal sojourn from cooking school in Europe to a tour of African cities to absorb the core ideas and fragrances of generations of cooks on that continent. Ironically, in centers of cultural dynamism in Africa itself, such as Addis Ababa, Lagos, Cape Town, Dakar, and Accra, the cultural dynamism, emerging elites with disposable income, and circulation of African cultural innovation in music, fashion, and commodities have brought about culinary hybridism on both a national and international scale. Africa's cooking pots have had a historical role, and now promise a new international contribution.

Epilogue

Some Good Comparative Readings

THIS BOOK covers an impossibly broad landscape of food, cooking, and culinary culture found within the African continent. And it leaves off the rich cooking traditions of North Africa and the Mediterranean world. Can a traveler moving across such a vast continent make sense of peoples who savor the pounded-yam *fufu* of Ghana and southern Nigeria, the spongy, sour *injera* of Ethiopia, or the *thiebou dienn* of Senegal? Can we really understand across generations how women who made and adapted those dishes dealt with the arrival of new ingredients as the world economy became increasingly more global in the twentieth century?

One question comes to mind: were the changes in the 1500–2000 era covered in this book a simple process of Africa's cooking becoming cosmopolitan, in other words developing an appreciation of other parts of the world? To a degree that is true, but it is not the simple matter of cultural addition that the term "cosmopolitan" implies. African cooks accepted the arrival of ingredients like canned tomato paste, bouillon cubes, new types of packaged rice, or pasta as regular items available in even small shops in rural areas. Yet there has also been a turning inward to recapture the central ideas of their own cooking, which have traveled across oceans and into the continent's own growing cities. Ethiopia's *tegabino shiro* (chapter 4) is a case in point, as is *thiebou dienn* (otherwise known as Jollof rice; chapter 5), which appears in Louisiana's jambalaya. The essence of those iconic dishes lies not just in the ingredients but also in the methods of cooking and the unique balance of the foods' textures that appear in many of the familiar ethnic menus in neighborhood urban restaurants in America and Europe.

This book is a beginning that invites historians of food and of cultural history to add African flavors and ideas as a meaningful contribution to the study of history. Food and cooking can join the history of music, dress, architecture, and language as one of the most illustrative measures of our world. The recipes here offer a certain type of voice, from those generations of cooks who otherwise remain silent. Yes, their world has changed, but they stir their pots, the world intervenes, and yet their ideas endure in the changing of what the world eats and in what part of that bears an African flavor.

In a book that takes on an entire continent, there are many questions that remain about local practice and historical evidence. These await the work of a new generation of culinary historians who can work in detail in specific areas with the skills of language and participant observation. My experience in Ethiopia has allowed me insight into that place, but elsewhere I have been more of an intensely interested traveler. The questions that need asking and the sources for addressing them might include the following:

- Can we set about collecting oral testimonies from women who learned their culinary craft a generation ago?

- With Ethiopian cuisine as a model, what national cuisines have emerged and what are the signature dishes recognized by global audiences?

- Can we read modern recipes for African influences in ingredients (e.g., powdered shellfish) or techniques (e.g., one-pot rice dishes)?

- Can economic historians pore over shipping records to identify when and where the earliest ingredients from the industrial world, such as canned goods, imported rice, bouillon cubes, pasta, and high-fructose corn syrup, arrived in African ports?

The history of food as cooking and sensual experience overall is a new subfield that is growing rapidly. For Africa, however, the process has scarcely begun. Cookbooks themselves make interesting reading as historical texts, but few historians are aware of their value for that purpose. In the area of cookbooks in ethnic cuisine, African occupies the smallest of spaces in even the most innovative bookshops or library collections.

Cookbooks themselves make interesting reading as historical texts, but few are aware of their own value for that purpose. It is worth it here to begin a list with some classic texts that directly address food and cooking as a topic of history. One of the oldest, and most readable, is Reay Tannahill's *Food in History* (1973). Tannahill's was really the first of its kind for a general readership, but she gives Africa exceedingly short shrift. She offers one page on "Arab Cooking" and comments for Africa that "cooking is only an art where food is consistently plentiful. . . . When shortages are a part of everyday life, filling the stomach is the only art." That is a telling statement in many ways, since it denies Africa its history of food as an aesthetic experience. Her disdainful comment probably applies more to her assumptions about social class than to Africa as a geographic setting. Taking a broader view of food and history, and more theoretically provocative, are Felipe Fernández-Armesto's *Food: A History* (2001) and the edited volume by Jean-Louis Flandrin and Massimo Montanari, *Food: A Culinary History from Antiquity to the Present* (1996). Both of these books are the work of serious historians and treat food as a serious topic. Neither, however, addresses Africa as a cultural or geographic context, except as a Mediterranean periphery. Reading between the lines in these works does, however, offer some insights into where Africa ought to fit and where new writing ought to appear, and they frame the place in food writing that Africa may soon occupy.

Of recent popular literature on food, the work that offers the most open-ended potential approaches to Africa's inclusion are journalist Michael Pollan's provocative books *The Botany of Desire* (2001) and *The Omnivore's Dilemma* (2006) because they see food and cooking as a historical process reflecting wider trends of human action at a global level. Though he does not focus on Africa, Pollan's writing on nature, human tastes, and the sensual at least invites the kinds of questions raised in this book. New writing on African foods and taste is likely to reflect some of his approaches.

Food and cooking as culture and as markers of cultural identity in world societies have in the past been the concern more often of anthropology than of history. It is not surprising, therefore, that we find some of the best comparative reading in that area. The most powerful and readable ideas are from Sidney Mintz, including *Sweetness and Power* (1985) and *Tasting Food, Tasting Freedom* (1996). For Africa, the classics are Jack Goody's *Cooking, Cuisine, and Class* (1982) and Jane Guyer's *Feeding African Cities* (1987). While both of these books are classic comparative studies and required reading for any would-be anthropologist of Africa, neither one directly engages the issue of food as either cooking or cultural knowledge. Goody, astonishingly, dismisses the idea of an African cuisine altogether. On the anthropology of diet in Africa, only Audrey Richards in 1939 presented serious evidence about cooking and the sensibilities of African woman about the mechanics and meaning of food. I cite her work here extensively, but she is worth reading in full. More recent writing about Ghana has actually done the best job of telling us what African cooking means. Gracia Clark's *Onions Are My Husband* (1994) tells us about the meaning of cooking in modern society in Ghana, and Claire Robertson's *Sharing the Same Bowl* (1983) tells about women's life and food in Accra as a window into both history and society. Those two works offer a glimpse of the context of recipes that we find in those compiled cookbooks that we occasionally find in bookshops in Africa's capital cities and on the shelves of used bookstores in London, Boston, or East Lansing, Michigan.

The best writing on African cooking and cuisine comes in the form of continent-wide presentations on the diaspora, or on diaspora cooking itself. Fran Osseo-Asare's *Food Culture in Sub-Saharan Africa* (2005) is informative, and has recipes that convey her enthusiasm for the topic. Jessica Harris is probably the most widely read writer on African cooking; her goal is to present a comprehensive list of recipes with a decidedly West African tilt. *The Africa Cookbook* (1998) understandably shares her personal journeys as a modern traveler in Africa, rather than adopting a historian's search for meaning. Vertamae Smart-Grosvenor's *Vibration Cooking* (1992) adds a powerful measure of passion into the idea of cooking and African influence on black folk in North America.

Judy Carney's *Black Rice* (2001) has been a pathbreaking insight into Africa's contributions to the techniques and substance of rice that links the farmer to the trader to the cook. It also gives us the idea of cooking as a form of knowledge, and women's knowledge at that. Her new work, *In the Shadow of Slavery: Africa's Botanical Legacy in the Atlantic World* (2009), takes us even further.

The most important book that combines the art of the cook and a serious consideration of African cooking traditions is Marcus Samuelsson's *The Soul of a New Cuisine: A Discovery of the Foods and Flavors of Africa* (2006). An Ethiopian adopted as a young child by Swedish parents, Samuelsson took his formal European training as a chef and success as a New York restaurateur on a tour of African cities. His book, in a coffee-table format with beautiful color photos, shows a keen appreciation of the ingredients of Africa's cooking. At the same time, however, he misses cornbread as a signature product of the American South and suggests making injera with yogurt and whole wheat flour to simulate the essence of texture achieved only in Ethiopia itself. His book, nonetheless, demonstrates a sense of the adaptability of African cooking to new ingredients available in new settings, and offers a fine sense of place that includes the New World as well as the Old.

A further body of writing that reveals the substance and meaning of food in Africa is in its rich modern literature, which is not consciously historical. Chinua Achebe's *Things Fall Apart* appears several times in this work. It has been the most widely read African novel for a generation. But there is, of course, much more. Chris Albani's *Graceland* ends each chapter with an Igbo recipe, one of his mother's. African women's writing, including Buchi Emecheta's *The Joys of Motherhood* and Mariama Bâ's *So Long a Letter*, will offer rich insights for studies of both history and literature. Beyond literature, Osuman Sembene's films (Mandabi or Xala) feature eating as a recurrent theme, whether as pleasure or as a marker of corruption. In its own way, each of these books and renderings of African culture, including recipe lists and cookbooks, can take the reader further into the deeper structures and meanings of Africa's traditions of cooking. I urge the reader to think of them as historical and to enjoy the results.

Appendix

Recipe List

Notes

Introduction: African Food and African History

The first epigraph to this chapter is from Felipe Fernández-Armesto, *Food: A History* (London: Macmillan, 2001), 5.

1. Here I disagree fundamentally with food historian Fernández-Armesto, who argues that "sauces generate a learned tradition of cooking because the recipes are complex and hard to remember: they therefore have to be written down and become a privilege of the literate." Fernández-Armesto, *Food: A History*, 131. Malian and Somali griots and poets have long proven the capacities of human memory for preserving and adapting oral performance. The Greek poet Homer, after all, recounted his stories orally and reports meals of Ithaca prepared without written recipes.

2. For this ill-informed assertion, see Linda Civitello, *Cuisine and Culture: A History of Food and People* (New York: John Wiley, 2003), 218.

3. Goody thus contrasts his idea of African foodways as socially undifferentiated with the Chinese "house of Chao," which defined the cooking of China. Jack Goody, *Cooking, Cuisine, and Class: A Study in Comparative Sociology* (Cambridge: Cambridge University Press, 1982), 40–96; also see Sidney W. Mintz, *Tasting Food, Tasting Freedom: Excursions into Eating, Culture, and the Past* (Boston: Houghton Mifflin, 1996), 93–105. On the Sung Dynasty's role in Chinese cuisine, see Michael Freeman, "Sung," in *Food and Chinese Culture*, ed. K. C. Chang (New Haven: Yale University Press, 1977), 143.

4. Priscilla Parkhurst Ferguson, *Accounting for Taste: The Triumph of French Cuisine* (Chicago: University of Chicago Press, 1994), 3.

5. Fernández-Armesto, *Food: A History*, 133.

6. Examples of this would include Ethiopia/Eritrea, Mande groups, Kwa language groups, and societies in southern Nigeria. I am grateful to Chelsea Shields-Strayer for this insight, offered in a 2007 seminar on the social history of food and cuisine held at Boston University.

7. Mintz, *Tasting Food,* 96.

8. Freeman, "Sung," 144. Freeman argues that Sung Chinese cuisine, for example, developed out of the traditions of several regions and an overarching elite culture. Is there an analogy for Africa there?

9. See, for example, *orike,* which refers to anthropomorphic maize plants, in James C. McCann, *Maize and Grace: Africa's Encounter with a New World Crop* (Cambridge, MA: Harvard University Press, 2005), 31–32. On the idea of iconic food references in the *Sundiata* epic, I am grateful to Natalie Mettler, whose work in the Bamanakan language and culture of Mali reveals the importance of food as cultural identity.

10. Vertamae Smart-Grosvenor, *Vibration Cooking; Or, the Travel Notes of a Geechee Girl* (New York: Ballantine, 1992), 4–6.

11. Maya Angelou, *A Song Flung up to Heaven* (New York: Random House, 2002), chap. 2.

CHAPTER ONE   Seasons and Seasonings
Africa's Geographic Endowments of the Edible

1. One North American example of this phenomenon is the dish Boston baked beans, a iconic regional winter specialty made simply from what remained in the New England larder in the dark days of winter: dried beans, salt pork, molasses (from the West Indies trade), and onions from the root cellar.

2. Audrey Richards, *Land, Labour, and Diet in Northern Rhodesia: An Economic Study of the Bemba Tribe* (London: Oxford University Press, 1939), 41–42.

3. Diana Wylie, *Starving on a Full Stomach: Hunger and the Triumph of Cultural Racism in Modern South Africa* (Charlottesville: University of Virginia Press, 2001), 44–45.

4. Jared Diamond, *Guns, Germs, and Steel: The Fates of Human Societies* (New York: W. W. Norton, 1997), 98–100, 138–42. This analysis, of course, assigns the North African littoral to the Mediterranean ecological zone rather than to tropical and subtropical Africa. For an assessment of African innovations in grains (sorghum and millet) and root crops (yam) see chapter 2.

5. See Stanley Alpern, "The European Introduction of Crops into West Africa in Precolonial Times," *History in Africa* 19 (1992): 14–23.

6. Alfred Crosby, *The Columbian Exchange: Biological and Cultural Consequences of 1492* (Westport, CT: Greenwood, 1972). Crosby later expanded his assessment of its full global impact in *Ecological Imperialism: The Biological Expansion of Europe* (Cambridge: Cambridge University Press, 1986).

7. See David Eltis, "The Volume and Direction of the Transatlantic Slave Trade: A Reassessment," *William and Mary Quarterly* 60 (2001): 17–46.

8. Judith Carney, *Black Rice: The African Origins of Rice Cultivation in the Americas* (Cambridge, MA: Harvard University Press, 2001), 164–66. Also see Eltis's cranky response to Carney's thesis about African rice.

9. Linda Civitello, *Cuisine and Culture: A History of Food and People* (New York: John Wiley, 2003), 218–20.

10. Felipe Fernández-Armesto, *Food: A History* (London: Macmillan, 2001), 159.

11. Interview with Zipporah M'Mwirichia, Meru, July 23, 2001, provided in Mary Ciambaka Mwiandi, "The Jeanes School in Kenya: The Role of the Jeanes Teachers and Their Wives in the Social Transformation of Rural Colonial Kenya, 1925–61" (PhD diss., Michigan State University, 2005), 109.

12. Vertamae Smart-Grosvenor, *Vibration Cooking; Or, the Travel Notes of a Geechee Girl* (New York: Ballantine, 1992), 4–6.

13. Arjun Appadurai, "How to Make a National Cuisine: Cookbooks in Contemporary India," *Comparative Studies in Society and History* 30, no. 1 (1988): 21–22.

14. Fernández-Armesto, *Food: A History,* 159.

15. See Madhur Jaffrey, *An Invitation to Indian Cooking* (New York: Penguin, 1973); Annabel Shaxson, Pat Dickson, and June Walker, *The Malawi Cookbook* (Zomba, Malawi: Government Printer, 1979); Marielle Rowan, *Flavours of Mozambique* (Maputo: Marielle Rowan, 1998); Laura Edet, *Classic Nigerian Cook Book* (London: Divine Grace, 1996).

16. Appadurai, "How to Make a National Cuisine," 21. For a range of curry dishes in Mozambique, see Rowan, *Flavours of Mozambique,* 16, 18, 21, 38.

17. Shaxson, Dickson, and Walker, *Malawi Cookbook,* 28–52.

CHAPTER TWO Staples, Starches, and the Heat of Atlantic Circulation

The first epigraph to this chapter is from Felipe Fernández-Armesto, *Food: A History* (London: Macmillan, 2001), 11.

The second epigraph is from Audrey Richards, *Land, Labour, and Diet in Northern Rhodesia: An Economic Study of the Bemba Tribe* (London: Oxford University Press, 1939), 52.

1. *Fufu* is a stiff paste molded by the eater into a ball, then dipped into sauce and swallowed, usually without chewing. It leaves a distinctive feeling in the stomach at the end of a meal.

2. Elizabeth J. Reitz, "Temperate and Arctic North America to 1492," in Kenneth F. Kiple and Kriemhild Coneè Ornelas, eds., *The Cambridge World History of Food,* 2 vols. (Cambridge: Cambridge University Press, 2000), 2:1278–1300.

3. Bomme Basemzanzi, *South African Indigenous Foods: A Collection of Recipes of Indigenous Foods, Prepared by Generations of Women* (Pretoria: IndiZAFoods, 2004), 71.

4. Christopher Ehret, *An African Classical Age: Eastern and Southern Africa in World History, 1000 B.C. to A.D. 400* (Charlottesville: University of Virginia Press, 1998), 5–14. Ehret argues for three zones: the Sudanic Agripastoral Tradition at the southern edge of the Sahara (for sorghum, pearl millet, and fonio—another African grain); the Cushitic Agripastoral Tradition of the Red Sea/Nile Valley area (for teff and finger millet); and the West African Planting Agriculture, which developed the yam.

5. For a good survey of the qualities and geography of sorghum in Africa, see "Sorghum in Africa," http://www.uea.ac.uk/cap/sorghum/Africa. Also see Kiple and Ornelas, *Cambridge World History of Food,* 2:1814.

6. On the comparative history of beers and distilled spirits, see Justin Willis, *Potent Brews: A Social History of Alcohol in East Africa, 1850–1999* (Oxford: Oxford University Press, 2002), and Emmanuel Akyeampong, *Drink, Power, and Cultural Change: A Social History of Alcohol in Ghana, c. 1800 to Recent Times* (Portsmouth, NH: Heinemann, 1996).

7. Pamela Greene, *Favorite Sierra Leone Recipes* (Freetown, Commercial Printers, 1970), 16.

8. Judith Carney, *Black Rice: The African Origins of Rice Cultivation in the Americas* (Cambridge, MA: Harvard University Press, 2001), 38–39.

9. Ibid., 15.

10. Ibid., 16.

11. See John Lobell, *The Little Green Book: A Guide to Self-Reliant Living in the 1980s* (Boulder: Shambhala, 1981). For nutritional information on rice see http://www.pechsiam.com/allabout_nutrition.htm.

12. Carney, *Black Rice*, 124–25.

13. Ibid., 114–116.

14. Ibid., 117.

15. Stanley Alpern, "The European Introduction of Crops into West Africa in Precolonial Times," *History in Africa* 19 (1992): 20–21.

16. Ehret, *African Classical Age*, 13. Cocoyam (*Colocasia esculenta*), also called taro, is an import that arrived in Africa via the Indian Ocean and, later, the Atlantic Rim and plays a supporting, but minor role in African cookery.

17. Chinua Achebe, *Things Fall Apart* (London: Heinemann, 1958), 24.

18. Gracia Clark, *Onions Are My Husband: Survival and Accumulation by West African Market Women* (Chicago: University of Chicago Press, 1994), 348–49; Claire C. Robertson, *Sharing the Same Bowl: A Socioeconomic History of Women and Class in Accra, Ghana* (Bloomington: Indiana University Press, 1984), 112.

19. Laura Edet, *Classic Nigerian Cook Book* (London: Divine Grace, 1996), 78.

20. Fran Osseo-Asare, *Food Culture in Sub-Saharan Africa* (Westport, CT: Greenwood Press, 2005), 18–19.

21. T. Edward Bowdich, *Mission from Cape Coast Castle to Ashantee*, ed. W. E. F. Ward (London: Frank Cass, 1966), 274–79.

22. James George Frazer, *The Golden Bough*, 2 vols. (London: Macmillan, 1890), 2:75.

23. Achebe, *Things Fall Apart*, 26.

24. Ibid., 24.

25. Annabel Shaxson, Pat Dickson, and June Walker, *The Malawi Cookbook* (Zomba, Malawi: Government Printer, 1979), 57.

26. M. D. W. Jeffreys, "The History of Maize in Africa," *South African Journal of Science* (March 1954): 198. In this quotation the common mistranslation of the Portuguese *milho zaburro* as maize (as opposed to sorghum, an indigenous African grain) is not a factor. The reference to *mehiz* and to the grain's resemblance to chickpeas points to maize as the cereal described.

27. M. D. W. Jeffreys, "How Ancient Is West African Maize?" *Africa* 33, no. 2 (1963): 121. Jeffreys cites a translation by Lains e Silva. Also see Frank Willett, "The

Introduction of Maize to West Africa," *Africa* 32, no. 1 (1962): 11. Robert Harms tells me that the French slaving ship *Diligent* called in at São Tomé in December–January 1731–32, where it took on cassava flour and "une Demy gamelle De mil" (a half barrel of maize/sorghum) as food for the middle passage. The latter may be maize rather than millet since maize is elsewhere described as a major provision for such vessels calling at São Tomé. It is not clear why the *Diligent* did not take on a larger consignment of maize, though perhaps the harvest was delayed and supplies were low.

28. Olfert Dapper, *Nankeurige beschrijvinge der Afrikaensche gewesten* (Amsterdam, 1668), 463. Quoted in Helma Pasch, "Zur Geschichte der Verbreitung des Maizes in Afrika," *Sprache und Geschichte in Afrika* 5 (1983): 189.

29. Dominique Juhé-Beaulaton, "La diffusion du maïs sur les côtes de l'or et des esclaves aux XVII et XVIII siècles," *Revue française d'histoire d'Outre-mer* 77 (1990): 188–90.

30. A. J. H. Goodwin, "The Origin of Maize," *South African Archaeological Bulletin* 8 (1953): 13.

31. James C. McCann, *Maize and Grace: Africa's Encounter with a New World Crop* (Cambridge, MA: Harvard University Press, 2005), 5.

32. For a full discussion of names for maize in African languages, see ibid., 33–38.

33. Thomas Astley, *A New General Collection of Voyages and Travels*, vol. 2 (London: Frank Cass, 1968), sec. 2.

34. Felix I. Nweke, John K. Lynam, and Dunstan S. C. Spencer, *The Cassava Transformation: Africa's Best-Kept Secret* (East Lansing: Michigan State University Press, 2002), xvii.

35. Ibid., 7.

36. Alpern, "European Introduction of Crops," 25–26; see also W. O. Jones, *Manioc in Africa* (Palo Alto: Stanford University Press, 1959), 62.

37. Jones, *Manioc*, 12; Nweke, Lynam, and Spencer, *Cassava Transformation*, 228n 9, 27–28.

38. Edet, *Classic Nigerian Cookery*, 23.

39. Nweke, Lynam, and Spencer, *Cassava Transformation*, 116–24.

40. Osseo-Asare, *Food Culture*, 149; Nweke, Lynam, and Spencer, *Cassava Transformation*, 124–26.

41. Marielle Rowan, *Flavours of Mozambique* (Maputo: Marielle Rowan, 1998), 20. This updated recipe calls for baking in an oven, but a traditional version would have used a single pot for braising.

42. Jean Andrews, "Chilli Peppers," in Kiple and Ornelas, *Cambridge World History of Food*, 1:281–87. From evidence on other crops (such as maize), it seems likely that capsicum's route may have included Venetian contact with the Ottoman Mediterranean and the eastern spice trade and India and thence to Africa's East Coast or up the Nile Valley.

43. Mary Umita Randelman, *Memories of a Cuban Kitchen* (New York: John Wiley, 1996), 104–5.

44. Andrews, "Chilli Peppers," 282.

CHAPTER THREE Taytu's Feast
Cuisine and Nation in the New Flower, Ethiopia, 1887

The epigraph to this chapter is from Gabra Sellase, *Tarika zaman za-dagmawi Menilek: Negusa nagast za-Ityopya* (Addis Ababa: Berhanena Salam Press, 1966 EC), 136–37; Guèbrè Sellassié, *Chronique du règne de Ménèlik II roi des rois d'Éthiopie,* ed. and trans. Tèsfa Sellassié and Maurice de Coppet (Paris: Maisonneuve frères, 1930), 229, 231. When there are discrepancies in the translation of these two texts, I have chosen my own translation of the Amharic texts.

1. See Harold G. Marcus, *The Life and Times of Menelik II: Ethiopia, 1844–1913* (Oxford: Clarendon Press, 1975), 222–25. Marcus bases his description of daily life and feast at court on interviews with a retired member of the kitchen staff.

2. The wood smoke would have been from juniper or acacia wood; eucalyptus arrived on Entoto only after 1894.

3. A. E. Pease, *Travel and Sport in Africa,* 3 vols. (London: Arthur L. Humphreys, 1902), also cited in Chris Prouty, *Empress Taytu and Menilek: Ethiopia, 1883–1910* (Trenton, NJ: Red Sea Press, 1986), 259–60.

CHAPTER FOUR Stirring a National Dish
Ethiopian Cuisine, 1500–2000

1. More recently, urban diets have included tomatoes, green beans, and cabbage where middle-class incomes allow.

2. See James C. McCann, *People of the Plow: An Agricultural History of Ethiopia* (Madison: University of Wisconsin Press, 1995), 49, and *From Poverty to Famine in Northeast Ethiopia: A Rural History* (Philadelphia: University of Pennsylvania Press, 1987), 172–73.

3. Manoel de Almeida, *Some Records of Ethiopia, 1593–1646,* ed. and trans. C. F. Beckingham and G. W. B. Huntingford (London: Hakluyt Society, 1954), 46. All of the spices listed here derive from areas outside of Ethiopia (in fact, outside of Africa). See Hansjörg Küster, "Spices and Flavorings," in *The Cambridge World History of Food,* ed. Kenneth F. Kiple and Kriemhild Coneè Ornelas, 2 vols. (Cambridge: Cambridge University Press, 2000), 1:431–37.

4. Daniel J. Mesfin, ed., *Exotic Ethiopian Cooking: Society, Culture, Hospitality, and Traditions* (Falls Church, VA: Ethiopian Cookbook Enterprises, 2004), 189.

5. Almeida, *Some Records,* 63. For raw meat in the seventeenth century see also Jerónimo Lobo, *The Itinerário of Jerónimo Lobo,* ed. and trans. Donald Lockhart (London: Hakluyt Society, 1984), 170–71. Widespread folk tradition claims, with considerable logic, that raw meat was favored by military encampments to avoid the smoke of campfires, which would reveal their location and size. The other dish is likely *dulet,* tripe sautéed in butter with hot green peppers, served often as breakfast the morning that a household has slaughtered a sheep or goat.

6. Mansfield Parkyns, *Life in Abyssinia: Being Notes Collected during Three Years' Residence in That Country* (London: Frank Cass, 1966), 214–15.

7. Aleksander Bulatowicz, *Z woskami Menelika II, Zapiski z podrozy do Etiopii* (Warsaw: Dialog, 2000), 72–73. I am grateful to my colleague Izabela Orlowska, who provided me with a translation from the Polish text.

8. Ibid., 72.

9. Pearce himself was a great consumer of raw beef. See Nathaniel Pearce, *The Life and Adventures of Nathaniel Pearce: Written by Himself during a Residence in Abyssinia from the Years 1810 to 1819 Together with Mr. Coffin's Account of his Visit to Gondar* (London: Henry Colburn and Richard Bentley, 1831), 95, 148.

10. Bulatowicz, *Z woskami*, 219.

11. Docteur E. Mérab, *Impressions d'Éthiopie: L'Abyssinie sous Ménélik II*, 3 vols. (Paris: H. Libert, 1921), 448–52.

12. Gabra Sellase, *Tarika zaman*, 122.

13. Lobo, *Itinerário*, 173. For lodging and board in town, see Francisco Alvarez, *The Prester John of the Indies: A True Relation of the Lands of the Prester John, being the narrative of the Portuguese Embassy to Ethiopia in 1540*, ed. and trans. C. F. Beckingham and G. W. B. Huntingford, 2 vols. (Cambridge: Hakluyt Society, 1961), 1:104–5.

14. C. W. Isenberg and J. L. Krapf, *Journals of the Rev. Messrs. Isenberg and Krapf, Detailing Their Proceedings in the Kingdom of Shoa* (London: Seeley, 1843), 432–33, 441–42. Yet Krapf also recounts an incident where he was refused hospitality in several houses until he was finally allowed to spend the night in an abandoned house and offered "a few loaves of bread and a little beer."

15. Parkyns, *Life in Abyssinia*, 73–74.

16. Isenberg and Krapf, *Journals*, 431–32.

17. The numbers of these public houses burgeoned in the growing city, established by divorcees or slaves and servants of the rich who converted their payments into businesses that offered food, lodging, and drink for cash. Mérab noted the overlap of pleasure and sustenance: "tout lupanar est un cabaret, ou tout cabaret est un lupanar" (all brothels are inn/restaurants and all inn/restaurants are brothels) (*Impressions*, 488–89).

18. Fan C. Dunckley, *Eight Years in Abyssinia* (London: Hutchinson, 1935).

19. Those hotels, however, did help introduce pasta as an alternative food for the middle class. Pasta al forno and spaghetti became staples of hotels and restaurants serving foreign food. For comparative discussions of the history of the restaurant, see Amy Trubek, *Haute Cuisine: How the French Invented the Culinary Profession* (Philadelphia: University of Pennsylvania Press, 2000), 31–41; Hans Conrad Peyer, "The Origins of Public Hostelries in Europe," in *Food: A Culinary History from Antiquity to the Present*, ed. Jean-Louis Flandrin and Massimo Montanari (New York: Columbia University Press, 1999), 287–94; and Jean-Robert Pitte, "The Rise of the Restaurant," in Flandrin and Montanari, *Food*, 471–80.

20. Without injera no meal was truly satisfying. For an equivalent sentiment for millet in central Africa, see Audrey Richards, *Land, Labour, and Diet in Northern Rhodesia: An Economic Study of the Bemba Tribe* (London: Oxford University Press, 1939), 46–52.

21. I am grateful to my Gondere colleague Asnakew Kebede for this observation.

22. The Time-Life volume on African food characterizes the Addis Ababa restaurant as "a Place Where One Can Eat as the Ethiopians Eat," suggesting the elite elaboration of food as the national norm. The author states that "a meal at the Addis Ababa offers not only a cuisine but a whole culinary tradition. Eating in Ethiopia is a highly ritualistic experience, from the washing of the hands that precedes a formal dinner to the service of coffee in ornate cups at its close." For photos and a narrative description of the food and ambiance of the Addis Ababa restaurant, see Laurens van der Post, *African Cooking* (New York: Time Life Books, 1970), 41–47.

23. EDU was the acronym of the Ethiopian Democratic Union, an exiled royalist party. Few of its customers even knew the official name on the small sign at its gate: "Entoto Restaurant." One *zegubegn* restaurant in Agaro had been opened by a retired military officer and was the only real restaurant in that coffee-rich town near Jimma.

24. Interview with Girma Belay, owner of Agare Genet Hotel, Burie (Gojjam), September 7, 2005. Tegabino shiro also often includes a *bozena* variation, with dried meat.

CHAPTER FIVE A West African Culinary Grammar

1. Chinua Achebe, *Things Fall Apart* (London: Heinemann, 1958), 69.

2. I thank Natalie Mettler for this keen observation. For the full story, see Djibril Tamsir Niane, *Sundiata: An Epic of Old Mali* (London: Longmans, 1965). Also see Natalie Mettler, "Oily Sauce, Salty Sauce: Food, Cooking, and Identity in the Mandekan Region of West Africa," African Studies Center Working Paper, Boston University, 2008.

3. Mungo Park, *Travels in the Interior Districts of Africa*, ed. Kate Ferguson Marsters (Durham: Duke University Press, 2000), 72.

4. Ibid., 73.

5. Afro-European groups that emerged on the coast in the sixteenth and seventeenth centuries created a distinct cultural mélange. See Walter Rodney, *History of the Upper Guinea Coast* (Oxford: Clarendon Press, 1970).

6. Wilem Bosman, *A New and Accurate Description of the Coast of Guinea: Divided into the Gold, the Slave, and the Ivory Coasts* (London: Frank Cass, 1967), 124.

7. Ibid., 123–25; quotation on 123.

8. Ray A. Kea, *Settlements, Trade, and Politics in the Seventeenth-Century Gold Coast* (Baltimore: Johns Hopkins University Press, 1982), 301.

9. Ibid., 312, 314–15.

10. Pieter de Marees, *Description and Historical Account of the Gold Kingdom of Guinea (1602)* (Oxford: Oxford University Press, 1987), 272. Marees does not describe the usual steaming process used for kenkey and other breads described in the twentieth century and in Wilem Bosman's late-eighteenth-century accounts. These other descriptions state that no ovens existed in West Africa. See also Claire Robertson, *Sharing the Same Bowl: A Socioeconomic History of Women and Class in Accra, Ghana* (Bloomington: Indiana University Press, 1984), 107–8; and Bosman, *New and Accurate Description*, 392.

11. Stanley Alpern, "The European Introduction of Crops into West Africa in Precolonial Times," *History in Africa* 19 (1992): 16–17.

12. Bosman, *New and Accurate Description*, 392–93.

13. Ibid., 438, 458–59.

14. Ibid., 392. For ship's list see editor's footnote in Ludvig Ferdinand Rømer, *A Reliable Account of the Coast of Guinea (1760)*, ed. and trans. Selena Axelrod Winsnes (Oxford: Oxford University Press, 2000), n30. It is unclear from this account if Muslim captives received any consideration in identifying the pork rations. Rømer himself advocated the use of beans, supplemented with prunes, rather than yellow peas at sea to promote health of the captives.

15. Judith Carney's work on New World subsistence strategies for Africans in *In the Shadow of Slavery: Africa's Botanical Legacy in the Atlantic World* (Berkeley and Los Angeles: University of California Press, 2009) shows remarkable adaptations to the new tropical environments of the Caribbean, Latin America, and the southern English colonies of North America.

16. Bosman, *New and Accurate Description*, 473.

17. See for example, Amy Trubek, *Haute Cuisine: How the French Invented the Culinary Profession* (Philadelphia: University of Pennsylvania Press, 2000), 11–30, 42–51; and Hans Jurgen Teuteberg and Jean-Louis Flandrin, "The Transformation of the European Diet," in *Food: A Culinary History from Antiquity to the Present*, ed. Jean-Louis Flandrin and Massimo Montanari (New York: Columbia University Press, 1996), 442–56.

18. For insights into this social process of class formation and effects on consumption, see Emmanuel Akyeampong, *Drink, Power, and Cultural Change: A Social History of Alcohol in Ghana, c. 1800 to Recent Times* (Portsmouth, NH: Heinemann, 1996), 47–69.

19. Margaret Field, "Gold Coast Food," *Petits propos culinaires* 43 (1993): 7–21. Field's survey of foods pre-dated Audrey Richard's study of Bemba diets by eight years.

20. The terms "soup" and "stew" are used interchangeably in West Africa. Neither Field nor any of my informants suggest any substantive difference.

21. Alfred Crosby, *Ecological Imperialism: The Biological Expansion of Europe, 900–1900* (Cambridge: Cambridge University Press, 1986), 2–3.

22. Claire Robertson, *Sharing the Same Bowl: A Socioeconomic History of Women and Class in Accra* (Bloomington: Indiana University Press, 1984), 115–17. Traveler T. J. Bowen reports that in the 1950s in Nigeria's Yorubaland "women were always engaged in preparing all sorts of dishes for sale to passersby." Also see Fran Osseo-Asare, *Food Culture in Sub-Saharan Africa* (Westport, CT: Greenwood Press, 2005), 33, 46.

23. Gracia Clark, *Onions Are My Husband: Survival and Accumulation by West African Market Women* (Chicago: University of Chicago Press, 1994), 356.

24. Ibid., 344–45; Robertson, *Sharing the Same Bowl*, 183.

25. Jack Goody, *Cooking, Cuisine, and Class: A Study in Comparative Sociology* (Cambridge: Cambridge University Press, 70.

26. Ibid., 78.

27. Examples of formula include Jessica B. Harris, *The Africa Cookbook: Tastes of the Continent* (New York: Simon and Schuster, 1998), 255; Laura Edet, *Classic*

Nigerian Cookbook (London: Divine Grace, 1996), 54; Tourist Company of Nigeria, *Nigerian Dishes* (n.d.), 15–16; Field, *Gold Coast Food,* 19.

28. Edet, *Classic Nigerian Cookbook* (London, 1996), 54.

29. Pamela Greene, *Favorite Sierra Leone Recipes* (Freetown: Commercial Printers, 1970), 38. A Sierra Leonean, Greene includes basic recipes and advice on nutrition and thrift in her cookbook dedicated to her husband, Fennel, who "enjoys my cooking." Dorinda Hafner's New World diaspora version of the Jollof rice recipe given here is more elaborate and explicit about method. See Dorinda Hafner, *A Taste of Africa* (San Francisco: Ten Speed Press, 1993). Hafner writes that Jollof rice's origins are a bone of contention, but that this version is her mother's.

30. http://www.oluolufoods.com. See also http://www.congocookbook.com; and Edet, *Nigerian Classical Cooking,* 68. Maya Angelou attributes it to Ghana. *A Song Flung Up to Heaven* (New York: Random House, 2002), chap. 2.

31. Osseo-Asare, *Food Culture,* 33.

32. Field, "Gold Coast Food," 17. Field was a trained chemist as well as a physician and anthropologist. The slippery balls of fufu are most often swallowed whole rather than chewed.

CHAPTER SIX Historical and Modern Cookery in the Maize Belt and Maritime Cultures of Eastern and Southern Africa

1. Laurens van der Post, *African Cooking* (New York: Time-Life Books, 1970), 200–201; Fran Osseo-Asare, *Food Culture in Sub-Saharan Africa* (Westport, CT: Greenwood Press, 2005), 145–46; Jessica B. Harris, *The Africa Cookbook: Tastes of the Continent* (New York: Simon and Schuster, 1998), 173–75; Zinta Konrad et al., *Tanti Ama's Cookbook* (Dakar: Dzika, 1982), 11.

2. Marcus Samuelsson, *Soul of a New Cuisine: A Discovery of the Foods and Flavors of Africa* (New York: John Wiley, 2006), xi–xiii, 140, 338. Maize does not appear at all in his index, and corn appears in a recipe for cornbread, which he erroneously attributes to West Africa.

3. James C. McCann, *Maize and Grace: Africa's Encounter with a New World Crop, 1500–2000* (Cambridge, MA: Harvard University Press, 2005), 9–15.

4. Marielle Rowan, *Flavours of Mozambique* (Maputo: Marielle Rowan, 1998), 20.

5. McCann, *Maize and Grace,* 104–11.

6. See ibid., 94–120.

7. Thomas Arbousett, *Missionary Excursion into the Blue Mountains,* ed. and trans. David Ambrose and Albert Brutsch (Lesotho: Morija Archives, 1991), 75. Here "Turkish corn" probably refers to sorghum (Indian corn is maize, and sweet reed may mean sorghum cane eaten as a snack).

8. Audrey Richards, *Land, Labour, and Diet in Northern Rhodesia: An Economic Study of the Bemba Tribe* (London: Oxford University Press, 1939), 91–93.

9. Ibid., 93–94. For a deeper historical view of cassava (manioc) see Jan Vansina, "Histoire du manioc en Afrique centrale avant 1850," *Paiduma* 43 (1997): 255–79.

10. Adapted from Bomme Basemzanzi, *South African Indigenous Foods* (Pretoria: IndiZAFoods, 2004), 65.

11. Richards, *Land, Labour, and Diet,* 94–96.

12. John Thornton, *The Kongolese St. Anthony: Don Beatriz Kimpa Vita and the Antonian Movement, 1684–1706* (Cambridge: Cambridge University Press, 1998), 15–16. In this period the grain for the nfundi may have been either maize or millet, though maize became dominant in later years.

13. Annabel Shaxson, Pat Dickson, and June Walker, *The Malawi Cookbook* (Zomba, Malawi: Government Printer, 1979), 21–23.

14. Adapted from Bomme Basemzanzi, *South African Indigenous Foods: A Collection of Recipes of Indigenous Foods, Prepared by Generations of Women* (Pretoria: IndiZAFoods, 2004), 35.

15. Adapted from ibid., 66.

16. Adapted from Harris, *Africa Cookbook,* 182.

17. Kenneth F. Kiple and Kriemhild Coneè Ornelas, eds., *The Cambridge World History of Food,* 2 vols. (Cambridge: Cambridge University Press, 2000), 2:1729.

18. Basemzanzi, *South African Indigenous Foods,* 37, 67, 79.

19. In Malawi, chopped green bird chilies appear on restaurant tables and a commercial line of Nali sauces is available as condiments.

20. Ann Gardner, *Karibu: Welcome to the Cooking of Kenya* (Nairobi: Kenway, 1993), 213–15.

21. Rowan, *Flavours of Mozambique,* 2.

22. Adapted from van der Post, *African Cooking,* 150–51. Cape Town cooks use the term "stockfish" to mean any white flaky fish, rather than salt cod as used in Europe and West Africa.

23. Adapted from van der Post, *African Cooking,* 119.

24. Ibid., 119, 122.

25. Adapted from Harris, *Africa Cookbook,* 232. Also see Shaxson, Dickson, and Walker, *Malawi Cookbook,* 42 for a Malawi expatriate version of this recipe. Peri-peri sauce has also made a global/regional appearance as the primary taste of Nando's Chicken, a popular fast-food chain with branches now in South Africa, Zimbabwe, Angola, Botswana, Kenya, Ghana, Swaziland, Tanzania, Uganda, Mozambique, Zambia, and Senegal. Osseo-Asare, *Food Culture,* 81–82.

CHAPTER SEVEN Diaspora Cookery
African, Circulation, and the New World Pot

1. David Eltis, "Free and Coerced Transatlantic Migrations: Some Comparisons," *American Historical Review* 88, no. 2 (1983): 251–70.

2. For forceful arguments on the Atlantic world, see John Thornton, *Africa and Africans in the Making of the Atlantic World* (Cambridge: Cambridge University Press, 1992); and Paul Gilroy, *Black Atlantic: Modernity and Double-Consciousness* (Cambridge: Cambridge University Press, 1994); and Lorand Matory, *Black Atlantic Religion: Tradition, Transnationalism, and Matriarchy in the Black Atlantic World* (Princeton: Princeton University Press, 2005).

3. Sidney Mintz, *Tasting Food, Tasting Freedom* (Boston: Houghton Mifflin, 1996), 33–49. Mintz's chapter on the evolution of Caribbean cuisine in the context of slavery and social oppression is a provocative view of social relations and their meaning for food.

4. See Amiri Baraka [LeRoi Jones], "Soul Food." In *Home: Social Essays* (New York: Morrow, 1962); for this citation see Doris Witt, *Black Hunger: Soul Food and America* (Minneapolis: University of Minnesota Press, 1999), 82.

5. Grits originated in America. American Indians were blanching corn to make hominy, and making grits from the hominy, long before European colonization, a further reflection of the movement of food culture both ways across the Atlantic—in this case eastward. I am grateful to copyeditor John Morris for pointing out this important distinction between grits and other maize porridges. It is important to note that grits is different from hominy grits—an American practice, found rarely in Africa, in which the maize is soaked in an alkaline solution before the hull is removed.

6. Robert Dirks and Nancy Duran, "African American Dietary Patterns at the Beginning of the 20th Century," *Journal of Nutrition* (2001): 1882–84. This remarkable study also contrasts these two areas with Philadelphia and Washington, DC, where beef, mutton, and a greater variety of vegetables were far more prominent.

7. Vertamae Smart-Grosvenor, *Vibration Cooking; Or, the Travel Notes of a Geechee Girl* (New York: Ballantine, 142). The Gullah—or Geechee—people of the South Carolina island are an African American group with strong linguistic and cultural influence from Sierra Leone.

8. Adapted from several variations. For example, see www.recipezaar.com/Hatties-Creole-Jambalaya-44419.

9. There are many variations; for example, see www.whats4eats.com/fish/moqueca-recipe.

10. Mary Umitia Randelman, *Memories of a Cuban Kitchen* (New York: John Wiley, 1996), 104. She quotes nineteenth-century author Jose Maria del la Torre, *Lo que fuimos y lo que somos* (Who We Were and Who We Are). I am grateful to my DuBois Institute colleague Melina Papademos for this reference.

11. Gary Edwards and John Mason, *Onje Fun Orisa = Food for the Gods* (New York: Yoruba Theological Archministry, 1981), 89–91.

12. Adapted from La Cocina Cubana: "Moros y Cristianos," http://www.juan-perez.com/cocina/cocina.htm.

13. Most restaurants use a U.S.-grown *Eragrostis* variety that has the taste of Ethiopian-grown teff (*Eragrostis tef*) but does not ferment similarly and leaves a heavy feeling. Most restaurateurs add self-rising wheat flour or other additives to add the characteristic bubbles or "eyes" of the real thing. Proper *berberay* is often imported from Ethiopia since its bulk allows its affordable shipment.

14. "Bargain Dining," *Chicago Magazine,* November 2005, 116. Yemiru Chenyalew, who operated a restaurant in Chicago, explained to me that the small size of Chicago's Ethiopian community meant that the menu of his restaurant had to cater to an upscale Wrigleyville clientele rather than to Ethiopians.

15. Mekeda Ethiopian Restaurant Lunch Special (thanks to the management of the restaurant for providing me with this menu). This innovative and attractively decorated restaurant is located in New Brunswick.

Bibliography

Achebe, Chinua. *Things Fall Apart.* London: Heinemann, 1958.

Akyeampong, Emmanuel. *Drink, Power, and Cultural Change: A Social History of Alcohol in Ghana, c. 1800 to Recent Times.* Portsmouth, NH: Heinemann, 1996.

Almeida, Manoel de. *Some Records of Ethiopia, 1593–1646.* Edited and translated by C. F. Beckingham and G. W. B. Huntingford. London: Hakluyt Society, 1954.

Alpern, Stanley. "The European Introduction of Crops into West Africa in Precolonial Times." *History in Africa* 19 (1992): 20–21.

Alvarez, Francisco. *The Prester John of the Indies: A True Relation of the Lands of the Prester John, being the narrative of the Portuguese Embassy to Ethiopia in 1540.* Edited and translated by C. F. Beckingham and G. W. B. Huntingford. 2 vols. Cambridge: Hakluyt Society, 1961.

Andrews, Jean. "Chilli Peppers." In Kiple and Ornelas, *Cambridge World History of Food,* 1:281–87.

Angelou, Maya. *A Song Flung Up to Heaven.* New York: Random House, 2002.

Appadurai, Arjun. "How to Make a National Cuisine: Cookbooks in Contemporary India." *Comparative Studies in Society and History* 30, no. 1 (1988): 3–24.

Arbousett, Thomas. *Missionary Excursion into the Blue Mountains.* Edited and translated by David Ambrose and Albert Brutsch. Lesotho: Morija Archives, 1991.

Astley, Thomas. *A New General Collection of Voyages and Travels.* 4 vols. London: Frank Cass, 1968.

Bâ, Mariama. *So Long a Letter.* London: Heinemann, 1981.

Baraka, Amiri [LeRoi Jones]. "Soul Food." In *Home: Social Essays.* New York: Morrow, 1962.

Basemzanzi, Bomme. *South African Indigenous Foods: A Collection of Recipes of Indigenous Foods, Prepared by Generations of Women.* Pretoria: IndiZAFoods, 2004.

Bazabesh Fanta. *Yabaltna Mench.* Addis Ababa: Yashefun Se'l Asmael Sumar, 1998 EC (2005).

Better Life Programme (Nigeria) Plateau State. *Traditional Dishes, Snacks, Drinks and Herbs from Plateau State.* N.p., n.d. African Studies Collection, Mugar Library, Boston University.

Beye, Abdoul Khadre. *Étude de l'art culinaire senegambien traditionnel.* Vol. 1. Dakar: Clairafrique, n.d.

Biasio, Elisabeth. *Majesty and Magnificence at the Court of Menilek: Alfred Ilg's Ethiopia around 1900.* Zurich: NZZ, 2004.

Biarnès, Monique. *La cuisine sénégalaise.* Dakar: Sociètè Africaine d'Edition, 1978.

Bosman, Wilem. *A New and Accurate Description of the Coast of Guinea: Divided into the Gold, the Slave, and the Ivory Coasts.* London: Frank Cass, 1967.

Bowdich, T. Edward. *Mission from Cape Coast Castle to Ashantee.* Edited by W. E. F. Ward. London: Frank Cass, 1966.

Bulatowicz, Aleksander. *Z woskami Menelika II, Zapiski z podrozy do Etiopii.* Warsaw: Dialog, 2000.

Carney, Judith. *Black Rice: The African Origins of Rice Cultivation in the Americas.* Cambridge, MA: Harvard University Press, 2001.

———. *In the Shadow of Slavery: Africa's Botanical Legacy in the Atlantic World.* Berkeley and Los Angeles: University of California Press, 2008.

Chang, C. K., ed. *Food in Chinese Culture.* New Haven: Yale University Press, 1977.

Civitello, Linda. *Cuisine and Culture: A History of Food and People.* New York: John Wiley, 2003.

Clark, Gracia. *Onions Are My Husband: Survival and Accumulation by West African Market Women.* Chicago: University of Chicago Press, 1994.

Crosby, Alfred. *The Columbian Exchange: Biological and Cultural Consequences of 1492.* Westport, CT: Greenwood, 1972.

———. *Ecological Imperialism: The Biological Expansion of Europe, 900–1900.* Cambridge: Cambridge University Press, 1986.

D'Abbadie, Arnauld. *Douze ans de sèjour dans la Haute-Éthiopie (Abyssinie).* 2 vols. Vatican City: Biblioteca Apostolica Vaticana, 1980.

Dapper, Olfert. *Naukeurige beschrijvinge der Afrikaensche gewesten.* Amsterdam, 1668.

Diamond, Jared. *Guns, Germs, and Steel: The Fates of Human Societies.* New York: W. W. Norton, 1997.

Dirks, Robert, and Nancy Duran. "African American Dietary Patterns at the Beginning of the 20th Century." *Journal of Nutrition* (2001): 1882–84.

Dunckley, Fan C. *Eight Years in Abyssinia.* London: Hutchinson, 1935.

Edet, Laura. *Classic Nigerian Cookbook.* London: Divine Grace, 1996.

Edwards, Gary, and John Mason. *Onje Fun Orisa = Food for the Gods.* New York: Yoruba Theological Archministry, 1981.

Ehret, Christopher. *An African Classical Age: Eastern and Southern Africa in World History, 1000 B.C. to A.D. 400.* Charlottesville: University of Virginia Press, 1998.

Eltis, David. "Free and Coerced Transatlantic Migrations: Some Comparisons," *American Historical Review* 88, no. 2 (1983): 251–70.

————. "The Volume and Direction of the Transatlantic Slave Trade: A Reassessment." *William and Mary Quarterly* 60 (2001): 17–46.

Emechata, Buchi. *The Joys of Motherhood.* New York: G. Braziller, 1979.

Eyeoyibo, Mac Oma. *Cookery Book in Isekiri (Warri Kingdom).* Benin City: Mofe Press, 1993.

Fernández-Armesto, Felipe. *Food: A History.* London: Macmillan, 2001.

Ferguson, Priscilla Parkhurst. *Accounting for Taste: The Triumph of French Cuisine.* Chicago: University of Chicago Press, 1994.

Field, Margaret. "Gold Coast Food." *Petits propos culinaires* 43 (1993): 7–21.

Flandrin, Jean-Louis, and Massimo Montanari. *Food: A Culinary History from Antiquity to the Present.* New York: Columbia University Press, 1996.

Frazer, James George. *The Golden Bough.* 2 vols. London: Macmillan, 1890.

Freeman, Michael. "Sung." In *Food in Chinese Culture,* edited by C. K. Chang. New Haven: Yale University Press, 1977.

Gabra Sellase. *Tarika zaman za-dagmawi Menilek: Negusa nagast za-Ityopiya.* Addis Ababa: Berhanena Salam Press, 1966 EC.

Gardner, Ann. *Karibu: Welcome to the Cooking of Kenya.* Nairobi: Kenway, 1992.

Geertz, Clifford. *Negara: The Theatre-State in Nineteenth-Century Bali.* Princeton: Princeton University Press, 1981.

Gilroy, Paul. *Black Atlantic: Modernity and Double-Consciousness.* Cambridge: Cambridge University Press, 1994.

Gonahasa, Jolly. *Taste of Uganda.* Kampala: Fountain, 2002.

Goodwin, A. J. H. "The Origin of Maize." *South African Archaeological Bulletin* 8 (1953): 13.

Goody, Jack. *Cooking, Cuisine, and Class: A Study in Comparative Sociology.* Cambridge: Cambridge University Press, 1982.

Greene, Pamela. *Favourite Sierra Leone Recipes.* Freetown: Commercial Printers, 1970.

Guèbrè Sellassié. *Chronique du règne de Ménèlik II roi des rois d'Éthiopie.* Edited and translated by Tèsfa Sellassié and Maurice de Coppet. Paris: Maisonneuve frères, 1930.

Guyer, Jane. *Feeding African Cities: Studies in Regional Social History.* Bloomington: Indiana University Press, 1987.

Hafner, Dorinda. *A Taste of Africa.* San Francisco: Ten Speed Press, 1993.

Harris, Jessica B. *The Africa Cookbook: Tastes of the Continent.* New York: Simon and Schuster, 1998.

Ikpe, Eno Blankson. *Food and Society in Nigeria: A History of Food Customs, Food Economy and Cultural Change, 1900–1989.* Stuttgart: Steiner, 1994.

Illife, John. *Africa: History of a Continent.* Cambridge: Cambridge University Press, 2002.

Isenberg, C. W., and J. L. Krapf. *Journals of the Rev. Messrs. Isenberg and Krapf, Detailing Their Proceedings in the Kingdom of Shoa.* London: Seeley, 1843.

Isert, Paul Erdman. *Voyage en Guinée et dans les îles Caraïbes en Amérique.* Paris: Éditions Karthala, 1989.

Jaffrey, Madhur. *An Invitation to Indian Cooking.* New York: Penguin, 1973.

Jeffreys, M. D. W. "The History of Maize in Africa." *South African Journal of Science* (March 1954): 197–200.

———. "How Ancient Is West African Maize?" *Africa* 33, no. 2 (1963): 115–200.

Jones, W. O. *Manioc in Africa.* Palo Alto: Stanford University Press, 1959.

Juhé-Beaulaton, Dominique. "La diffusion du maïs sur les côtes de l'or et des esclaves aux XVII et XVIII siècles." *Revue française d'histoire d'Outre-mer* 77 (1990): 188–90.

Kea, Ray A. *Settlements, Trade, and Politics in the Seventeenth-Century Gold Coast.* Baltimore: Johns Hopkins University Press, 1982.

Kiple, Kenneth F., and Kriemhild Coneè Ornelas, eds. *The Cambridge World History of Food.* 2 vols. Cambridge: Cambridge University Press, 2000.

Konrad, Zinta, et al. *Tanti Ama's Cookbook.* Dakar: Dzika, 1982.

Kudeti Book of Yoruba Cookery, The. Rev. ed. Lagos: C.M.S. (Nigeria) Bookshops, 1961.

Küster, Hansjörg. "Spices and Flavorings." In Kiple and Ornelas, *Cambridge World History of Food,* 1:431–37.

Lobell, John. *The Little Green Book: A Guide to Self-Reliant Living in the 1980s.* Boulder: Shambhala, 1981.

Lobo, Jerónimo. *The Itinerário of Jerónimo Lobo.* Edited and translated by Donald Lockhart. London: Hakluyt Society, 1984.

———. *A Voyage to Abyssinia.* Translated by Samuel Johnson. London: Eliot and Kay, 1789.

Marcus, Harold G. *The Life and Times of Menelik II: Ethiopia, 1844–1913.* Oxford: Clarendon Press, 1975.

———. "The Organization of Menilek II's Palace and Imperial Hospitality (after 1896)." *Rural Africana* (Spring 1970).

Marees, Pieter de. *Description and Historical Account of the Gold Kingdom of Guinea (1602).* Oxford: Oxford University Press, 1987.

Massaia, Guglielmo. *I miei trentacinque anni di missione nell'alta Etiopia.* 22 vols. Rome: Tivoli, 1929.

Matory, Lorand. *Black Atlantic Religion: Tradition, Transnationalism, and Matriarchy in the Black Atlantic World.* Princeton: Princeton University Press, 2005.

McCann, James C. *From Poverty to Famine in Northeast Ethiopia: A Rural History.* Philadelphia: University of Pennsylvania Press, 1989.

———. *Maize and Grace: Africa's Encounter with a New World Crop, 1500–2000.* Cambridge, MA: Harvard University Press, 2005.

———. *People of the Plow: An Agricultural History of Ethiopia.* Madison: University of Wisconsin Press, 1995.

McQueen, Adele, ed. *The Liberian Way of Cooking.* Typescript. Monrovia: Committee on International Club Women's Project, n.d.

Mérab, E. *Impressions d'Éthiopie: L'Abyssinie sous Ménélik II.* 3 vols. Paris: H. Libert, 1921.

Mesfin, Daniel J., ed. *Exotic Ethiopian Cooking: Society, Culture, Hospitality, and Traditions.* Falls Church, VA: Ethiopian Cookbook Enterprises, 2004.

Mettler, Natalie. "Nafên: The Ingredients of Ethnic Identity in the Mande Region of West Africa." African Studies Center Working Paper, Boston University, 2008.

Mintz, Sidney W. *Sweetness and Power: The Place of Sugar in Modern History.* New York: Viking, 1985

———. *Tasting Food, Tasting Freedom: Excursions into Eating, Culture, and the Past.* Boston: Houghton Mifflin, 1996.

Mwiandi, Mary Ciambaka. "The Jeanes School in Kenya: The Role of the Jeanes Teachers and Their Wives in the Social Transformation of Rural Colonial Kenya, 1925–61." PhD diss., Michigan State University, 2005.

Ngude, M. *Mapishi Yetu.* Dar es Salaam: Longman Tanzania, 1978.

Niane, Djibril Tamsir. *Sundiata: An Epic of Old Mali.* London: Longmans, 1965.

Nweke, Felix I., John K. Lynam, and Dustan S. C. Spencer. *The Cassava Transformation: Africa's Best-Kept Secret.* East Lansing: Michigan State University Press, 2002.

Nyaho, E. Chapman, E. Amarteifio, and J. Asare. *Ghana Recipe Book.* Tema: Ghana, 1970.

Orlowska, Izabela. "Feasting and Politics: Ethiopian Gibir [Feast] and Its Functions." Workshop paper, Eating and Drinking in History, University of Edinburgh, 2008.

Osseo-Asare, Fran. *Food Culture in Sub-Saharan Africa.* Westport, CT: Greenwood Press, 2005.

Pankhurst, Richard. *Economic History of Ethiopia, 1800–1935.* Addis Ababa: Haile Sellassie I University Press, 1968.

Park, Mungo. *Travels in the Interior Districts of Africa.* Edited by Kate Ferguson Marsters. Durham: Duke University Press, 2000.

Parkyns, Mansfield. *Life in Abyssinia, Being Notes Collected during Three Years' Residence in That Country.* 1853. London: Frank Cass, 1966.

Pasch, Helma. "Zur Geschichte der Verbreitung des Maizes in Afrika." *Sprache und Geschichte in Afrika* 5 (1983).

Pearce, Nathaniel. *The Life and Adventures of Nathaniel Pearce: Written by Himself during a Residence in Abyssinia from the Years 1810 to 1819 Together with Mr. Coffin's Account of His Visit to Gondar.* London: Henry Colburn and Richard Bentley, 1831.

Pease, A. E. *Travel and Sport in Africa.* 3 vols. London: Arthur L. Humphreys, 1902.

Peyer, Hans Conrad. "The Origins of Public Hostelries in Europe." In Flandrin and Montanari, *Food,* 287–94.

Pitte, Jean-Robert. "The Rise of the Restaurant." In Flandrin and Montanari, *Food,* 471–80.

Plummer, G. *Ibo Cookery Book.* Lagos: C.M.S. Bookshops, n.d.

Pollan, Michael. *The Botany of Desire: A Plant's-Eye View of the World.* New York: Random House, 2001.

———. *The Omnivore's Dilemma: A Natural History of Four Meals.* New York: Penguin, 2006.

Prouty, Chris. *Empress Taytu and Menilek: Ethiopia, 1883–1910.* London: Raven Educational Services; Trenton, NJ: Red Sea Press, 1986.

Qalamawarq Gezaw. *Yagurage Megeb Esrar: Ka46 Aynet Balay Endala Yawqalun?* [Guide to Gurage Food: Do We Know More than 46 Types?]. Addis Ababa: n.p., 1999.

Randelman, Mary Umitia. *Memories of a Cuban Kitchen.* New York: John Wiley, 1996.

Rattray, R. S. *Ashanti.* 1923. New York: Negro Universities Press, 1969.

Richards, Audrey. *Land, Labour, and Diet in Northern Rhodesia: An Economic Study of the Bemba Tribe.* London: Oxford University Press, 1939.

Robertson, Claire C. *Sharing the Same Bowl: A Socioeconomic History of Women and Class in Accra, Ghana.* Bloomington: Indiana University Press, 1983.

Rodney, Walter. *History of the Upper Guinea Coast.* Oxford: Clarendon Press, 1970.

Rømer, Ludvig Ferdinand. *A Reliable Account of the Coast of Guinea (1760).* Edited and translated by Selena Axelrod Winsnes. Oxford: Oxford University Press, 2000.

Rowan, Marielle. *Flavours of Mozambique.* Maputo: Marielle Rowan, 1998.

Samuelsson, Marcus. *The Soul of a New Cuisine: A Discovery of the Foods and Flavors of Africa.* New York: John Wiley, 2006.

Samuel Tefera. *Zamanawi Ya megeb zegejet* [Modern Cookery]. Addis Ababa: n.p., 2001.

Shaxson, Annabel, Pat Dickson, and June Walker. *The Malawi Cookbook.* Zomba, Malawi: Government Printer, 1979.

Smart-Grosvenor, Vertamae. *Vibration Cooking; Or, the Travel Notes of a Geechee Girl.* New York: Ballantine, 1992.

Tannahill, Reay. *Food in History.* New York: Stein and Day, 1973.

Teuteberg, Hans Jurgen, and Jean-Louis Flandrin. "The Transformation of the European Diet." In Flandrin and Montanari, *Food,* 442–56.

Thornton, John. *Africa and Africans in the Making of the Atlantic World.* Cambridge: Cambridge University Press, 1992.

———. *The Kongolese St. Anthony: Don Beatriz Kimpa Vita and the Antonian Movement, 1684–1706.* Cambridge: Cambridge University Press, 1998.

Tourist Company of Nigeria. *Nigerian Dishes.*

Trubek, Amy. *Haute Cuisine: How the French Invented the Culinary Profession.* Philadelphia: University of Pennsylvania Press, 2000.

Van der Post, Laurens. *African Cooking.* New York: Time-Life Books, 1970.

Vansina, Jan. "Histoire du manioc en Afrique centrale avant 1850." *Paiduma* 43 (1997): 255–79.

Willett, Frank. "The Introduction of Maize to West Africa." *Africa* 32, no. 1 (1962): 1–13.

Willis, Justin. *Potent Brews: A Social History of Alcohol in East Africa, 1850–1999.* Oxford: Oxford University Press, 2002.

Witt, Doris. *Black Hunger: Soul Food and America.* Minneapolis: University of Minnesota Press, 2004.

Wylie, Diana. *Starving on a Full Stomach: Hunger and the Triumph of Cultural Racism in Modern South Africa.* Charlottesville: University Press of Virginia, 2001.

Index

Abijian (Côte d'Ivoire), 128
Achebe, Chinua, 184; on yam in Ibo culture, 41, 43–44, 109, 135
Accra, 110, 115; culinary hegemony of, 130–131; cultural dynamism in, 179; woman and culture of food, 128. *See also* Ghana; Gold Coast
açorda soup (shrimp and egg soup, Angola), 158
Addis Ababa, 13; culinary culture, 91; growth as capital, 97, 179; site of 1887 feast, 65; social life at court, 90; as spiritual center, 77
African America, 166–69. *See also* diaspora
African cuisine (cookery), as distinctive, 8; Africa-themed restaurants, 30
agricultural history of food, 22; innovation in Africa, 23, 34
ajiaco Criollo (Cuban Creole stew), 60, 172–73; recipe, 173
Akan, 121. *See also* Asante; Kwa
alcohol: production of with grain, 35; for *talla* and white lightning in Ethiopia, 102. *See also* beer
Algeria (French colony), 29; ratatouille (Algerian), 29; version of couscous, 112–13
Angelou, Maya: on orality of cooking, 12
Angola, 27, 30; Angolan chicken, 164
ants, 22, 149
Appadurai, Arjun (anthropologist): on Indian cuisine, 29. *See also* cookbooks
Arab cookery, 25; pilaf rice preparation, 39
Asante: elite culture, 119; evening meal, 129–30; feast, 120; food in public life,

120; on Odwira yam festival, 42, 43; political history, 3, 28, 41
ash: American soaking of maize in, 33–34; ashcake in African American cooking, 168; as salt substitute in central Africa, 34, 153. *See also* nixtamalization; salt
Asian migrants, 128
Asian rice: as staple food, 8–9. *See also Oryza sativa*
Atlantic Ocean (Atlantic Rim): culinary traditions of, 42, 119; effect on African cooking, 9, 22, 136; effect on movement of slaves, 25–27; as trade network, 8, 24, 25–27, 166. *See also* Columbian Circulation

bachelors: cooking by, 9
baguettes: appearance in African cities, 3, 27. *See also* bread
bananas, 8, 33, 156. *See also* enset (*Ensete ventricosum*); plantain
Baraka, Amiri, 167, 169
barley: as large-seeded grass species, 22; as part of Mediterranean world, 24; replaced by maize in Ethiopia, 101. *See also* beer
beans, 79, 136; fava, 90; French, 155; frozen, used in recipes, 151; in Gold Coast cooking, 126–27; in West Africa, 117. *See also* black-eyed peas; chickpeas; cowpeas; legumes; pulses
béchamel (sauce), 29, 156
beef, 91–92; dried, 104; dried, in "ayako," 173; raw, in Ethiopia, 85–86, 98

palm wine, 117, 120. *See also* wine
pasta, 3. *See also* spaghetti
patten doya (Nigerian yam pottage), 42
peanut, 135; in central African relishes, 145, 146, 151; oil, 111; West African key ingredient, 116. *See also* groundnut
peppers, 3, 58–61; "aji-aji" Caribbean origins, 60; black pepper, 60, 81, 154; Ethiopia, early shortage in, 86; Ethiopian pepper (*berbere*), 72–73; Ethiopian pepper pastes, 73; malagueta, 73; in West African cooking, 116; in West African dishes, 131–32. *See also* capsicum; malagueta pepper; *peri-peri* sauce
peri-peri sauce (pepper sauce, Mozambique), 158–59. *See also* capsicum; peppers
Persian Gulf, as food trade network, 8
plantain: compared to grains and root crops, 56, 139; cultivation, 57; *dodo* (fried plantain), 57; as element of common cuisine, 109–10; as *fufu*, 33; in Gold Coast cooking, 123–24; as starchy staple, 33, 55–58; nutritional value, 57. *See also* banana; *matooke*
polenta, 34, 104, 13
pork, 166; in soul food, 166–68
porridge, 153; central African types, 145; Ghana, 129; guinea-corn and millet, 130; maize, 7, 33, 37, 137–39; names for, 137–38
potatoes, 4, 33, 155; sweet potato, 124, 131, 145; in West Africa, 118
poultry, 31. *See also* chicken
pounded yam, 5, 7; in diaspora cooking, 163; as element of common cuisine, 109–10. *See also fufu*; yam
pozole. *See* hominy; maize; nixtamalization
processing: of cassava, 52, 53, 143; of rice, 39
pulses, 78. *See also* beans; chickpeas; lentils; *shiro wet*
pumpkin, 112, 140

qwanta (dried meat), 104

ratatouille (Algerian), 29
recipes: as accumulated knowledge, 110; as a form of memory, 3; as primary historical sources, 11–12
Red Sea, as food trade network, 8, 24–25, 67; for Ethiopia, 101

relishes, 144–53; in Bemba diet, 20, 144–47. *See also* stews
restaurants: Addis Ababa Restaurant, 100; in diaspora, 175–79; in Ethiopia, 95–97, 100, 104; Makeda Restaurant (New Brunswick, NJ), 178–79
rice: as African domesticated food crop, 27, 38; African "red," 39; Africa's contribution to New World cooking methods, 26–27; "Carolina gold," 40; compared to wheat and maize for nutrition, 38–39; converted, 40; *Cristianos y Moros* (black beans and rice, Cuba), 174; culture, development of in the Americas, 26–27; as large-seeded grass species, 22; long-grain types, 40, 170; Mediterranean methods for, 39; New World preparation of, 39; as staple, 7, 37–40, 139; Uncle Ben's, 27, 40. *See also Oryza sativa; Oryza glaberrima*
Richards, Audrey (anthropologist), 32, 120; cooking as social anthropology,18; women's knowledge of cooking, 141
ritual: Eucharist, 68; and meaning of food in Ethiopia, 67–68; for yam in Asante and Nigeria, 44

sadza, 138. *See also* maize; porridge
Sahara, 24; culinary culture, 113; trans-Saharan trade, 40, 111
Sahel: food production in, 22, 110
Saint Louis (Senegal), 114, 131
sale of food in public places, 5. *See also* hospitality; restaurants; snacks
salt: forms in Ethiopia, 82; potash salt, 147; scarcity in southern African cooking, 141, 144; as trade item, 3
salt cod, 133. *See also* stockfish
samosa, 31, 106
samp. *See* maize; porridge
Samuelsson, Marcus, 8, 139, 179
seasoning, in central Africa, 146–47
seasons: of Bemba diet, 18–19; contrast in wet and dry, 18; hungry season, 18; rhythm of, 17–22; of Serengeti Plain, 18; of Zulu diet, 21–22
seeds, 3; borrowed from European settlers, 116; exchange by women, 111; large-seeded species, 22; for peppers, 60
Senegal: as distinctive cuisine, 7, 131; *mafé*, 132
Serengeti, seasonal migration of wildlife, 18

CPSIA information can be obtained
at www.ICGtesting.com
Printed in the USA
LVHW100355221122
733353LV00003B/11

9 780896 80272